Bloom's Modern Critical Interpretations

Albert Camus's
The Stranger
New Edition

Edited and with an introduction by
Harold Bloom
Sterling Professor of the Humanities
Yale University

**BLOOM'S
LITERARY CRITICISM**
An Infobase Learning Company

Bloom's Literary Criticism
An imprint of Infobase Learning
132 West 31st Street
New York NY 10001

Library of Congress Cataloging-in-Publication Data
  Albert Camus's The stranger / edited and with an introduction by Harold Bloom. — New ed.
    p. cm. — (Bloom's modern critical interpretations)
  Includes bibliographical references and index.
  ISBN 978-1-60413-580-0 (hardcover)
  1. Camus, Albert, 1913–1960. Étranger. I. Bloom, Harold.
  PQ2605.A3734E8335 2011
  843'.914—dc22
                          2011018174

Bloom's Literary Criticism books are available at special discounts when purchased in bulk quantities for businesses, associations, institutions, or sales promotions. Please call our Special Sales Department in New York at (212)967-8800 or (800)322-8755.

You can find Bloom's Literary Criticism on the World Wide Web at
http://www.infobaselearning.com

Contributing editor: Pamela Loos
Cover design by Alicia Post
Composition by IBT Global, Troy NY
Cover printed by Yurchak Printing, Landisville PA
Book printed and bound by Yurchak Printing, Landisville PA
Date printed: July 2011
Printed in the United States of America

10 9 8 7 6 5 4 3 2 1

This book is printed on acid-free paper.

All links and Web addresses were checked and verified to be correct at the time of publication. Because of the dynamic nature of the Web, some addresses and links may have changed since publication and may no longer be valid.

Contents

Editor's Note

My introduction upholds that Camus was essentially an essayist, even in his narrative fictions. David Sprintzen opens the volume with an exploration of the reader's tenuous relationship to the ambiguous figure of Meursault. Jack Murray then takes up the novel's notions of closure or lack thereof.

Larry W. Riggs and Paula Willoquet-Maricondi consider how acts of writing shape the narrative, followed by Robert R. Brock's suggestion that the underdeveloped characters were created to serve the author's allegorical and political motivations in writing the novel.

Gerald Prince notes how the work, with its dual perspectives, is a meditation on the accuracy of narrative representation, after which Colin Davis points to the novel's vicariousness and complicity with the murder it describes.

Adrian van den Hoven continues the exploration of murder and motive in Camus and in Sartre's *Dirty Hands*, followed by John Foley's discussion of Meursault as the absurd center of a novel of ideas. The volume concludes with Arthur Scherr's appraisal of the Christian themes coursing through the work.

Introduction

Albert Camus wrote and published *L'Étranger* before he was thirty. Only forty-six when he was killed in a car crash, Camus might seem an unfulfilled novelist, except that he was always essentially an essayist, even in his narrative fictions. *The Stranger* (which loses little in the eloquent translation of Mathew Ward) inflicts a considerable wound at first reading. I have just reread it after twelve years, and am a touch saddened by its imaginative inadequacy, yet remain moved by its protagonist's pragmatic innocence. Meursault may be an odd version of Voltaire's Candide, but Jean Paul Sartre's insight remains correct, and *The Stranger*, no comedy, clearly has its affinity with Voltaire's "philosophical" fables, *Candide* and *Zadig.* An emblematic rather than enigmatic figure, Meursault compares poorly with Dostoevsky's fierce nihilists or with Kafka's guilty obsessives. An admirer of Melville and of Faulkner, Camus could not begin to match the terrifying Shakespearean inwardness of Captain Ahab or of Darl Bundren (*As I Lay Dying*). Lucid, severe, and engaging, *The Stranger* nevertheless is a tendentious work, one that knows too well what it is about, and what its effect upon the reader will be.

"We have to labor and to struggle to reconquer solitude." That is Camus in his *Notebooks* in September 1937, when he was going on twenty-four. We need not consider Camus the most authentic spokesman of aesthetic solitude in the century just past—that distinction belongs to Franz Kafka, rightly considered by W. H. Auden to have been the Dante of his age. Kafka, desperate for happiness, found next to none. Camus, who thought of himself as happy, can seem a minor moralist when compared to Kafka or to Freud. And yet Camus became the most representative intellectual of the 1950s, both in France and throughout the West. He stood for individualism: moral,

aesthetic, social, political, and for the ultimate value of each person's consciousness, however absurd (or absurdist) such consciousness might be.

And yet time has dimmed Camus, particularly as a literary artist. Forty years after his death, we read him as an incarnation of the 1950s, not as a seer of Eternity, like Kafka or like Samuel Beckett. On the scale of a James Joyce or a Marcel Proust, Camus's fictions fade out of existence. Is Camus now more than a nostalgia, and is *The Stranger* still a poignant and persuasive narrative? A period piece can have its own value, but time at last will efface it.

I first read *The Stranger* in 1948, when I was eighteen, and was strongly moved. Returning to it in 1988, I was rather disappointed; time seemed to have worn it smooth. Reading it a third time, I find I hover between my two earlier critical impressions. The book's stance refreshes me, as it previously did not twelve years ago, even though I cannot recapture the curious vividness *The Stranger* seemed to possess more than half a century back. *Then* it seemed tragic, though on a minor scale, an aesthetic dignity I could not locate in 1988. Tragedy today clearly is too large a notion to apply to Meursault. Camus regards him as essentially innocent, but if Meursault is nature's victim, or society's rather than of some element in his self, then who would think him tragic? And yet Camus presents Meursault, extreme though he be, as a valid self, one that ought to survive. This is a subtle test for the reader, since Meursault is just barely sympathetic. At first, indeed, Meursault's is an inadequate consciousness as, dazed by the North African sun, Meursault murders a man, gratuitously, and evidently without willing himself to do so. Though he never feels or expresses remorse for the murder, Meursault changes as he undergoes legal judgment and approaches execution. Everything had been all the same to Meursault; he had seemed incapable of wanting anything very much or wanting it more than another thing. As he awaits death, Meursault affirms a version of self: the knowing pariah who wants only the enmity of the state and the people.

Camus makes Meursault into someone we are in no position to judge, but that is an aesthetic risk, because can we still care when we are not competent to at least reach for judgment? Christianity is massively irrelevant to *The Stranger*, and to all of Camus's work. Secular humanism, now out of fashion, is affirmed throughout Camus, and I am touched by the desperate minimalism of Meursault. To see that even Meursault ought to be allowed to go on is to see again the obscenity of capital punishment. The United States, these days, executes on a fairly grand scale. In 2000, *The Stranger* ironically becomes a strong parable against the death penalty. Meursault is not as yet an impressive person as his book closes, but he *has* begun to change, to feel, to choose, to will. To destroy him is more than a societal blunder, in Camus's view. Meursault's life has been an absurdity, but to take away his life is even more absurd.

DAVID SPRINTZEN

The Stranger

A man devoid of hope and conscious of being so has ceased to belong to the future, and no gospel keeps its meaning for him (MS, 31; E, 121, 1436).

Who Is This Stranger?

"Mother died today. Or maybe it was yesterday, I don't know. I received a telegram from the rest home: MOTHER DECEASED. BURIAL TOMORROW. VERY TRULY YOURS. It doesn't say anything. Maybe it was yesterday" (STR, 1).[1] Not exactly the normal reaction of a son to the news of his mother's death. What kind of person responds in this matter-of-fact way? Are we not at first put off by such casualness? Perhaps even scandalized by our initial encounter with Patrice Meursault?

Is not this Meursault a stranger to our normal feelings and expectations? We sense a distance. Not that he seeks to scandalize or offend. Far from it. He is rather quite unassuming, almost shy. He wants neither to offend nor to be hated. Expressing an air of naïveté, he often experiences an undercurrent of uneasiness as to what is expected of him. Occasionally he is moved to apologize without quite knowing what he is guilty of. When asking his boss for two days off to attend his mother's funeral, for example, he feels that he "ought not to have said that to him." Or, when sensing the reproach of the director of the rest home, he begins to explain himself.

From *Camus: A Critical Examination*, pp. 23–40, 285–87. Copyright © 1988 by Temple University.

A subtle tension thus pervades our relation with Meursault from the first. Between the complete unassuming naturalness of his actions and observations, on the one hand, and his insensitivity to normal feelings and expectations, on the other, a gulf emerges that makes it quite difficult for us to coordinate our emotional response to him. We are drawn to identify, even sympathize, with him. And yet how can we not feel a condemnation begin to arise within us to which we are not yet able to give expression?

In short, we are disoriented, perhaps even slightly offended, by our encounter with a being who shows no sign of sharing normal human feelings. Nor does he attest to any normal aspirations. Slowly we are familiarized with his world, even led to see our own world through his eyes. Stripped of our normal "conceptual lenses," we see that world increasingly as arbitrary, capricious, pretentious, even hypocritical. By the time of the trial we may even find ourselves tempted, if not actually inclined, to side with Meursault against the prosecutor and jurists who inhabit the world that was ours at the beginning of the novel. However short-lived that experiential voyage may prove to be, the stylistic accomplishment is remarkable.

Perhaps Meursault is Camus's portrait of the being he might have become had not M. Germain, to whom he dedicated his Nobel Prize address, rescued him from the life of physical plenitude and spiritual exhaustion that was the lot of lower-class French Algerian youth. Recall Camus's friend Vincent, mentioned in *Summer in Algiers*, whose direct and uncomplicated lifestyle and morals, though lacking in love, suggest a closeness to the vital and sensuous qualities of existence.[2] Meursault resides in that shrunken present rich with sensations that lead nowhere. But that must not be misunderstood. He is not without feelings or morals. He feels for Salamano, is moved by the testimony of Celeste, and feels concern for several individuals, including the magistrate. Throughout his ordeal, he treats everyone with consideration and is even able to see the point of view of the prosecutor. He simply refuses to interpret his experience or to give it a significance beyond what is immediately present to the senses.

A lively sensitivity to the play of light and shadow colors his day. The weather, qualitative changes in experience and in the modulations of nature practically enrapture him. He takes them as they are, asking and expecting nothing more. At the same time he remains practically blind to the socially established meanings with which others embellish events.

Nowhere is this more evident than in his relation with Marie. Like Vincent, he knows nothing of love and cares nothing for the institution of marriage. But when Marie smiles in a certain way he is attracted to her and wants her. His desires are not without warmth, but they lack premeditation or foresight. They are spontaneous responses to sensuous qualities and reflect little if any conceptual interpretation or social propriety.

The fascination of Meursault and the young journalist with one another may also be seen in this light. Camus became a journalist as a result of having by chance had Louis Germain as his teacher. And so with the novel. Had Meursault not been compelled by familial poverty to give up his education and abandon his career aspirations, he might have found himself in the audience covering a murder trial. Thus their fascination with each other suggests the chance nature of their destinies and their reciprocal being for one another. In the journalist Meursault sees the person he might have become, fascinated with the person the journalist Camus might have been.

And similarly with the problems of poverty with which Camus's early sensibilities were clearly marked. For it is poverty that keeps Patrice Meursault from pursuing his education and would have done likewise for young Albert. The testimony of his friends about never being invited into his home bears witness to an anguished sensitivity, as does his evocative discussion of the novel *La Douleur*, which had such a profound impact upon him. Camus's first effort at a full-length novel, *A Happy Death*, is quite explicit on the destiny of those condemned to poverty, whatever the natural gifts of their environment. Without money with which to buy the time to be happy, *that* Meursault would have been condemned to the exhausting rigors and spiritual depletion of the 9-to-5 job, which, however necessary to make ends meet, leads only to a wasted life and meaningless "natural death."

Who then is this Patrice Meursault who so innocently disconcerts us? A clerk without ambition, who rejects his boss's offer of advancement and a position in Paris. A man who will marry Marie if she wishes, but who considers marriage no big deal. Obviously intelligent, but having been compelled by poverty to give up schooling, he concluded that ambition was a waste of time and effort. All that mattered was living one day at a time, accepting the pleasures offered, and expecting no more.

Having given up the future, his life follows the trajectory of the moment: job, acquaintances, social routines, climate. Even his language, with its simple factual statements, its lack of connectives, its concentration on sensations and images, bears witness to the pervasiveness of the present. Events happen and Patrice responds. Camus observes: "He limits himself to *responding to questions*. At first, these are the questions which the world asks us every day—[at the end] they are the chaplain's questions. Thus, I define my character negatively" (TRN, 1923).

Such is the person we encounter at the outset. It is not clear what effect the death of his mother had on him. Judging by his explicit response, it would seem to have had no effect, other than to mildly annoy his employer and thus cause some discomfort for Patrice. Yet it is here that the narrative begins. The opening lines suggest that Meursault began writing the chronicle shortly

after receiving the note from the rest home—perhaps as a diary or a random collection of notes. The exact status of the narrative is not clear or consistent. Pursuing internal clues would lead one to conclude either that he kept a running account of his life from then on, making somewhat regular entries after the day's or week's events, or that everything was essentially written from the perspective of a post-sentence reevaluation of his life. Or perhaps it is simply an oral report of his life given at sporadic moments to an impartial observer. In any case, the entries in the first part of the narrative tend to be more direct, more in the style of an immediate, noninterpretative reporting of events in temporal sequence, whereas those of the second part involve greater editorial selectivity. If we take seriously this change in perspective as the narrative proceeds, we would probably be led to a conclusion emphasizing its temporal elaboration. In any case, the world we see is the world Patrice is conscious of seeing *as he sees it*. The meaning of these events is, in the first instance, the meaning of these events to *him*. And it is to that meaning that I now turn.

Meursault's World

What then is the world that is revealed to us through this stranger's eyes? One in which events just happen. Of course, a habitual pattern carries us from day to day. But there does not seem to be any logic to the pattern. "Rising, streetcar, four hours in the office or the factory, meal, streetcar, four hours of work, meal, sleep, and Monday Tuesday Wednesday Thursday Friday and Saturday according to the same rhythm" (MS, 12–13). Expressions, movements, modes of dressing and of carrying oneself strike the observer as do colors, lights, sounds, and temperature. Social and natural events merge and interpenetrate, without priority or distinction between them. The social is rather but an aspect of the natural. There is but one unitary present, with the world of habit being altogether natural and inevitable for Meursault.

It is from this perspective that the world is revealed to us in the first part of the narrative. Nothing significant seems to happen. Each event takes place on the same metaphysical plane. If one thing is singled out for attention rather than another, that is only because it momentarily grabbed Patrice's attention. No hierarchies of value are recognized. Occasional lyrical passages relieve the emotional tedium like shafts of radiant sunlight bursting through the skies of an otherwise overcast day. But that is their only significance. Each of the first five chapters concludes essentially with the observation "that, after all, nothing had changed" (STR, 19).

With the killing of the Arab, however, "it all began." Meursault understood that with that shot he "had broken the harmony of the day, the marvellous silence of a beach where [he] had been happy" (STR, 50). The natural order is shattered. The cyclical time of a habitual life immersed in nature is

transfigured by a single event. All later events now take on the meaning of either leading up to or following from it. If the metaphysical ground of the first part is cyclical nature, that of the second is historicized nature, nature subjected to the organization and interpretation of society. Rather than eternal repetition, events now become the children of the past and the parents of the future, in a linear history that leads either to death or to transfiguration. Each life becomes a unique journey, each event a transition. This metaphysical transformation demands an appropriate existential one. Patrice can no longer act as if his life will be eternal repetition. The unity of nature and history is sundered, and historically socialized reason emerges to insist on a different kind of accounting.

Under the pressure of events, this realization begins to dawn on Patrice. First, in jail, he is called upon to recount the events at the beach. He is questioned about his past and initially draws a blank, noting that he has lost the habit of self-interrogation. Thinking about his past is the beginning of an experiential transformation by which he comes to locate himself in a linear historical world, which location is the precondition of his being able to take personal responsibility for his life.

With this dawning recollection of his past, a sense of perspective emerges. The flatness of the experiential landscape undergoes seismic transformation. Preferences are recognized and valued. An emerging selectivity stylistically transforms the narrative. Criteria of value are suggested. The sensually given is subject to reflective appraisal, and the previously implicit ethics of quantity begins to acquire an appreciation of experiential qualities that only conscious attention can bring. This qualitative self-appropriation of life comes to consummation in the encounter with the chaplain, when the values by which Meursault had lived are reflectively articulated and defended. Thus completes the reconstruction of his experience. From the reconstitution of his memory to the reaffirmation of his life, Meursault has achieved a reflective grasp of the life he has lived, and has found that it was good. He has also realized that to have so lived was to have rejected the expectations of the established social order. Thus a de facto rebel becomes a de jure one. An explicit articulation of these emerging values confronts a chaplain who embodies the rejected order. But I am jumping ahead of my story.

The world was initially composed of natural and social habits—habits of things and of people. Each had its regularity and its unique sensuousness. Patrice observes and responds. He never asks why, what ought to be done, although he does comment upon connections between events—why, for example, the people in the streets on Sunday behave as they do. He thus reveals an ability to analyze facts for their connections, but no interest in exploring purposes or goals. Occasionally he notes the purposes of others—as

with Raymond's desire to get even—but for him, and for us through his eyes, this is but another fact that he observes and to which he responds.

Social conventions also lose their privileged status and appear not to differ from natural occurrences. Like voyagers from another planet, we are often left to wonder at the natives' strange behavior, their dance of social etiquette and the mirage of their personal beliefs. A feeling of purposelessness textures the narrative, pervading Part 1. A feeling of strangeness is subliminally generated in the reader by the contrast between the pure contingency of the events recounted and our subterranean sense of their familiarity and ordinary meaningfulness. This contrast is brought explicitly to the fore in Part 2 by the establishment's insistence on the purposefulness of its world. "The meaning of the book consists precisely in the parallelism of the two parts," affirmed Camus (TRN, 1924).

The use of the disconnected compound past (*passé composé*)—of which so much has been made in critical studies since "Sartre's Explication de l'Étranger"—tends to reduce each fact to an irreducible and unconnected given, thus strengthening this emerging sense of the absurdity of the human situation when it lacks any aspiration to order. Clearly this is Camus's intention. That our world is governed by chance is brought home so much more forcefully when presented by and realized in the life of one who is so unassumingly natural and unself-conscious. A simple individual, without depth or contrivance, presents our world to us in a way that reveals it as being without deeper significance. Confronting such a world tends to make people uncomfortable. "Do you want my life to have no meaning?" the magistrate cries. Whatever his intentions, Patrice's way of living is felt as threatening to society's institutions, beliefs, and aspirations.

Estrangement

The social order from which Meursault is so estranged is the world of ambition and the desire for advancement that his employer expects, as well as the decorum and grief to which all at the burial bear witness. It is the wearing of black as a show of mourning, and the sustained sadness that forbids the beginning of a liaison on the day following the burial of one's mother, not to say the sacrilege of viewing a Fernandel film. It is also the expectation that one ought to cry at the funeral of one's grandmother, about which Camus personally felt such conflict and hypocrisy. And it is certainly viewing love as a serious matter and treating marriage as an important social institution. Here we glimpse the deeper social meaning to which normal people cling with ferocious tenacity. The rituals and ceremonies, the institutions and practices, by which society daily reenacts the drama of its cosmic significance are grounded in a system of values and beliefs that give shape to a

living that might otherwise hover precariously close to the abyss of nothingness. Not to speak of the offices, hierarchies, and prerogatives by which the power and self-esteem of the few may be protected from the desires of the many.

The personal appropriation of that ritualized belief system defines and valorizes an individual's place, giving us our sense of what it is important to do, to strive after, to avoid, and to become. People act in the belief that some things matter more than others, and because they feel that it is worth the effort. This is quite normal. Precisely so.

Meursault had in fact given up on these beliefs when he gave up his ambition. We can take him to have been an intelligent working-class French Algerian whose social development was short-circuited by the need to leave school and get a job. We may even conjecture that this necessity followed upon an upbringing in which circumstances—perhaps including his more than average intelligence—had conspired to keep him somewhat apart from others, not fully integrated into social norms and practices. All this might of course have described Camus himself to some extent.

In any case, giving up ambition and, by implication, the belief system by which it is sustained, Meursault settles into a style of life in which inarticulate personal needs and satisfactions dictate spontaneous responses to the demands of nature and others. He goes along with the flow of habits and events. Such is the path of least resistance, except when his inclination moves him otherwise. And why act differently when "it's all the same to him"?

But then the beach, where "the trigger gave way [and Meursault] . . . understood that [he] had broken the harmony of the day, the marvellous silence of a beach where [he] had been happy. Then [he] pulled the trigger four more times on the motionless corpse where the bullets buried themselves effortlessly. And it was as if, with these four brief shots, [he] was knocking on the door of misfortune" (STR, 50). What could have been simpler or more natural? Heat, exhaustion, the beating of the sun, the shaft of light, the threatening confrontation—and the body tightens up to defend itself: The hand clenches the revolver, and the trigger gives way. With perhaps a touch of exasperation, even annoyance, at the intrusion of the threatening other into this already oppressive situation, the tension previously held coiled within his body bursts forth with those four fatal shots, as if it had been waiting for that moment of release.

All of which is, in one sense, no great deal. Oppressive conditions give rise to tension. The tension is released, and life goes on. Yet a person was killed. Surprisingly perhaps, the authorities initially show little interest in Meursault. As they become aware of his strangeness, their attitude changes. He does not "live by the rules." He does not think like ordinary people. He

does not pay his respects, but seems indifferent to everything that is usually taken seriously. Is not such an attitude offensive? Who is this person, to treat cavalierly what we hold so dear? How can he act this way? There must be something the matter with him. Otherwise there would have to be something the matter with us for taking so seriously that which is not worthy of such respect. If we can't get him to see the error of his ways, thus acknowledging the Truth of ours, we must treat him as a traitor to the human community, and make him pay for his transgression.

Thus a transformed portrait of Meursault emerges. Initially he had simply appeared to be a bit odd, certainly not offensive or brutish. But he didn't want to see his mother's body, he smoked at her funeral, he rejected a chance to move to Paris, and he didn't take marriage seriously. He even seemed inordinately sensitive to trivial matters but awkward, even dense about the norms of social behavior. Now that queerness becomes perversity, indifference metamorphoses into insensitivity, and passivity into calculated criminality. No longer will Meursault's life be allowed to follow the trajectory of inclination and habit. The socialized demand for coherence and purposefulness now takes control. What may well have been lurking in the background now takes center stage, insisting that events conform to its terms. The portrait of a cold-blooded, ruthless murderer takes shape. And why *did* Meursault fire those four extra shots into the body of a corpse, asks the prosecutor, if not to make sure that the job was well done?

Returning to the beach and Meursault's description of what took place, the *why* seems about as relevant as asking a plant why it grows toward the light. Genetics, habit, and inclination seem sufficient. The *why* presupposes a world of purposeful beings who act for more or less premeditated reasons. But is that what took place on the beach?

> I walked slowly toward the rocks and it felt like my forehead was swelling and pulsating under the sun. All this heat pressed down on me. . . . I gritted my teeth, clenched my fists in my pants pockets. My jaws would contract with every sword-like reflexion that darted up from the sand, from a bleached shell, or from a piece of broken glass. . . .
>
> As soon as [the Arab] saw me, he raised up a little and put one hand in his pocket. Naturally my hand closed around Raymond's revolver which I hadn't removed from my jacket. . . . A whole beach vibrating with the sun was surging behind me. I took a few steps toward the source. . . . The scorching sun attacked my cheeks and I felt drops of sweat forming in my eyebrows. It was the same sun as on the day I had buried Mother and, as then,

my forehead hurt and all my veins were pulsating underneath my skin. Because of this heat which I could no longer stand, I took a step forward. . . . The Arab took out his knife and pointed it at me in the sun. The light flashed on the steel and it was like a long blade attacking me on the forehead. At the same instant, the sweat that had been forming in my eyebrows ran down all at once over my pupils, covering them with a warm, thick veil. . . . I felt nothing more then but the cymbals of sun on my forehead, and, indistinctly, the bursting blade of light from the sword continually in front of me. This burning sword was eating away at my eyelids and digging into my aching eyes. It was then that everything reeled. . . . It seemed to me that the heavens had opened to their full extent in order to let it rain fire. My entire being became tight and I closed my grip on the revolver. The trigger gave way (STR, 48–50, modified).

No interpretation, no motive, no conscious revolt is apparent. Only the quasi-instinctive, perhaps physiological, response of a natural animal to an oppressive situation. Under the pressure of the sun, he tenses up and the trigger yields. The Arab, the sun's rays striking off the blade of the knife, the taut grasp of the revolver—all are part of one natural environment whose elements are in tension with one another. Whom can one ask for a motive? The environment is returned to equilibrium by the removal of a nexus of tension. That is all.

But Meursault is a human being and a member of society, and its officials soon see that much more is at stake than simply the killing of an Arab by a French Algerian—about which, it should be noted, little official concern was likely to have been expressed at that time. "For the magistrate," writes Barrier, in his perceptive study of *The Stranger*, "a consciousness which is so non-human represents the grave threat of dismantling the entire edifice of values upon which the very order of society is based" (Barrier, 69).

Two points should be noted here. Meursault is portrayed as a brute, a person so cold and calculating as to smoke at his mother's funeral, begin a liaison on the following day, and commit pre-meditated murder without the least feeling of remorse. Such a "moral monster" would of course be a threat to any order. But Meursault is still more threatening, for he does not even recognize, not to say acknowledge, the values and norms by which the fabric of society is woven together. If he would repent and admit guilt, he would at least implicitly legitimize the claim of those values. Even a murderer can be pardoned—far more easily, Camus suggests, than one who not only refuses to acknowledge social norms, but fails even to perceive their existence. His

refusal thus constitutes a sort of inarticulate metaphysical rejection by which he places himself beyond the horizon of the normal social world. As a spiritual alien upon whom accepted social absolutes make no claim, his being can only appear to the "good people" as a threat to the values and beliefs that are dear to them.

But why, one might ask, must the officials insist upon portraying Meursault as a ruthless killer, one who is morally guilty of matricide? Why must such evil motives be imputed to him in the first place? Why must society—in the persons of the magistrate, defense attorney, and prosecutor—refuse in principle to see him as he is?

We might reflect here upon the problem faced by the early Christians who had to come to terms with the Jews' rejection of Christ as the Messiah. With unbelieving pagans a more energetic propagation of the faith would have sufficed. But the challenge posed by the Jews was of another order. To them the revelation had been given. How can one account for the rejection of a faith that seems both self-evident and salvific? If Christians were not to doubt their faith's evidence, truth, or significance, what were they to make of the Jews' rejection? Either the Jews were ignorant innocents—like children or, perhaps, brutes—or they were willful, insensitive, and possibly downright evil.

Similarly, Meursault is too intelligent to be dismissed as a fool, but his attitude directly challenges the certainty with which the established order confronts the cosmic abyss. By imputing an evil nature to him, the prosecutor can both bring him within the normal cosmic drama and explain the specific reason for his behavior. Let's look at this logic. "To understand is, above all, to unify. The mind's deepest desire, even in its most elaborate operations, parallels man's unconscious feeling in the face of his universe; it is an insistence upon familiarity, an appetite for clarity. Understanding the world for a man is reducing it to the human, stamping it with his seal" (MS, 13).

A motive, no matter how malevolent, bespeaks an intelligible individual. A motivated act is an intelligible act; its world, a familiar world. To insist upon there being a motive—to insist so unself-consciously that the possibility that there might not be one does not *even* arise—while, at the same time, characterizing that motive as the willful rejection of humane sensibilities, here truly is the "best of all possible worlds." Presented with a criminal who is metaphysically comprehensible but morally reprehensible, society may, at one and the same time, reaffirm its cosmic drama and purge itself momentarily of any repressed and taboo inclinations that threaten to shatter it.

What would it mean to accept Meursault as he presents himself? How would we make sense of a world in which chance was pervasive, and in which natural processes predominated to no purpose? Would not a recognition of the essential arbitrariness of the social order and its hierarchies circumscribe

the domain of meaning, rendering it contingent and without direction? And what of the "justice" system? And the organization of power and social prerogatives? Is it any wonder that an "evil" Meursault is more intelligible and less threatening than a impulsive one?

> A world that can be explained even with bad reasons is a familiar world.... On the other hand, in a universe suddenly divested of illusions and lights, man feels an alien, a stranger. His exile is without remedy since he is deprived of the memory of a lost home or the hope of a promised land. This divorce between man and his life, the actor and his setting, is properly the feeling of absurdity (MS, 5).

Meursault is thus inadvertently the most dangerous of rebels, for he rejects the metaphysical foundation of normal social order.[3] As a de facto rebel who becomes conscious of his rebellion only at the end, he must be "put in his place." Society must either obtain his complicity or his destruction. That is the way with absolutes. They brook no opposition.[4]

Barrier correctly observes that for Camus "Meursault is innocent of the *moral* crime of which he is accused and the society guilty for condemning him for such a crime" (Barrier, 74). Rather, Meursault's revolt, involving as it does a reaffirmation of the manner in which he lived his life, contains for Camus elements essential to the establishment and maintenance of human dignity.

Consciousness and Death

Having been indicted for "not playing the game," Meursault will no longer be allowed to freely follow the flow of his feelings. Viewed as a criminal, he will learn deprivation. At first, quite naturally his attention turns toward his immediate surroundings. But that is not long sustaining. Cut off from the world, he is forced back upon himself. Robbed of access to space, and confronted with the fact that he can no longer take the future for granted, he begins to think about his past life—and especially Marie.

With the slow awakening of his memory, a new depth of being emerges. He begins to appear as a being "for himself." Rather than just being there, his life appears as something to be lived, valued, retained, reconstituted, reaffirmed, and, perhaps, redirected. It is to be reflectively taken in hand, to be consciously molded in accord with his personal evaluation of what matters. Memory fuels self-consciousness, as habituated passivity gives way to lucid affirmation. This subterranean transition develops throughout Part 2, reaching its culmination in the encounter with the chaplain. At first, he is called upon to recount his life. Repeatedly he must retell the story of the beach

confrontation. Then, as days turn into weeks and months, the rhythm of the days fades into the monotony of an unchanging present. With the turn inward, the being that he is "for himself" begins to emerge, fascinating him. He finds a reflected image of himself in a mirror. He is drawn to the journalist who suggests the being he might have been. The automaton woman reappears—that being who is completely other than himself—and there seems to be a mutual fascination with each other: she, for whom every action is rationally precalculated and purposeful; he, for whom none had been. It is as if the journalist and the automaton woman are the mirrors wherein Meursault may see the range of beings he might have been.

As Meursault comes to self-awareness, the narrative undergoes stylistic transformation. In place of the seemingly unedited description of chance events in temporal order, we now have the selective reporting of particular events. Long periods are now condensed into a few paragraphs, while a single significant day requires its own chapter. Important encounters are presented in detail, while others drift into obscurity. And judgments emerge, almost unintentionally. But it is the encounter with the chaplain following the condemnation to death that is required to make this existential transformation explicit.[5]

Without doubt the thought of death can remarkably concentrate one's attention. Today and tomorrow can be taken as they come only so long as one expects them to keep coming. Once the death sentence is handed down, the image of the guillotine looms over our horizon, threatening decisively to sever our relation with our future possibilities. And so with Patrice.

> No matter how hard I tried to persuade myself, I could not accept that insolent certitude. Because, in the final analysis, it came to a disproportion between the judgment on which the certitude was based and its imperturbable course, from the moment when this judgment had been pronounced. The fact that the sentence had been read at eight o'clock rather than at five, that it might have been something entirely different . . . it seemed to me that all of this took away from the seriousness of such a verdict (STR, 89–91).

And yet, however chancy the process leading up to the judgment, "from the second it had been given, its effects became as sure, as serious" as the most palpable and inescapable of facts.

Doubtless, there is something absurd in the disproportion between the haphazard and contingent nature of daily existence and the certainty of the punishment's execution. Confronted with this absurdity, Meursault's initial response is typical.

What interests me just now is if I can avoid the machine, if there can be a way to escape the unavoidable.... I don't know how many times I've asked myself if there are any cases of condemned men who were able to fool the machine, who were able to disappear before the execution.... I scolded myself for not having paid enough attention to the accounts of executions.... There, perhaps, I might have found accounts of escape. I would have learned that in at least one case, the wheel had stopped, that in its never-ceasing momentum, hazard and chance, one time only, had caused a change in the normal order of things. One time! In a way, I believe that would have sufficed for me (STR, 89).

Patrice is struggling here to find grounds for the "leap of faith." Faced directly with death, his passionate will to live becomes explicit in his search for a way out. "What mattered was the possibility of escape, of being able to jump out of the path of inevitability, a crazy course which offered all chances of hope." Here, through his struggle, we encounter the fundamentals of the human condition that constitute the problematic of *The Myth*.

Only after having confronted the facts of his impending execution will he allow himself the luxury of hoping that his appeal might be granted. That thought let loose a "surge of blood that ran through my body, causing tears to come to my eyes. I needed to work at moderating my cries of ecstasy, to reason with them so to speak" (STR, 94).

It is precisely at such a moment that the chaplain entered, after having thrice been rejected by Meursault. This missionary for Jesus, who exudes the self-satisfaction of those who "know" themselves to be "in the Truth," incarnates a religious hope built upon acquiescence in the sacrifice of innocence. For the nonbeliever, however, who feels the full weight of finitude bearing down upon him, the chaplain's complacent acquiescence in, and even complicity with, this capricious and unjust order of things is ultimately unbearable. Having struggled vainly to reconcile two contradictory visions of his future, Meursault's outrage finally coalesces in an explosive rejection of rationalized injustice. As the chaplain literally pins Patrice to the wall, chastising him for his attachment to this life, and challenging him to deny that he had come to hope for another, de facto rebellion finds articulate expression, retrospectively justifying his previous life. Having made explicit the link between the leap of faith and the rejection of life, Meursault can no longer contain the rage welling up within him. The only after-life for which he could hope would be "a life where I could remember this one" (STR, 98). No, the chaplain was not his "father: he was with the others." And what is this "truth" he is offering but

a path of illusions built upon renunciation? Meursault will not acquiesce in this life-denying myth. His truth had been of this earth, and it will remain so.

He had lived by the impassioned and transitory values of this life. "I had been right. I was still right" (STR, 98). So what if they were finite? He had not been wrong. He may have failed to reflectively appreciate the life he had lived. He may have let that life slide along, rather than consciously giving shape to it. But he had not betrayed it. If he had lived in a way that involved de facto alienation from social norms, *that* had not been a mistake. "Far from his being deprived of all sensitivity, a profound, because tenacious, passion animate[d] him" (TRN, 1920). He had glimpsed a truth that involved rejection of normalized hypocrisy. "It was but a negative truth—the truth of being and feeling—but one without which no conquest over self or world will ever be possible."

It thus becomes clear what Camus meant when he referred to Meursault as the sole Christ we deserve today. For this sacrificial figure's innocence is born out of social and even metaphysical naïveté, upon which altar he will be crucified. Unlike Jesus, however, who can accept his death in resignation, asking his father to "forgive them for they know not what they do," Meursault rejects such resignation. Acceptance of the unjust suffering of innocents—for Camus, the rock upon which Peter's church is built—can be counterposed to the revolt that bursts forth like a mighty stream, drowning the chaplain in its righteous indignation and passionate reaffirmation. Perhaps it makes sense for one who believes in a salvific afterlife to be so forgiving, but that makes only more poignant the loss of this life for which Meursault can find no redeeming features. Resignation and forgiveness only add insult to injury, compounding injustice with complicity. No, rather than forgiving them, Patrice wants his revolt confirmed in the cries of hatred with which he hopes to be greeted by a crowd of spectators on the day of his execution.

From the death of his mother to his impending execution, passing through his killing of the Arab and society's condemnation of him, *The Stranger* reveals a more sophisticated development of that transition from natural to conscious death that had been the basic structure of *A Happy Death*. What could be more natural for Meursault than the dying of an elderly woman who had lived out her life? Thus his response. But such nonchalance with respect to natural processes leaves us totally prey to chance and to the dissolution of human meanings. Thus the death of the Arab, but one more natural event for Meursault. And yet, it was by his hand that the trigger was pulled, a point of which the authorities make much. Consciousness was a participant in and contributor to this death, even if only by inadvertence. Such will *not* be the case for society. It intends consciously and quite deliberately to kill Meursault for transgressing the moral bounds of its world. For these bounds constitute

society's response to the existential challenge of finitude. However unjust this sentence, the chaplain intercedes on behalf of accepting it as the price that must be paid if belief in the transcendent significance of human life is to be sustained. Patrice rebels so vehemently because death is not an entree into another life but the end of this one, and we should not so easily acquiesce in its realization. Death will come, inevitably, but we need not—must not—assist it. Not by inadvertence and certainly not by conscious decision. As for rational justification of such complicity, that is an evil of another order. We must rather draw forth from this dawning recognition of human finitude a renewed appreciation for what life has to offer. A passionate will "to exhaust the field of the possible" must replace our "longing for immortal heights."

A Cryptomythic Tale

If Meursault is not guilty of murder, nevertheless a human being *is* dead and Meursault *did* pull the trigger. Although not guilty of having *willed* the slaying, he *is* guilty of permitting himself to become an accessory in the destruction of a human life. Actually, his guilt seems to lie precisely in his *not* having willed anything.[6] Lacking lucidity, Camus seems to be suggesting, we are ever in danger of entering into complicity with the forces of destruction. Consider the drama of "The Misunderstanding" or the citizens of Oran at the onset of *The Plague*. Human revolt at this stage of Camus's development primarily consists in the struggle to maintain a lucid awareness of our condition. Meursault at the crucial moment fails to take control of himself, to maintain the necessary human distance from the forces of nature. He succumbs passively to union with nature—at the expense of the human.

This failure is similar in source to the temptation that Camus speaks of in his contemporaneous essay "The Minotaur, or the Stop at Oran."

> The Minotaur is boredom. . . . These are the lands of innocence. But innocence needs sand and stones. And man has forgotten how to live among them. At least it seems so, for he has taken refuge in this extraordinary city where boredom sleeps. Nevertheless, that very confrontation constitutes the value of Oran. The capital of boredom . . . is surrounded by an army in which every stone is a soldier. In the city, and at certain hours . . . what a temptation to identify oneself with those stones, to melt into that burning and impassive universe that defies history and its ferments! That is doubtless futile. But there is in every man a profound instinct which is neither that of destruction nor that of creation. It is merely a matter of resembling nothing (LCE, 130).

The stranger, it might be thought, bespeaks an inner call of our being, a countercultural invitation to return to a precivilized innocence, free of the burdens of individuality and conscience. One might think here of Freud's death instinct, the purported desire to return to our inorganic origins that constituted for Freud such a profound threat to the requirements of civilized living. Freud is, of course, not alone in speculating upon such presocial needs, desires, or longings. Whatever their scientific warrant, the pervasiveness of attention to them suggests that these reflections are giving expression, however inadequate the form, to very significant human concerns. At an archetypal level, Meursault might remind us of Rousseau's noble savage, whose innocence has not yet been sullied by sophistication and social pretention. There is, however, a price to be paid for such natural innocence, of which both the killing and society's response give us a sense.

Two further points about the dramatic significance of this cryptomythic tale need to be noted. First, there seems to be some ambiguity in the novel concerning the positive aspects of Meursault's character. Many have taken him to be bored with, and generally indifferent to, living. Certainly he shows no enthusiasm for all those futures we hold so dear. Similarly for matters of social etiquette. At the same time, he is fascinated by the behavior of the automaton woman—to the extent of trying to follow her when she leaves the restaurant—while he carefully attends to events at the home, at the trial, or, on Sundays, in the street in front of his balcony. Further, he evinces an enthusiasm for swimming, for hopping on the truck to take off for the port with Emmanuel, and, of course, for Marie Cardona. The "normal" reading of his character as indifferent to life may tell us more about the readers than about the person being interpreted. Such a reading of Meursault may be further confirmation of the extent to which we readers predicate the significance of *our* lives on the meaningfulness of belief systems that are being placed in question by him. Thus we would be finding him guilty in a manner similar to that of the jurors.

Whether or not Camus is successful in making this point, however, his intent should not be in doubt. "Meursault is not . . . a derelict for me, but a poor and naked man, in love with the sun which leaves no shadows. Far from his being deprived of all sensitivity, a profound, because tenacious, passion animates him, the passion for the absolute and for truth. *It concerns a truth which remains negative*, the truth of being and feeling, *but one without which no conquest of self and world will ever be possible*" (TRN, 1920, my italics).

The second point concerns the mythic significance of Oran. Given the previous description of the quality of Oranian life, the selection of Oran as the location for the outbreak of plague should not come as a surprise. The citizens of Oran, in their passive innocence, their boredom, their lack of lucidity, succumb to the temptations of habit. They are a sort of collective Meursault

without the inarticulate passion, captives of the forces of nature and habit, waiting for whatever may befall them. The plague, a symbol of the unreasonable in nature that constitutes a permanent threat to the realm of the human, gains supremacy in proportion to the degree to which the inhabitants have abandoned the spirit, with its vigilant lucidity. A failure not unlike that of which Meursault is guilty.[7]

From Rebellion to Conduct

With Meursault confronting death and opening up, "for the first time, to the tender indifference of the world" (STR, 100), Camus has completed his dramatization of the development of the human spirit from complete immersion in the natural/social world to the emergence of the self-conscious and self-possessing individual.[8] What remains is for such an emergent being to find a way to live. What meaning can a Meursault thus come unto himself find in his life? And what positive relations can he establish with his fellows? In this context we can appreciate the evocative explorations of the human condition encountered in *Nuptials*, and then the more argumentative theoretical exposition set forth in *The Myth of Sisyphus*. We would not be misled in viewing these works as the developing expressions of the being that Meursault has become.

I have already delineated the essential parameters of the Camusian vision. As natural animals we are extensions of the natural world with which we instinctively feel at one. But as conscious beings who can reflectively grasp the structure of that world, and of our distinctive place in it, we must recognize that our humanity is built upon the partial separation from nature of the realm of the human. We must, without imperiling our ties to nature, distance ourselves from its random course. And we must to some extent take upon ourselves the responsibility for the life we live. We must come to terms with our past and our future, incorporating into our lives the meaning that emerges from reflective appreciation of our finitude. We do not have unlimited time! Our potentially joyful union with nature will eventually be shattered by death. The "must" here is of course an ethical one. Meursault's rejection of the chaplain's consolations is not essentially negative. "There is a refusal which has nothing in common with renunciation.... If I obstinately refuse all the "later-ons" of the world, it is as much a matter of not renouncing my present riches.... Everything that is proposed to me is an effort to discharge man of the weight of his own life.... Between the horror and the silence, the certitude of a death without hope ... I understand that all my horror of dying comes from my jealousy for living" (*Noces*, LCE, 76).

At this point, Camus explicitly refuses to view the absurd as a justification of resignation—as it had been for Sartre in "The Wall," of which Camus

was quite aware at this time.[9] In response to the chaplain's invitation to resignation, Meursault recapitulates Camus's response before the religious inscriptions in Florence: "'One must,' said the inscription. But no, and my revolt was right. This joy which was in process, indifferent and absorbed like a pilgrim on the earth, I had to follow it step by step. And, for the rest, I said no. I said no with all my strength. . . . I did not see what uselessness took away from my revolt and I know well that it added to it" (*Noces*, LCE, 99). The revolt here articulated still lacks clarity as to what is being rejected—death, or the nihilistic resignation drawn therefrom—as well as a positive direction. Yet it has given forceful expression to the decision to affirm life in its present richness.

The conclusion of *The Stranger* is thus a beginning. Meursault now understands "why [his mother] had pretended to start over." We have come full circle. "Freed of the illusions of another life," our world has been returned to us fresh, inviting, uncertain, awaiting the significances we can give to it. The burdensome metaphysical and social rationalizations that fogged our vision and clogged our senses have been lifted. No wonder that sense of liberating release to which Meursault gives expression in opening up "for the first time, to the tender indifference of the world" (STR, 100).

There can be little doubt that Camus personally felt the oppressive weight of social expectations and conventions, even to the extent of exhibiting traits of which he was not at all proud. The normal and expected, even the admired and rewarded, can often be quite violative of our self-respect and personal integrity. We can both play up to those expectations and at the same time be disgusted by so doing. The struggle to find acceptance, along with the distaste for such a need, can play havoc with a desire to be true to oneself. This tension plays like a basso continuo to the explicit themes of Camus's life and work. Thus Meursault's revolt is not only the metaphysical rejection of social hypocrisy, but also the personal purgation of the temptation to play by the rules—even to be the dandy—and the reaffirmation of the individual's right, experienced by Camus almost as a characterological duty, to bear witness in one's actions to the truth of one's experience.

Meursault's revolt thus consummates a series of rejections:

- Of resignation in the face of death's inevitability.
- Of acceptance of the meaninglessness of a life without transcendence.
- Of any "leap of faith" in an afterlife *at the expense of* the only life we are given with certainty.
- Of the rituals of habit through which one's life is reduced to a meaningless routine—often rationalized in terms of a hoped-for life hereafter.

- Of the oppression of normal social order in which we are expected to be, feel, and behave in accordance with the "rules of the game."

The Stranger thus charts a pathway toward self-conscious affirmation, providing the metaphysical ground from which the positions first struggled with in *Two Sides of the Coin* and *Nuptials* and then reflectively articulated in *The Myth of Sisyphus* could emerge.[10] It has cleared away the theoretical terrain, while existentially instantiating the necessary personal perspective. *The Stranger* is the zero point, comments Camus (TRN, 1924). . . .

Notes

1. All references to the English edition of *The Stranger* are to the excellent translation by Kate Griffith, published by the University Press of America in 1982. This version is far better than the more popular one by Stuart Gilbert.

2. Recall the discussion of Vincent in Chapter 1.

3. Quoting from Camus's essay "Between Yes and No," Barrier comments perceptively, "A philosophical Meursault: 'yes, everything is simple. It is men who complicate things. Let no one tell us stories. Let no one say to us of a man condemned to death: "He is going to pay his debt to Society" but "He is going to have his neck cut."'" Barrier goes on to say, "What the author refuses are the abstract ideas with which one discreetly covers the concrete, palpable horror of the existent fact" (Barrier, 77).

4. We might consider the similar situation confronted by Kaliayev in "The Just," . . . The explicit effort of the police chief, Skouratov, and the Grand Duchess to extract Kaliayev's complicity in their values is an effort to undermine the base of his opposition and thus to destroy his rebellion. The rebel must feel the rightness of his cause. He must experience both indignation and justification. The most effective counter by which society can incapacitate rebellion involves its delegitimation. With respect to an individual insurgent, a potent strategy consists in reducing social protest to the status of a personality disorder, thus inducing guilt. This counter-revolutionary effort is explicitly presented in the dialogue between Nada and The Fisherman in "The State of Siege," while its logic is explored more fully in *The Fall*. That work probes the existential foundation of the personal effort to destroy rebellion's roots in autonomous self-expression by inducing pervasive guilt.

5. "In the last chapter of the book," writes Barrier, "before the arrival of the chaplain, it clearly seems as if the narrator is struggling to reconcile two incompatible attitudes in the face of death, and everything takes place as if he were repeating to himself: 'In a sense it is too horrible to think about. But in another sense, since it must be thought about, let's be reasonable'" (Barrier, 76).

6. While a bit unclear about the meaning of "l'absurde," Mlle. Germaine Brée goes to the heart of the matter when she observes: "The very essence of *l'absurde* in his case is that out of indifference he linked forces with violence and death, not with love and life. . . . He fails to ask any questions and thereby gravely errs. In *L'Étranger* Camus thus suggests that in the face of the absurd no man can afford passively just

to exist. To fail to question the meaning of the spectacle of life is to condemn both ourselves, as individuals, and the whole world to nothingness" (Brée, 117). There is reason to question the use of the word "indifference" here. Furthermore, it is an overstatement to suggest that human beings *must* question the spectacle of life, lest life be rendered meaningless. Many people lead rather normal and not unrewarding lives without engaging in a great deal of philosophical reflection, while objective circumstances seem to have much to say about when and to what extent inquiry is initiated. We are not dealing with an all or nothing here, nor with an intellectualist bias about the importance of reflection. More to the point is the consideration that the significance of an individual life and the degree to which it can be given meaning depend in large part upon one's ability to break through the tedium of encrusted habit. The call for lucidity in the face of death is only an invitation to make the most of that which is given to us.

7. Actually, the initial complicity of Oran's citizens with the rule of plague is not at all unlike the collaboration of the people of Cadiz with *The Plague* in "The State of Siege." In both of these encounters with the plague, however, there are significant differences from the situation of Meursault, and the resolutions differ accordingly. In response to the natural evil in *The Plague* the citizens establish community action teams that take us beyond the essentially individual level of response to the absurd studied in *The Stranger*. In the play, on the other hand, the evil has become social, and the response thus takes us to a more complicated political level in considering the nature of revolt.

8. We might think of *The Stranger* as Camus's literary portrayal in cameo of Hegel's *Phenomenology of the Spirit*.

9. Camus's review of "The Wall" appeared in *Alger Republicain* on March 12, 1939. It criticized Sartre precisely for taking the absurd as a conclusion, not as a starting point (cf. LCE, 203–6).

10. *The Stranger* depicts the process by which an individual may come to consciousness of his condition; *Nuptials* explores this perspective as an attitude. While the world may be the home within whose bosom we are born, *Nuptials* poignantly expresses our emerging realization of the tenuousness of our occupancy. The power of nature, the inexorable flow of time, the experiential distance that inevitably separates human lives from each other, these shatter illusions as to the permanence of our residence. "There are two convictions about which the prose of *Nuptials* winds all of its themes," writes Thomas Hanna.

> The first is that nature or the world is distinct from and foreign to the understanding and desires of man, but is at the same time his home where he is fascinated, surpassed, and finally conquered. This conviction is developed in the Tipasa and Djémila sections. The second conviction is that death is the final and inescapable destiny of all men, and that man must adjust his life and actions to this inescapable destiny. The second conviction is the core of the last two sections entitled *Summer in Algiers* and *The Desert* (Hanna [I], 8).

By dwelling upon these "inescapable facts" of which Meursault had become conscious, *Nuptials* takes in hand "the geography of a certain desert" (*Noces*, 99; LCE, 105), outlining the boundaries of human action. It seems like the stranger reflecting upon his life and finding it good, when Camus writes:

There is a feeling actors have when they know ... they have made their own gestures coincide with those of the ideal character they embody. . . . That was exactly what I felt: I had played my part well. I had performed my task as a man, and the fact that I had known joy for one entire day seemed to me ... the intense fulfillment of a condition which, in certain circumstances, makes it our duty to be happy. Then we are alone again, but satisfied (LCE, 71).

In responding to the priest, Meursault had said that he had no use for, nor could he conceive of, another life unless it was filled with the qualities of this one. In this he was echoing an attitude already expressed in *Two Sides of the Coin* (cf. LCE, 50).

Nuptials depicts the terrain within which the stranger is condemned to live, inviting us to take up residence in the only home that can be truly ours.

"This clearly involves undertaking the survey of a certain desert . . . accessible only to those who can live there in the full anguish of their thirst. . . . Only then is it peopled with the living waters of happiness" (*Noces*, 99–100; LCE, 105, slightly modified).

JACK MURRAY

Closure and Anticlosure in Camus's L'Étranger: Some Ideological Considerations

Le sens du livre tient exactement dans le parallélisme des deux parties.
(*Carnets II*, 30)

On the formal level, the novel, in its very nature, tends toward sprawl, unconnectedness, and even anarchy, and it must therefore transcend such perils if it is to achieve the closure dictated by the canons of classicism or realism. Closure is not simply a formal matter, but because of the necessary logical connectedness that it imposes on all the narrative content of any particular work, it becomes an ideological matter as well. Its principal danger is that it may impose a monological construal or reading of the events recounted, whereas a move away from closure would advance into chaos where no coherent reading would be possible at all. Few works in the modern period illustrate both the formal and ideological dimensions of the problem at issue here better than Albert Camus's *L'Étranger*. While firmly installed within both the realist and classical traditions, the novel nonetheless enacts an extensive debate between two contending sides over closure, underscoring the contention by an elaborate displacement process that must be designated as allegory. Because the crucial matter of the murder dictates that the dialectic set up between either side inevitably becomes trapped in its own illogic, the reader who endeavors to interpret the text finds himself in the position of the author's Sisyphus: just at the point when he feels that

From *Symposium* 46, no. 3 (Fall 1992): 225–40. Copyright © 1992 by the Helen Dwight Reid Educational Foundation.

25

he is approaching some final construal, he must begin the whole interpretive task over again.

At first sight, the work appears totally coherent and harmonious and recalls the compact economy of a Gidean *récit*.[1] Because of this, the seeming randomness and disjointedness of the first part are only a calculated literary illusion. Moreover, its scattered parts quickly join together in a whole after the arrest and during the trial, for it is then that the purpose of their narration becomes clear (see Van den Heuvel 69; Banks 15).[2] On an even more formal level, the text is divided into two fairly even halves with a blank page marked "II" dividing them. Castex demonstrates that the first five of the six chapters of the first part are answered by the five chapters of the second part, the extra sixth chapter actually being a pivot between the two sections (103).[3] Furthermore, the complete antithesis in character of the two parts, if anything, only enhances their clear interconnectedness in a thematic closure (if not a narrative one). Uri Eisenzweig, for example, qualifies the world described in the first five chapters as "Paradise," relativized thus by the irruption of Time after the fatal shot fired in the pivotal chapter six, which converts what has preceded into radical anteriority. The second part becomes that of the Law (of the Father), but a continual mirroring process assures a symmetrical relationship with the first part (71–75 and passim). Carl Viggiani specifies the nature of this relationship when he sees in the second section an ironic recapitulation of everything that has happened in the first part (885).

In this study I shall modify Viggiani's statement by proposing, instead, two contending construals of the same series of narrative elements, Meursault's and the prosecutor's. If the murder is not in doubt, there is a considerable difference of opinion between the two figures over the relevance to it of a series of episodes preceding it: the protagonist's behavior at the mother's funeral and his actions in the days following. Meursault sees no connection whatsoever, whereas the prosecutor most emphatically does (see McCarthy 68). In the latter instance, one may say that the prosecutor imposes radical narrative closure on the elements over against Meursault's position (the "anti-closure" one) that they are unrelated, adventitious, and inconsequential—a position, in short, that leans toward narrative "anarchy."[4] If one adheres to the standard narratological line that the *histoire* or *fable* must consist of a string of events in which each constitutes a transformation that leads causally to the next (Prince 17–18), then only Meursault's involvement with Raymond, the altercation with the Arabs, and the murder itself (with the consequent imprisonment, trial, and death sentence) are connected.[5] By contrast, if one believes that character produces destiny, then recounting episodes in which the protagonist's character is revealed through his behavior has some relevance to the

final outcome (see Rimmon-Kenan 35). Necessarily, a disagreement on these issues has ideological overtones that transcend the purely formal.

A useful context for shedding light on the formal aspect of the debate is Claude Bremond's disagreement with narratologists in the Proppian tradition. His principal charge against them is that they organize the sequence of actions in terms of the end (20), although it might be fairer to speak of the rigidity of the order of the "functions." André Abbou, for example, seems to invoke the Proppian tradition when he uncovers, in *L'Étranger*, three functions reminiscent of the medieval tale: (1) "le mandement et l'avertissement", (2) "la poursuite de la quête et le sacrilège", and (3) "le retour à l'histoire et la transfiguration" (245; see also 247–50). Propp and his followers, in Bremond's view, tend to eliminate all variations or possibility of narrative deviation in favor of an almost mechanical sequence of episodes or events (22). In their place, Bremond proposes a nondetermined series of narrative segments, each one of which has a beginning, middle, and end but at every stage offers a bifurcation where the narrative subject may go one way or another, where things may get better for him or worse, and episodes ensue (32–33 and passim). In short, his perspective follows a given character along from moment to moment in the course of his successive acts without anticipating what their end will be. Bremond adds (92) that, more often than not, the subject is not active but passive before the events in which he is enfolded (he *suffers* them). Obviously, in the case of anything so decisive as a murder, it is crucial to determine whether the accused has simply fallen into it (in a passive way) or has committed it as an inevitable consequence of a depraved or fallen nature that has driven him to it. This is what is at stake in *L'Étranger*.

In the context just cited, the prosecutor's construal might be said to cast Meursault's story in light of the end (the murder), while Meursault follows Bremond's pattern of chance alternatives presenting themselves to him as each somewhat random episode succeeds the next until a sequence is gradually formed that goes from bad to worse. Meursault definitely depicts himself as one who unwittingly undergoes what befalls him, whereas the prosecutor sees him as cynically and criminally active in all the actions and patterns of behavior that he attributes to him. Because Meursault's account comes before the other and is conveyed in the first person, it has a psychological advantage over the other rendering on the reader, for the reader will be inclined to see Meursault's presentation as the correct one and the prosecutor's offering as a distortion.[6] Moreover, the latter must be relayed by Meursault as narrator, and the reader should not be blind to the caricatural way the prosecutor and the other figures in the court are portrayed.[7] Needless to say, the very excess of the prosecutor's version makes Meursault seem moderate and impartial

by comparison (Barrier 72). Such an effect is indispensable if he is to be transformed into victim and martyr in the reader's eyes.

When we take up Meursault's version of what happened,[8] we see that, while it follows the conventional chronological pattern already mentioned, it does so in an often artfully haphazard way.[9] This is but the beginning of the move toward anticlosure. For example, Meursault's account contains many elements that are extraneous to the events leading up to the murder, elements that pertain to the ordinary routines of his everyday life, to background material, etc. The latter have the effect of making the strictly narrative elements (i.e., those events that really do lead up to the murder) appear more relative in importance, if not actually devalued, so that they seem not to be the strongly marked (and transformational) events customary in closely structured narrative. The description of, and insistence on, routine, in particular, produces such an effect. The dominant perspective of routine means that unusual events such as the mother's death become only interruptions in the mechanical repetition of Meursault's life and either constitute unsettling intrusions or else do not have any clear importance at all at the time of their occurrence. In general, all this is consonant with a narrator who suffers events as they come along.

The text, moreover, displays a skillful use of verb tenses at the beginning (and elsewhere in isolated incidences), particularly that of the present tense, which suggests a curious moment of narration. The first paragraph and the first three (or four) sentences of the second one, for example, are oriented toward a present time that makes everything seem to be happening now (see Banks 17). Such a temporal orientation takes advantage of the imperfect or unfinished aspect of the current moment; just as in Bremond's pattern, things may go this way, or that. Gerald Kamber, among others, has noted that the *passé composé*, much used subsequently in the novel, is affected to the extent that it derives its effect from the present cast of Meursault's account established at the outset (389; also Banks 19; Fitch 13; McCarthy 22; Van den Heuvel 69).[10] He adds, moreover, that the tense produces a staccato rhythm that enhances the sense of discontinuity in the narrative line (393). When we see the tenses at work in short declarative sentences reminiscent of the American novel, the effect of disjunction is complete.[11] Through such manipulation of verb tenses, then, chance and randomness establish themselves at the opening of the text and set a kind of pattern in the reader's perception of what follows when, in fact, the text shifts to the more conventional past tenses of narrative.

Another way that the text creates discontinuity is through the fairly constant insertion of sensory or pictorial details—snapshots, one might say— that are like curious instances of Roland Barthes's *effet de réel*. Eisenzweig has insisted on the nonlinear effect of these images, their photographic, or even

instantaneous, aspect in contrast with the homogeneity of the linear account of things that closure will not allow to fall apart into unconnected fragments (13). They are *live*, one might say, but inevitably their effect in a narrative is to produce formal disruptions that constitute a break in the production of meaning (16). In practice, this means that the narrative process itself is constantly distracted by notations that call attention away from it. The result is a further devaluation of the episodes being recounted.

Certainly the most outstanding example of such a procedure is the famous Sunday afternoon Meursault spends in his apartment just wandering around smoking and looking out the window. To the extent that a narrative segment is supposed to advance the action, one may say that this particular one, if anything, is an "anti-event," because it produces nothing at all. As Eisenzweig has put it, causality and even argumentation have no part to play here (17). At best, the passage is structured by the chronological movement of the day, the coming and going of the same characters out in the street, the diagnostic activities associated with different times of the afternoon. Meursault himself ties this interval in with the context of the nonevent when he says (1142): "J'ai pensé que c'était toujours un dimanche de tiré, que maman était maintenant enterrée, que j'allais reprendre mon travail et que, somme toute, il n'y avait rien de changé."[12] Because, strictly defined, narrative cannot exist without transformation, this must be construed as an anti-narrative statement that has an important bearing on the matter of closure.

The explicit mention of the mother's funeral in the text just quoted is a clear signal to the reader to downgrade it in importance as an event. One notes that the account of the funeral, like that of the Sunday afternoon, involves the chronological progression of the day, the dry notation of sights and sense impressions, and the substitution of what might be called self-absorbed ritual for activity producing specific narrative consequences. Similarly, in chapter five we have a chronologically ordered enumeration of supposedly chance events that interrupt an otherwise normal working day for Meursault. One of the events is Raymond's telephone call inviting him to spend the following Sunday (the day of the murder) at the beach as guest of his friend, Masson. Because this is definitely part of the *machine infernale* in which Meursault turns out to be caught, it is hardly unimportant. And yet, it has gained no significance here as Meursault recounts it, and the on-moving present of the moment of narration, in conjunction with the dominance of routine, serves to depreciate it still further.

The key episode of the novel, of course, is the murder itself, which takes place in the sixth and final chapter of Part I. To the extent that Meursault's routine includes going to the beach on Sundays and enjoying himself, the

weekend idyll is preserved. Yet the day is continually interrupted by the unusual or the obstructive. Meursault sleeps late and badly, doesn't have any breakfast, and is uncomfortable in the heat and sun. The Arabs who follow after his group are an ongoing irritant, if not worse, so that he has considerable difficulty in returning to an idyllic perception of the day. The bright light and heat, a heavy meal with wine, the trouble the Arabs bring with them lead him to seek relief and escape from the oppression.

During the climactic scene when Meursault shoots the Arab, the narration insists on the kind of bifurcation of which Bremond speaks, thus enhancing the view that the murder is a product of pure contingency and could easily not have happened at all (see Sartre 106). Twice Meursault describes himself as having reflected at the time that he could have fired or not fired the revolver (1166), simply turned around and not walked up to the spring where the Arab was (1167–68). Once he had taken the crucial extra step toward it, he saw that such a move was stupid (1168) and was at the root of all that happened subsequently. Here is where Viggiani sees the intervention of destiny in Meursault's story (888), for, at the moment when he hears the detonation of the gun, he says: "c'est là, dans le bruit à la fois sec et assourdissant, que tout a commencé" (1168). It would be possible to see, in this presentation of the encounter between contingency and fate, an effort to downgrade the importance of will or motivation (if only that of self-defense). But one is more reminded simply of Bremond's observation that the narrative agent is more often a patient, simply enduring what befalls him.

What is easily forgotten is that a crucial element motivating the narrative (or antinarrative) structure of Meursault's account in Part I is the need to put the reader on his guard against the prosecutor's "distorted" account of the events that will be presented during the trial in Part II (see Castex 81). Put another way, where Meursault is concerned, the first account in the text seeks to "légitimer ses conduites" (Goldschläger-Lemaire 185), or, as Gerald Kamber puts it, advance an "instruction judiciaire" (388). It is for this reason that the text begins with the mother's funeral, even though Meursault's way of representing it impresses on the reader its lack of any bearing upon the murder. What he offers, then, is a rebuttal before the charge. At the same time, his account provides details that discount or contradict the accusations or interpretations that the prosecutor will make. One is almost tempted to see a self-serving purpose in this, except for the fact that Meursault is so candid that he provides details which, had his antagonist known them, would have damned him further. Establishing himself as a totally outspoken and selfless character, Meursault offers exonerating details about himself that must be exploited by the reader, who will likely be inclined to see the protagonist as victim, if not martyr.

To summarize Meursault's version of the story, one might argue that it is presented according to an essentially cyclical view of life based on the alternating routines of work and leisure, on the passage of the day or week. Its temporal orientation tends to be in the present moment; his version is prospective, one might say, rather than retrospective, let alone reflective. In this respect, Meursault keeps finding himself in new Bremondian bifurcations, but he tends not to make too much of the alternatives they propose, because his awareness of contingency is related to his cyclical view of time (as opposed to destiny). Hence, he admits to Marie that, if it had been another woman instead of her, he would probably have accepted to marry her as well (1156), and, in his outburst against the chaplain at the end, he says that he could always have lived another way than the way he had, done this rather than that, etc. (1210). In the contention with the prosecutor over the meaning of established facts, then, it will turn out that what is at stake is not cavil over their meaning but something of a far deeper nature. Meursault himself is proposing a construal of his past experiences that avoids the threat of closure at almost every turn ("almost" because of the irreversible consequences of the murder).

Turning to the prosecutor's version of Meursault's story, it is obvious that he is working from a prepared scenario whose closure becomes clear as he proceeds with his examination of the witnesses. Here we have a striking instance of how the judiciary's way of functioning is totally determined by the written, as Eisenzweig's general argument would have it: the (guilty) subject is created by a text that one assumes the prosecution has culled from a vast pile of transcripts, notes, and affidavits, to say nothing of a whole tradition of comparing individual behavior with previous example. The witnesses summoned to the courtroom must either confirm the scenario or suffer ridicule, or worse, for their failure to assent. In short, the prosecutor wants only to convey a hermeneutic view of all the episodes now familiar to the reader by showing that Meursault killed the Arab because of his fundamentally criminal nature (he is a "monstre moral" [1193]). This is the closed field of meaning (the closure) that structures the prosecutor's account, and he has only to fit the narrative or descriptive fragments offered by the witnesses into this scheme, so that Meursault's taking up an adulterous relationship the very next day after the funeral and his subsequent complicity with Raymond in the "squalid" episode of the mistress, might be construed as leading inevitably to the murder. In short, between the funeral and the murder there is "une relation profonde, pathétique, essentielle."

In the confrontation of anticlosure and closure, one might say that, against the more disjunctive account analyzed earlier, we have the prosecutor's overdetermined rendition. Not only does Meursault's monstrously criminal nature dictate that every episode, however trivial it may seem, participate

in the production of the final outcome, the murder; there also must be a connection between what the prosecutor describes as Meursault's moral murder
of his mother and the upcoming trial of a parricide, so that, in the prosecutor's hyperbolic reasoning, the first crime produces the second. There is no
place in his version for the kind of chance action or the prospective outlook
that Bremond's view of narrative invites. This is especially brought out by his
sarcastic reaction to the way Raymond keeps attributing everything to chance
in his responses. "Le procureur a rétorqué que le hasard avait déjà beaucoup
de méfaits sur la conscience dans cette histoire" (1193). Instead, the prosecutor's vision of what has transpired illustrates the anti-Bremondian view of a
story as a rigidly constructed narrative determined by its end. Hence, unlike
Meursault's prospective view of things happening in a purely contingent way
within a cyclically ordered existence, the prosecutor's outlook is retrospective,
deterministic, and, as noted, overdetermined. One might well attribute his
interpretation to the requirements of the antagonistic nature of the trial as a
confrontation, but he is also moved by the extreme moral indignation of the
ideologue that, in turn, opens up the novel to the ideological debate that is
its principal effect.[13] Through all of this, episodes that had few connections,
and often little value or importance, in Meursault's account have now been
subordinated to a hermeneutic that unites them all in function and value.

Since the hermeneutic is essentially an ideological construal of the same
set of events, episodes, and behavioral patterns that have already been presented in the text from a conflicting perspective, any analysis of the debate
must address the ideological implications of the disjunctive nature of the one
account and the extreme closure characteristic of the other.[14] The implicit
problematic at stake here has been admirably investigated by Leo Bersani in
his essay, "Le réalisme et la peur du désir." Bersani attributes to nineteenth-
century realism a strong tendency toward closure that serves as both a formal and implicitly ideological response to the potential anarchy of narrative
sequence always threatening the novel and a parallel socio-historical trend
toward anarchy in a more political sense, to say nothing of unintelligible social
and political fragmentation. In this context, a reliance on closure, as on other
formal restrictions (matching what was happening in French literature in the
seventeenth century when there were similar fears of social chaos), expresses
an authoritarian impulse that corresponds to efforts to preserve established
social institutions against the perceived threat of formal lawlessness and dissolution (57).

L'Étranger shows how the incompatibility between closure and formal
laxity may become a displaced contention between conservative and insur-
rectionary forces. It even conveys the bone of the contention as Bersani perceives it: over individual desire in its conflict with René Girard's "inauthentic

community of desire," the latter being one where people merely desire what they think all others want (58). Not only does Meursault's spontaneous pursuit of his own desires, to say nothing of his fairly systematic nonconformity, threaten the society surrounding him, but it also requires the sheen of intelligibility provided by the prosecutor's overdetermined characterization of him, framed within a narrative dominated by extreme closure. In Bersani's view, desire cannot be contained by the strictures of realist narrative, with its demand for fast-paced consecutiveness and formal coherence, but constantly threatens it with disjunction and formal disintegration (65). In the realist narrative, a hero borne along by desire necessarily becomes a social rebel whom society will inevitably subject to a "ritual of expulsion," because he is by his nature an intruder or stranger in the world represented in the text (66–67). Certainly, Meursault answers such a description; and it is certain, too, that we are dealing here with a Romantic narrative paradigm, one that numerous critics have uncovered in Camus's hero.[15] At any rate, on the formal level, although it is inexact to call the prosecutor's characterization of him "realistic," it is accurate to say that Meursault's disjunctive account of his own actions imperils the coherence and intelligibility that Bersani sees as indispensable to realism.

In other words, a problem arises because realism, like classicism, requires fairly strict narrative logic to satisfy the demands of rational plausibility. In his article "Camus's Stranger Retried," Girard shows how much the novel fails the test, in this domain. The principal stumbling block, as he sees it, is the idea of an "innocent murder," a feature that produces a "logical flaw" in the very narrative structure of the novel itself (523). What the text ends up showing is that "the hero is sentenced to die not for the crime of which he is accused and which he has really committed, but for his innocence, which this crime has not tarnished and which should remain obvious to all people at all times, as if it were the attribute of a divinity" (523–24). It is only fair, however, to recall that, as Camus has ironically stated it, the prosecutor's chief argument is similarly flawed: "tout homme qui ne pleure pas à l'enterrement de sa mère risque d'être condamné à mort" (1928), a position that also sentences Meursault for something else than the actual crime. In either case, the illogic of the basic argument becomes a stumbling block for any effort at finding a totally comprehensive explanation or interpretation, so that one is required to begin all over again. Typically, the murder itself keeps popping out of the closet where it has been vainly relegated, and it must once more be taken into account.

The text itself encourages such moves toward elucidation, and Girard's own statement implies that this is accomplished by the passage from the realist level to the allegorical. In the novel, such a change of register is brought about by the prosecutor himself, who transforms Meursault, his life, and his

acts into an allegorical text through the application of his rigid hermeneutic. Any hermeneutic, like all other types of interpretive discourse, has been allied with allegory by Northrop Frye (89).[16] In this context, Bersani has noted the frequent allegorization of the individual in highly composed formal genres such as classicism or realism (53), although it might be better to temper this with Frye's insistence that, when allegorization occurs, it is often because the novel has lapsed into romance and the characters have been turned into archetypes (304). Such a move constitutes a displacement process that recalls Freud's shift of the "psychic accent" (336, 338) wherein the true meaning becomes centered elsewhere than on the surface level of the text, as in Part I of *L'Étranger*. Certain seemingly trivial details, in the process, attain the unexpected intensity of major ideas, despite their initial feeble potential (Freud 246). In this way a deflection of thought takes place. Such an allegorization process seems indispensable, if there is to be a riposte to the prosecution's demonization of what is otherwise presented as an absolutely humdrum life. The first part, read in and for itself, will not suffice, nor will the reader's own corrective musings as he peruses the excessive discourse of Part II with his own impressions in mind of what has gone before. The prosecutor's allegorization, in other words, necessitates a counter-allegorization.

Two specific details within the text suggest how such a process takes place: the *juge d'instruction* calling Meursault "monsieur l'Antéchrist" (1176), and the prosecutor accusing him of being morally accountable for the parricide the same court is about to judge. Clearly, there is a tie between the illogic of the latter's courtroom depiction of the protagonist and a parallel allegorization of him. Identification as the antichrist will affect the more general matter of Meursault's anomalous position within society and the more specific one of his position in respect to Christ.[17] Philip Thody notes how Camus, pressed by literary journalists, contributed considerably to the promotion of his protagonist as such an archetypal figure (67). In this respect, an important paratextual element—namely, Camus's preface of 1955 for the American school edition of *L'Étranger*—is the statement that Meursault is "le seul Christ que nous méritons" (1929). Formally, then, allegorization involves a hyperbolization, as well as symbolization, of the basic qualities of the individual represented.

The problem now is to place Meursault-as-Christ within the framework of the ideological contention at work in the novel. It is not difficult to enumerate a few qualities that Meursault has in common with Christ: his simplicity, his nonjudgmental openness to others, particularly those rejected by society (e.g., Raymond). He even possesses the same unresisting tendency to let matters take their course, which motivates that part of Christ's story leading to the Passion; and his execution has certain parallels with the Crucifixion

(see Banks 56). As far as the narrative is concerned, the failure of Jesus's own people to recognize him as Christ or the Messiah is an important ingredient in his martyrdom. Therefore, to the extent that the reader is invited to see an intertextual tie between the stories of Meursault and Jesus, he will necessarily consider him a martyr and even a Christ who also is not recognized. (The judge calling him antichrist thus betokens misrecognition.)

Another intertextual tie that the mention of Christ ensures is to Dostoyevsky's "Grand Inquisitor" in *The Brothers Karamazov*. Although the Christ of Dostoyevsky's account is simply chased away rather than sacrificed, his silence and his refusal to defend himself during the Inquisitor's harangue is repeated in Meursault's like behavior during his many interrogations. More important, however, is the threat represented by the "freedom" Dostoyevsky's Christ-figure brings to the world, a freedom the old Inquisitor believes is more than mankind can bear. Instead, mankind needs servitude to authority. Clearly, Dostoyevsky's manipulation of the Christ story (in what must be called an allegorical fantasy) epitomizes Bersani's perception of a confrontation between authoritarianism and alleged anarchy. When we turn back to Meursault, he incorporates Christ's insurrectional kind of freedom as well, if we recall Christ's free-wheeling attitude toward the Law and even established social custom. There is something almost systematic about Meursault's defection from standard institutions and conventions, often brought out in his confrontations with figures standing as spokesmen for them: not only the director of the old people's home or the various magistrates but even his employer, who expects his offer of a better job in Paris to elicit the ambition expected of anyone in contemporary society. To these may be added Meursault's nonconformist attitudes toward love, marriage, to say nothing of a mother's death. Through a process of intertextuality, Dostoyevsky's model allows a pattern to emerge in which an ensemble of attitudes and behavioral traits take on a kind of ideological affirmation through the identification with Christ. The pattern thus assures that the reader will understand the deeper point at issue in the text in the framework of a well-established intellectual context of Western literature and thus be more aware of Meursault's positive ideological resonance.

To understand, however, how such an allegorization eludes any final interpretation, we must again confront the same recurrent (and always troublesome) paradox: the event from which Meursault's Christ-like martyrdom emerges is his quite un-Christ-like killing of the Arab. Through the displacement process of allegory, this violent act tends to become merely an absurd act inaccessible to explanation and thus transformed into a simple narratological given without any importance in its own right (Van den Heuvel 53–54). We are left with Girard's "innocent murder." Such a downgrading of what, in

a more purely realist rendering, would be the key episode in the account is effected by the sanctification of the protagonist through the Christ context (with the parallel villainizing of his adversary, the prosecutor). Lost in such sleight-of-hand, in addition to the murder itself, is the latent issue of the ethnic identity of the victim, particularly important in the Algerian setting where the land is a former French colony and Meursault a potential symbol of the colonizers.[18]

Instead, the Arab, at best, and again through allegorization, is simply transformed into the embodiment of that force which, like other disagreeable contingencies in the course of the protagonist's existence, serves as an obstacle to his ongoing effort to live entirely on the level of desire. Ironically, one could point out that the murder both confirms the perils of the kind of anarchy brought on by desire and illustrates the danger posed by a man so candid about what does or does not matter (according to a nonconformist value system founded on desire). But the irresistible appeal of Camus's antihero, impervious to the detestable nature of his act, creates a situation of undecidability that sends the reader off again on the enterprise of establishing some final interpretation of the text that will exonerate Meursault (or at least the author for his choice of an Arab as victim; see McCarthy 71–72).

The problem disclosed here may be illustrated by the increasingly difficult reception L'Étranger has undergone since 1960, the year of the author's death. The resistance in France, particularly by those on the left, to the Algerian War and their consequent sympathy for the rebelling Arab population inspired disgust with the way the murder of the Arab is so quickly lost sight of in the novel, and it opened the way toward construing Camus as a racist. (This was abetted, of course, by the author's anomalous position during the late 1950s on the deteriorating political situation in his homeland, a position that satisfied no one.) More considered statements, however harsh, such as those by Conor Cruise O'Brien (1970) and, more recently, John Erickson (1988), have identified a colonial unconscious in Camus that formed natural limits to what he could believe or feel about Algeria and Arabs or even what he could write in his works. However this may be, the scandal of the murder itself has now become compounded by the shock produced by the racial identity of the Arab victim, to say nothing of the tendentious nature of his description in the novel. Within the Camus field itself, we have a conflict between Philip Thody's "racialist" reading of the novel (1979) and Dorothy Bryson's riposte (1988) in which, in her effort to free Camus of the charge of racism, she is forced to uncover a deeply recessed intention on the author's part within the novel to condemn his hero for his inhumanity. While both contenders in this debate tend to institutionalize Camus as an Author who is morally responsible for the content of his work, whether racist or antiracist,

they nonetheless emphasize (even vehemently) the ideological contention at work in the text.

They do so by responding to the formal patterns that I have examined in the present study. Thody, for example, speaks of "a narrative in which ... the completely innocent experience of events in the first half of the novel is interpreted as overwhelming evidence of guilt in the second" (64). Bryson elaborates a "chiasmic pattern" where "initially nonspecific guilt in the eyes of the reader ... is transformed into the necessary innocence of Absurd Man even as a contrary charge is being effected in terms of the bourgeois society of the text" (272). She even mentions the "spuriously naive parataxis" of the first part of the text that is "indispensable to the creation of the scandal that is Meursault" and its contrast with the restored causality of Part II where a "malign motivation" is attributed to him "on the essentialist level" (273). She places the contrast between Meursault's disjunctive account and the prosecutor's overdetermined one in the context of E. M. Forster's distinction between "story" and "plot." Both critics recognize the ideological inflation that the protagonist undergoes through the kind of allegorization process I have already described, Bryson underscoring the intertextual ties with Christ (227n). In short, the very important issue of the ideological resonance in the choice of an Arab victim in the novel is replayed in the same formal structure exploited by earlier readers for the uncovering of quite different readings and issues.

In conclusion, Camus's *L'Étranger* is an outstanding example of how the potential for formal anarchy residing in the novel as a genre relates to the far deeper ideological issues that Leo Bersani has brought to light. Closure invites anticlosure in a kind of dialectical face-off. In the process, the prosecutor's hyperbolically structured construal of Meursault's acts becomes a negative ideological pole against which Meursault's own disjunctive account becomes the positive one. The hyperbolization, in turn, signals a shift from the realistic to the allegorical plane whereby the sense of ideological contention becomes intensified and an interpretive effort is required on the reader's part. Because of the basic illogic that hyperbolization tends to foster, Camus's text does not produce a clear and single meaning but, instead, continues to demand new attempts at exegesis particularly because of the obstacle of undecidability posed by the murder. Each effort, one suspects, will somehow remain unsatisfactory. I hope to have shown that such a result is to be derived from the potential incoherence that always threatens the novel as a form and prevents it from totally becoming one with the effort toward formal coherence and monological meaning that closure implies. In this context, Meursault's account of his own acts, to say nothing of his ideological attitude toward them (summarized in his outburst at the chaplain at the end of the novel), converts the text into one that, in continuing to question its own

formal structure, becomes the vehicle for discussing any number of the major debates of modern times.

NOTES

1. While pointing out this parallel, Gerald V. Banks also insists on the differences between Camus's handling of the form and Gide (13–14). In this article I shall hold to the working premise that *L'Étranger* is a *novel*, although it is only right to point out that there has been much debate about its exact genre, let alone its proper conformity to the genre chosen (see Barrier 16).

2. Pierre-Georges Castex, who uses the author approach to the novel, suggests a tantalizing course that the genesis of the novel may have taken—namely, Camus's having to link together three quite disparate and plainly unrelated bits of narrative: a character condemned to die who refuses all consolation; a mother's funeral; a tough man and his fight with his mistress's brother (17–26). From this angle, Camus may well have found himself in the typical creative dilemma faced by any writer who must assemble a coherent and unified body out of such *disjecta membra*—in other words, attain closure. Alain Costes looks on the fragments as literary versions of obsessive phantasms that occur throughout Camus's earliest writings (57–62).

3. Brian T. Fitch stresses the stylistic difference between chapter six and the chapters that have gone before, particularly the intrusion of highly metaphorical language (42–44).

4. The formal issue is also construed by some commentators in the framework of parataxis versus syntaxis, Meursault's account being highly paratactic. See Goldschläger and Lemaire, 186. As for the ideological side, Sartre laid down the opposition between the two construals as "le flux quotidien et amorphe de la réalité vécue" against "la recomposition édifiante de cette réalité par la raison humaine et le discours." The reader will consider the flux so convincing that he will be unable to recognize it in its transposed form at the trial where it has been fed through prefabricated verbal structures (110–11).

5. Gerald V. Banks divides the sequence involving Raymond into eight stages, each one of which accelerates and increases Meursault's active involvement in his neighbor's plot (49).

6. Eisenzweig puts this the other way around: the falsity of the prosecutor's account, to the extent that it has a specular relationship with the other account (i.e., as a form of *mise-en-abyme*), necessarily reflects on the status of the first one—makes it "true" (7). Oddly, such a perception of Meursault does little to make him more sympathetic to the reader: he tends to remain too much an unknown quantity (see Fitch 36).

7. This detail has been noted by many critics. Sartre himself pointed out the secret humor of the novel and suggested similarities with the *conte philosophique* (116). See also Banks 55; Barrier 69–70, McCarthy 71. Fitch develops Sartre's suggestion even further, seeing in Meursault's focalization of the trial a calculated and Candide-like innocence that transforms the whole judicial procedure into a satire on social structures (60, 62–64).

8. A considerable amount of ingenious discussion has endeavored to cast his version (which takes up the first part of the novel) as a *journal intime*. Such an interpretation has had to concentrate on the play of temporal references and verb

tenses in the individual chapters, because there are no conventional textual markers indicating the form (e.g., dates at the head of each textual division, etc.). I agree with Maurice-Georges Barrier (27–28) that such efforts are useless and that we are dealing with a stylistic or mere literary procedure enabling the reader to experience the events of Meursault's life as he lives them. Patrick McCarthy, of course, finds an unexpected lode, when he suggests that Meursault's account, to the extent that it borrows from the *journal intime*, parodies, and thereby criticizes, the form itself, one highly favored by other authors who had gone before Camus at the prestigious house of Gallimard, publisher of *L'Étranger* (26, 99).

9. Renée Balibar, for example, cites the temporal incoherence of the third paragraph of the first chapter of the novel (113). To this must be added Barrier's notation of the way each of the first five chapters begins in the morning with awakening or with Meursault at work, and ends with evening (92).

10. Obviously, the topic of the *passé composé* as used in *L'Étranger* has been exhaustively studied. Interesting analyses include Barrier (16–19, 27n), Jere Tarle, and Renée Balibar.

11. Sartre was the first of many commentators to see a tie between Camus's style in *L'Étranger* and the American novel, a tie underscored by the author's skillful use of the *passé composé* (p. 117).

12. Significantly, Sartre identifies this statement as the reader's first encounter with the Absurd in the novel (104).

13. According to Pierre V. Zima, using at once a narratological and ideological framework, the prosecutor refuses to consider Meursault a nonsubject without any narrative program but, to the contrary, a responsible subject who confirms Althusser's principle that "l'idéologie interpelle les individus en sujets." This explains his use of a dualist scheme (characterized by a premeditated teleology based on "evil" as opposed to Christian "good" [94]) in which to place the events, actions, and narrative sequences concerning Meursault-as-subject.

14. I am dealing with the ideological dialectic at work *within* the text. Therefore, I will not take up the basically extrinsic matter of Meursault as the "absurd hero," living a life according to a prior realization of the Absurd, matters that relate *L'Étranger* back to *Le Mythe de Sisyphe*, an interpretive trend set by Sartre's famous explication of the novel. It should be pointed out, however, that McCarthy's following comment on the Absurd has a bearing on the matter of randomness versus causality (84): "Since there is no causality, experiences must be listed rather than rearranged into an order." Zima adds that the devaluation of all elements in the subject's life leads to a radical critique of all ideological discourse (91).

15. Some critics are quite specific. Castex, for example, sees a parallel between Meursault's waiting for death and Stendhal's highly Romantic rendition of the same scene for his hero Julien Sorel (43). Others stress more general patterns. Fitch, for instance, speaks of the Romantic conflict between society and the individual to be seen in the novel (56), whereas Eisenzweig relates to a Romantic attitude— Meursault's perception of contingency or inconsequentiality in matters in which others see profound significance (132–33). Girard develops the Romantic ties at greatest length (even discounting the connection with the satirical *conte philosophique* altogether): Chatterton, in particular, but also the Romantic side of Dostoyevsky (526–27) and Kierkegaard (528).

16. Eisenzweig quotes Harald Weinrich's comment (in his work *Tempus*) that, in their nature, the proceedings of a trial inevitably become commentary about what

has already happened, so that whatever narrative elements they contain are subordinate to that (142n).

17. Philippe Hainon has examined the question of the use of familiar history or legend to frame the main narrative in a realist work, thus contributing to its direction and overall meaning (136–37). My contention would be that such a procedure could also help transform it into allegory.

18. McCarthy has bravely taken this delicate matter up and says that "it is hard to imagine that the author [of important newspaper articles on the plight of the Arabs] could have chosen to write a novel where an Arab is murdered, without brooding on his choice of a victim" (11). He develops this issue at some length (55–62), adding that, at any rate, the great success of the novel was at the expense of the colonial issue, for Meursault was transformed into "a universal figure rather than a pied-noir" (97).

Works Cited

Abbou, André. "Le Quotidien et le Sacré: introduction à une nouvelle lecture de *L'Étranger*." In Raymond Gay-Crosier, Jacqueline Lévi-Valensi, eds., *Albert Camus: oeuvre fermée, oeuvre ouverte?* Actes du Colloque du Centre Culturel International de Cerisy-la-Salle. *Cahiers Albert Camus 5*. Paris: Gallimard, 1985. 231–65.

Balibar, Renée. "Le passé composé fictif dans *L'Étranger* d'Albert Camus." *Littérature* 7 (1974): 102–19.

Banks, Gerald V. *Camus: L'Étranger*. London: Edward Arnold Ltd., 1976.

Barrier, Maurice-Georges. *L'Art du Récit dans L'Étranger d'Albert Camus*. Paris: Nizet, 1962.

Bersani, Leo. "Le réalisme et la peur du désir." In Roland Barthes, Leo Bersani, Philippe Hamon, Michel Riffaterre, Ian Watt, *Littérature et réalité*. Paris: Seuil, 1982.

Bremond, Claude. *Logique du récit*. Paris: Seuil, 1973.

Bryson, Dorothy. "Plot and Counter-Plot in *L'Étranger*." *Forum for Modern Language Studies* 24(3): 272–79.

Camus, Albert. *Théâtre, récits, nouvelles*. Paris: Gallimard, 1962.

Castex, Pierre-Georges. *Albert Camus et «L'Étranger»*. Paris: José Corti, 1965.

Costes, Alain. *Albert Camus ou la parole manquante*. Paris: Payot, 1973.

Dostoyevsky, Fyodor. *The Brothers Karamazov*. Trans. Constance Garnett. New York: Random House, 1950.

Eisezweig, Uri. *Les Jeux de l'écriture dans L'Étranger de Camus*. Paris: Lettres Modernes, 1983.

Erickson, John. "Albert Camus and North Africa: A Discourse of Exteriority." In Bettina L. Knapp, ed., *Critical Essays on Albert Camus*. Boston: G. K. Hall, 1988. 73–88.

Fitch, Brian T. *Narrateur et narration dans L'Étranger d'Albert Camus: Analyse d'un fait littéraire*. 2nd edition. Paris: Lettres Modernes, 1968.

Freud, Sigmund. *The Basic Writings*. New York: Random House, 1938.

Frye, Northrop. *Anatomy of Criticism*. Princeton, N.J.: Princeton UP, 1971.

Girard, René. "Camus's Stranger Retried." *Publications of the Modern Language Association* 79(4): 519–33.

Goldschläger, Alain and Jacques Lemaire. "Technique narrative parataxique et psychologie des personnages dans *L'Étranger* d'Albert Camus." *Neophilologus* 61 (1977): 185–93.

Hamon, Philippe. *Introduction à l'analyse du descriptif*. Paris: Hachette, 1981.

Kamber, Gerald. "Diction et contradiction dans un texte de *L'Étranger*." *Neophilologus* 55 (1971): 387–99.

McCarthy, Patrick. *Albert Camus: The Stranger*. Cambridge: Cambridge UP, 1988.

O'Brien, Conor Cruise. *Camus*. London: Fontana/Collins, 1970.

Prince, Gerald. *A Grammar of Stories*. The Hague: Mouton, 1973.

Rimmon-Kenan, Shlomith. *Narrative Fiction: Contemporary Poetics*. London: Methuen, 1983.

Sartre, Jean-Paul. *Situations I*. Paris: Gallimard: 1947.

Tarle, Jere. "Sur l'emploi du passé composé dans *L'Étranger* d'Albert Camus: De la grammaire à l'écriture et au style." *Studia Romanica et Anglica Zagrebiensia*, 25–26 (1968): 87–101.

Van den Heuvel, Pierre. "Parole, mot et silence: Les avatars de l'énonciation dans *L'Étranger* d'Albert Camus." *La Revue des Lettres Modernes* 632–36 (1982): 53–88.

Viggiani, Carl. "Camus's *L'Étranger*." *Publication of the Modern Language Association* 71 (5): 865–87.

Zima, Pierre V. "Indifférence et structures narratives dans *L'Étranger*." In Paul-F. Smets, ed. *Albert Camus*. Bruxelles: Éditions de l'Université de Bruxelles, 1985. 88–98.

LARRY W. RIGGS AND
PAULA WILLOQUET-MARICONDI

Colonialism, Enlightenment, Castration: Writing, Narration, and Legibility in L'Étranger

Camus' *L'Étranger* (1942) has been examined from many critical points of view. In some ways, the most interesting interpretations are those that can be broadly characterized as psychoanalytic. These usually focus on the issues of separation, parricide, and guilt in the novel. What is proposed here is an approach that goes beyond these analyses by combining the issue of what might be called "narratability" with some psychoanalytic insights, focusing first on the key incident in Meursault's story when he involves himself in *writing*. The major "Acts" of Meursault's tragedy are all defined by *writing*: the telegram announcing his mother's death, the letter he writes for Raymond, Marie's letter to him in prison, and the reporters' notes during the trial.

Our analysis also enables us to link another of the novel's underlying themes—fragmentation and colonization of the environment—with our examination of Meursault's movement toward narratability and condemnation. The unbearable intensity of the sun throughout the novel is a token of this fragmentation. *L'Étranger* links writing, judgment, and colonization with fragmentation of the natural environment. The evocation of the funeral establishes this link: Meursault describes the hearse carrying his mother's body as resembling "un plumier" 'an inkwell' (25); he sees the other people at the wake as judges; the European-style ceremonial dress of the participants in

From *Studies in Twentieth Century Literature* 16, no. 2 (Summer 1992): 265–288. © 1992 by *Studies in Twentieth Century Literature*.

the funeral put them at odds with the desert setting.[1] Colonial culture places persons in conflict with their environment.

The world wherein the story unfolds is obviously a colonial one. Raymond Sintès' relationship with his Arab mistress is a small-scale reproduction of colonial Algeria, as is, perhaps, old Salamano's relationship with his dog. It is also, then, both a major literal cause of Meursault's fate and a symbol for the entire complex of "causes" at work in Algeria. As Jean Gassin has it: "Dans *L'Étranger*, les rapports vrais entre Français et Arabes sont exactement dépeints. . . ." 'In *L'Étranger*, the true relations between French and Arabs are accurately portrayed' ("Camus Raciste?" 278). Meursault's story, which begins in earnest with the letter he writes for Raymond to the latter's mistress, recounts his recruitment as both a subject and an object of colonization. Indeed, it seals his conscription into the world of subject/object relations in general. Meursault becomes a self capable of narration as he discovers and participates in power as the principle of relationships in this modern, colonial world. Camus makes clear, in *L'Étranger*, the way in which inquiry and explanation, whose original purpose was to neutralize the irresistible power of fate, have become modern equivalents of fate. Narrative is the representation of time and character in terms of causality. As an object of judgment and as a character in a novel, Meursault will be the creature of such representation.

To become capable of narrating is both to become a colonist and to be colonized. It requires a subject/object relationship *within* the self. Becoming a subject capable of narrating one's life is also becoming an individual who behaves and understands in ways that lend themselves to being *read*. Meursault will wind up as the criminal whose act legitimates the administrative and judicial institutions that rule Algeria and condemn him.

Creating conflict and recruiting individuals into "historical" conflicts are keys to social, cultural, and political differentiation and organization. Meursault's story is, from the beginning, one of self-awareness arising from fragmentation, conflict, and guilt. The death of Meursault's mother is followed immediately by an incident in which he experiences the crushing power of the sun. His drowsiness on the way to and during the funeral is largely an effect of the sun's overwhelming strength. Throughout the story, the sun is associated with oppressive weight and with cutting instruments (Andrianne 167–69). It symbolizes both illumination and reduction, or the essence of modern Western "knowledge" (Hall 37).

To structure nature into a hierarchy of literal and symbolic functions is to organize and hierarchize persons, activities, beliefs, and knowledge. The initial fragmentation of nature into separate entities with separate symbolic meanings inaugurates this process. René Andrianne emphasizes that "sur la nature, l'action du soleil n'est pas moins oppressante que sur les hommes" 'the

sun's effects are no less oppressive on nature than on men' (166–67). The "cosmic parents"—sun and sea—are sundered, leaving man in an inadvertently self-imposed exile and inaugurating an endless, self-defeating effort to return to the "source."

The creation and perpetuation of power is the purpose which this process is designed to accomplish, and power over nature is a disposition of the real and symbolic environments that is convenient to the powerful (Lewis 69). Power over the environment is also fundamentally a function of what is suppressed. Creation of a fragmented world depends on the primordial suppression of unity. Understanding, the assignment of meaning, depends on fragmenting the world—tearing it apart—in order to reconstitute it with culturally, ideologically, defined linkages. As Julia Kristeva has it, interpretation—the assignment of meaning—is always an act of violence (Gallop 27). Unfortunately, as Edward T. Hall puts it, our civilization has emphasized fragmentation and analysis at the expense of our brain's integrative functions (9).

Meursault inscribes himself within a course of events and a narrative—as well as within a colonized world—by serving as a conduit for *another's* desire and hatred. His "autonomy" and responsibility are derivative. He is colonized as he takes his position among the colonizers. The writing is the sign of initiation into the symbolic order, the order defined by another's disposition of symbols and, consequently, of a fragmented world's elements. He becomes the instrument that reproduces a separation of which he is and will be the victim. He is colonized by colonialism, and by the symbolic disposition of the world inherent in French culture in Algeria, as he allows a particular colonialist to make use of his skill with language. The violent, alienated style of Raymond's relations with his mistress replaces definitively the unity of mother and child, of person and environment.

Writing As *Con-scription*: Initiation, Individuation, Castration

There are a number of ways in which Meursault's composition of the letter for Raymond Sintès connects with contemporary literary and psychoanalytic theories about language and, particularly, about writing. Meursault inadvertently takes his place—literally *inscribes* himself—in a conflictual drama (which thereby becomes *his* drama) when he associates himself with Raymond in the latter's dispute with his Arab mistress. At the trial, the prosecutor speaks of the letter as being "à l'origine du drame" 'at the origin of the drama' (146). It is out of this conflict that the narrative of Meursault's "fate" develops. The writing of the letter prefigures both Meursault's (equally inadvertent) later taking up of the gun with which he will kill an Arab and his inexorable evolution toward a situation that makes him capable of writing the narrative the reader reads. It seals his birth into language.

The night of initiation during which Meursault writes the letter is a watershed in the development of both his life and his consciousness. He is initiated into narrative consciousness by the same act that involves him in the events that will be narrated. He thereby begins to become the self that will be capable of writing the story. Writing makes him a differentiated, conscious self with an individual, tragic fate. His destiny will be that of a writer, as well as that of an ordinary individual and of a character in a novel.

As he takes up the pen, which is certainly an instrument of power, Meursault "stands in for the father": he allies himself with the male Raymond *vis à vis* the feminized "Mauresque" woman, and with the French position in relation to Arab Algeria. Inadvertently—and it is important to emphasize the *passivity* with which Meursault approaches this *act*—he becomes the instrument, but also in a sense the subject, of violence toward the Arab woman and toward the feminized Arabs in general. Meursault says of the letter that "je l'ai écrite un peu au hasard" 'I wrote it without giving it much thought' (54).

In a real sense, writing the letter is a gesture that involves Meursault in reproducing and legitimating the violent separation of Algeria into Arab and French poles. Raymond's choice of Meursault as *porte-parole* or scribe both informs the reader that Meursault has some skill as a writer and inaugurates the latter's inexorable "climb," or fall, to narrative consciousness about his life. This incident also may be related to Camus' own experience of writing *in* and *as* French. As Camus says in his *Essais*: writing is "un déchirement perpétuellement renouvelé . . ." 'a perpetually repeated sundering' (1090). If we take *L'Étranger* as it is presented—as a hypothetical first-person narrative—then it can have been written only in the interval between condemnation and execution. We will argue here that Camus presents individuality in our civilization, and particularly the writer's individuality, as the *aftermath* of a predetermined crime.

Further analysis along these lines discloses more of this incident's importance as a focus of meanings for the novel. Until this night with Raymond, Meursault has conspicuously refused any place in a "rational," "progressive" narrative or biography. He is not married; he frustrates his boss by refusing to desire advancement in his career; love is of no interest to him; he does not participate in the ceremonies of ritualized grief; he does not even find Paris attractive. Meursault does not experience the needs and desires called for by the current social norms. He does not pursue fragmentary and fragmenting objects and "satisfactions." His pleasure in Marie and in the unity of sun and sea, and his intense thirst on the fatal day, are the only experiences of strong pleasure and desire that he recounts.

In a sense, of course, Meursault will be tried and convicted for pleasure: acquiring a mistress and seeing a Fernandel film are not among the approved

activities of one whose mother has just died. So, Meursault must be "digested" into a different but equally comprehensive story: that of the criminally heartless pleasure-seeker.

Meursault's failure to cry at his mother's funeral is perceived as a withholding of what is due. He does not lend his body and its functions, in this case his tears, as pen, ink, and paper for the ritual repetition and legitimation of the code. Ceremoniousness emphasizes that the code is, precisely, a culture's repetition to itself of the stories or myths whose message is the culture's uniquely legitimate claim to true understanding. Reality must be made to "recite" the Law. Individual lives must produce only recognizable dramatized copies of society's accepted stories. The "individuality" of a particular destiny is merely a kind of rhetorical device.

Heretofore, Meursault has truly appeared as an *étranger* 'outsider'; he does not perform in a way that expresses desire for integration into the social system or complements others' performances in the ritual reproduction of the governing social ideology. Indeed, *this* is what he will be judicially condemned for. Clearly, his mother's death has inaugurated a concentration of pressures toward conformity, but until he writes the letter, Meursault remains socially "indigestible." He does not fall within the norm of autonomy, the norm of the self as a progressive narrative, characteristic of cultures that take themselves to be "advanced" (Heller and Wellbery 8–11). As Michel de Certeau has said, modernity *is writing* (168). Writing is prediction and control. It is also separation and isolation.

As it is recounted, the writing of the fateful letter is both Meursault's self-inscription in the ideologically and physically divided world and a profound challenge to ordinary understanding of how one becomes a subject. Special competence in a language, and particularly competence as a writer, is regarded in Western culture as conferring authority. Meursault thus acquires a certain authoritativeness and responsibility as he inadvertently becomes Raymond's ally and the ally of colonialism. Writing the letter is of a kind with firing the gun. In both acts, Meursault stands in for another and adopts a violently dominant position. He both confirms the cultural/ideological *status quo* and violates its laws. He makes *marks* that determine the course of his story or the meaning that will be read into his life.

Meursault takes his place in a causal chain by writing the letter, but he is writing *another's* message. This message is the expression of another's aggression and desire. Thus, in terms of Jacques Lacan's style of psychoanalysis, Meursault becomes a "subject" by taking up language as a means of expressing desire and aggression. However, he is actually only serving as a conduit for another's desire. To use language, and particularly to write, is to be colonized by an alien "voice." The subject is always an instrument. Meursault functions,

in his personal "fate," as a scribe, reproducing a message passed to him by another. However, what he reproduces is also the inscription of his own destiny. As far as Meursault is concerned, the trial will, in effect, be the definitive utterance of the discourse within whose terms Meursault already inscribes himself when he writes the letter. This colonization by another "voice" reaches its extreme when Meursault evokes the experience of hearing his lawyer speak about the murder in the first person (159).

The letter is, too, a perfect example of what we have learned to call the "flight of the signifier": it is a linguistic product whose ultimate provenance is lost in an infinite regress, and whose eventual effects and meaning are far beyond its "author's" control. Raymond, a symbolic father-initiator, is himself merely the creature of a certain division of the social world. He is no more the "ultimate" source of what the letter expresses than Meursault. However, Raymond *takes himself* to be the originating subject of his acts, even as he merely passes on the social pattern. This is a mistake Meursault will steadfastly refuse to make.

As Meursault acquires a role, a narrative position, and thus a "fate," that fate makes him a co-performer in the colonial drama. He becomes the colonial administration's "partner" as he becomes Raymond's ally. Colonization appears, then, on two levels here: there is the obvious, literal colonization of Algeria with its native population and even its landscape by the French; there is also "colonization" in the form of others' presence *within* the acts whereby individuals "make" their individuality. Once Meursault allows himself to be involved in Raymond's conflict, he cannot escape the pattern of self-perpetuating rituals that is civilization in "French" Algeria. Not only is he the object of this "game," but his criminal—and apparently autonomous—act provides both pretext and legitimacy for the process that will destroy him as it becomes the narrative and the "meaning" of his life. Like Raymond, the judicial system speaks in terms of rules and legitimacy but, in the end, possesses only violence. Raymond beats his mistress, he says, in order to *punish* her (52).

It makes perfect sense, then, that the evening with Raymond is recounted in terms suggesting that it functions as a ceremony of initiation (47–56). On the night of the letter, Meursault and Raymond eat *boudin*—blood sausage—and drink wine. Raymond also says that he has beaten the woman "jusqu'au sang" 'until she bled' (51). It is clear that this is a *blood* ritual. After Meursault has written the letter, Raymond begins to *tutoyer* him 'address him in the familiar form'. Meursault does not object to this. He acquiesces—passively, as usual—in Raymond's implication that a bond has been formed.

This night of initiation consummates Meursault's colonization by, and entry into, the male, or, more properly, masculine style of subjectivity. Several times during the course of their conversation, Raymond emphasizes that they

are men, and that they are going to be "copains" 'pals'. After the letter is written, Raymond says that men always understand one another (55). The letter expresses a violently hostile attitude toward the Arab woman. Meursault
already knows that Raymond has beaten her bloody. He has even heard that
Raymond "vit des femmes" 'lives off women' (47). If so, Raymond lives off
women—Arab women—as the colonists live off Algeria. The writing of the
letter can thus be seen as consummating the separation from the female and
the destruction of unity inaugurated by the death of Meursault's mother. Her
death is turning out to be both the literal death of a particular person and
the end of a kind of relation to the world. It also begins the fragmentation of
nature and the quest for reintegration which become more important themes
as the story unfolds.

Meursault is pressured to take a narrative perspective on his own life.
The *Juge d'instruction* 'investigating judge' expects Meursault to demonstrate
this kind of awareness by acknowledging a need for Christ's redemption. The
Juge exclaims that believing all men believe in God is what gives meaning to
his life. Meursault's unbelief is thus explicitly made a threat to meaning, and
this is another attempt to assimilate him into a system of self-reinforcing
ideological assumptions.

If it is true, as John Freccero asserts, that there is a "male" or masculine
form of narrative and particularly of autobiography, and if that sort of narrative emphasizes conflict, separation, and linear development, then Meursault
becomes a male narrator as he becomes a male subject. He will be unable,
finally, to refuse completely the stance of transcendental subjectivity that
characterizes traditional autobiography and narrative as well as "normal" personality development.

In fact, of course, male individuation in most cultures involves emphatic
separation from all that is female. This separation is often consummated in
a night of bloody initiation—as with Raymond's blood sausage and wine.
Thus, Meursault's ability to tell his story as a first-person narrative appears
to be a function of this brutal, but for him inadvertent and unwelcome, differentiation. He becomes a fully individuated male as he becomes a *writer*.
He thereby enters into the *déchirement* (sundering) of which Camus spoke.
Moreover, Meursault's role as a French colonialist male will be consummated
by the murder.

As he takes up the pen—perhaps inevitably in order to express another's
desire and hatred—he becomes the creature of the writing tool he has taken
up, and his life begins to acquire a fateful order that will permit its linear narration. In the broadest sense, of course, the "tool," which is also a weapon, is
language itself—in Meursault's and Camus' case French, which in Algeria is
the language of separation or *déchirement* in its colonialist form. The use of

any tool always requires performance of a quasi-ritual behavior. The tool-user is processed by the tool. In the case of writing, one is obliged to specialize in reproducing the entire world inherent in a language and culture.

When he writes the letter, Meursault places himself in a story, or a tradition of stories, as old as the violent overthrow of earth goddesses by sky gods (Ruether). He is conscripted—drafted—into the discourse that tirelessly articulates tasks and roles whose purpose is repetition. Some of these tasks are, of necessity, crimes. The discourse rejects stories it does not already contain. Ultimately, then, the power that destroys Meursault is the same as the one that beats the "Mauresque" woman, or Salamano's dog. The body—most dramatically and definitively Meursault's body—is both the page on which the copies of dominant stories are written and the writing implement.

There is a link between the "empowerment" of a writer, as Camus evokes it for us, and the psychoanalytic concept of castration. Stephen Ohayon has said that the "theme of solar castration" (194) is strong in the novel. We usually think of writing as expressing one's uniqueness. In fact, however, as Meursault writes, and as he shoots, he is leaving the traces that will replace him, that will permit his reduction to legibility. These are the gestures that will justify his transportation into the space of judgment, and of narrative; they will allow his conversion into a case. During the trial, when Meursault has the urge to speak, his lawyer will say "Taisez-vous" 'Be quiet' (151). Meursault feels that "Tout se déroulait sans mon intervention" 'Everything was happening without my participation' (151). He is silenced, manipulated—castrated.

Meursault's ultimate fate—decapitation—will certainly be the ultimate castration. Progressive narration is a struggle to achieve *separation*. To succeed in this struggle is to be marked; to be distinguished is to be torn, to inscribe oneself in a system of symbols and subject/object relations, and also to be a surface which is *written upon*. This passage prepares us to see Meursault's story as a profound challenge to the myth of individual autonomy—even the autonomy of the writer. "Mastery" of language (and this is Western civilization's most admired kind of mastery) is seen here as conferring something quite other than autonomy. Camus, like Lacan, suggests that it is through "mastery" of language that the "subject" comes into existence as yearning for something with which to fill a lack, or void. The break with the mother, and more generally with the female or feminine, that inaugurates the "narratable" existence of an "autonomous" individual is both factitious and fictitious, even as it is real: that is, it is only by a kind of trick that the individual appears to have, or to desire, autonomy.

Like any member of a culture, Meursault is an unwitting initiate, or recruit. His most fateful "act" is simply to become a substitute, a stand-in. He stands in for Raymond when he writes the letter, and also when he shoots

the Arab. During the trial, the court, in effect, makes him a stand-in for a parricide. This substitution emphasizes the fundamental interchangeability of individuals in modern societies, their ineluctable status as tokens in a comprehensive system of exchange. The use of writing is an initiation into another's disposition of symbols and relations—a *de facto* colonization. It is also entry into the world of semiotic exchange. The guillotine will convert Meursault's body into a *sign*, making it an object processed by a discourse and placed in the museum of approved meanings. Individuality is reduced to equivalence. Even crimes (and certainly bodies) have their significance assigned to them by the administration, and that significance can be altered at the administration's convenience.

So, writing the letter makes Meursault a participant in the fractured worlds of language, of symbolic manipulation and fragmented nature, and of colonialism. It is the event that "officially" launches the inexorable process whereby Meursault will ultimately appear to have what might be called a "social Oedipus complex" and to be a parricide. The process Meursault undergoes is strikingly like that described by Freud in *The Future of an Illusion* (38–42). This social Oedipus complex must be *provoked* in the child in order for the Law to function; it must be inculcated in each individual for the Law to be effective (see Poster 34–35). Moreover, it must exist in *identical form* in all individuals.

The Law has need of Crime—"sin is pleasing to God" (Freud 38); the threat of parricide must exist to legitimate the exactions of civilized life. Meursault's case will be explicitly linked to that of the parricide so that he can be seen to have acted *as if* he had had an Oedipus complex. It is the supposed desire to transgress the Law—to kill the father—that creates the individual as a threat to the social order as it makes him an individual. He is constituted as needing-to-be-controlled. The interchangeability, from the court's point of view, of Meursault and another criminal emphasizes the fact that uniqueness is an illusion; the individual, even or especially the criminal, is a signer to which the ruling culture or ideology assigns meaning as it will. Meursault will be described by the Prosecutor as "un gouffre où la société peut succomber" 'an abyss into which society could sink' (155). He is both manipulated as an unspeaking object and inflated and generalized into a symbolic bogeyman.

In a very real sense, Meursault will only *appear* to be the subject of the murder, just as he is only problematically the writer of the letter. The murder, like the letter, consummates another's violent hatred and reproduces an ideologically defined situation wherein violent hatred is indispensable as justification and perpetuation of an administration. The individual must *appear* to be the autonomous subject of criminal desire if Law is to appear both a necessary and a just control and sanction.

Violent confrontation across a rupture in the world's unity now defines Meursault's relations with the Arabs, the court, and the sun. He and the Arabs are antagonists because the organization—the writing—of thought and space in Algeria makes them antagonists. The "Algeria" he and the Arabs live in is a culturally, ideologically synthesized space. The landscape is composed of "mineralized" fears, lusts, and alibis.

Suppression of the female (or of the feminine), was necessary in order to inaugurate the differentiation Meursault experiences. With their names, customs, costumes, and power, the French have imposed another "Algeria": they have written over the original Algeria as if it were merely a blank page. This new place is one where unity is impossible. The French inhabit their own fears, desires, and rationalizations. The Arabs are reduced to silence, or feminized. They have no names and they do not speak. They certainly do not write, although they too must inhabit the written-over Algeria.

Enlightenment's Central Subject and Totalizing Eye:
The Hypertrophic Sun

It is useful to see the sun as the symbol of the symbolic and as the model for enforcement of hierarchical relations. The idea that nature is a political order, with the sun at the "top," sets up "nature" as a confirming reflection of the human political order. If the natural elements can be fragmented and opposed to one another, with the sun above and the "feminine" ocean below, and if, indeed, they are seen as inherently so fragmented and hierarchized, then it appears necessary and appropriate that the same be done with people. More-over, the "integration" of natural "elements" into a coherent symbolic system legitimates the order claiming to reflect and be reflected by the symbolic integration. The sun therefore functions here in a way that recalls Louis Althusser's mythical "central subject" (170) which is constituted by the pretense that an ideology is organized around a central truth: the sun is both a symbol and *the* symbol of symbolization, both a truth and the keystone of Truth. It is the capstone of a hierarchy and the "proof" that that hierarchy is "true."

The fateful privileging of the masculine, or of separation, is shown by Camus to be fundamental in the fragmented, fate-ridden world Meursault must inhabit. Having perceived the importance of this letter, we can better appreciate Camus' presentation of the tragic process, one of whose central elements turns out to be *writing*, in its broadest sense.

Colonialism is a regime of supposedly transcendental positions and generalizations. It functions as a system of writing—a language. The Arabs have no names because they exist in colonial Algeria only as a dark and threatening generality; they are background material. They exist to justify the tautologies that the colonialist authorities repeat to themselves. Even Meursault's crime

is converted from one against an individual and an Arab into one against the *French* authority system and customs. The Arabs embody the mythical lazy, uncivilized "African" (Pratt) who, along with the "hostile" natural environment, justifies—even seems to call for—the colonial culture's transforming presence. It is into *this* language that Meursault will be conscripted.

From the beginning, when Meursault receives the news of his mother's death by telegram and when he is crushed by the sun while walking along the paved road with the funeral party, the issues of writing and spatial inscription are fundamental. The body of the world is written on, as are the bodies of persons. Living beings thus become signs, serving as the medium in which the dominant ideology reiterates itself. Meursault's "acquisition" of a coherent identity and an "individual" fate is really just the use of his life to repeat an old "story." Asphalt is a kind of ink, an instrument of fragmentation, and an organizing medium. As such, it is part of the novel's exploration of *marking*, as are the knife, fists, bullets, blood, judgment, guillotine, and literal writing that figure so prominently in the story.

Already in the beginning, Camus suggests the absence of "escape routes" (Lyotard 8) in this comprehensively written-upon environment. The Law seizes bodies in order to make them its "text" (de Certeau 139). The sun is like the lamp that lights the surface being written upon. It is specifically the mother's funeral that focuses the sun's intensity and makes it oppressive. This will be an even stronger theme during the trial than at the funeral. It is important to emphasize that this funeral is a ceremony, and a French/Catholic-style ceremony. Everyone wears black. No concessions are made to the physical facts of the Algerian environment. Catholic symbolism and ceremony have been transported into this environment wherein they are experienced as uncomfortable self-sacrifices. The same will be true at the trial: there, too, the principals and the spectators will be oppressed by the sun's heat, which is exaggerated by their clothing. The exercise of a mutilating, killing power is disguised as self-abnegation.

The colonialists' tendency to experience their presence in Algeria as both a necessary "civilizing" influence and a noble self-sacrifice on their part is legitimated and perpetuated by this refusal to adapt their costumes and ceremonies to the environment. The semiotics of their dress and behavior constantly emphasize their separation from nature. Indeed, nature appears hostile to their culture. Their rapacity—their own "primitive" urges—is hidden by their status as national heroes of self-sacrifice, battling with a "harsh" nature and a "primitive" people. Asking for the death-penalty, according to the Prosecutor, is a "pénible devoir" 'painful duty' (157). Mastery disguised as self-sacrifice—power exercised "on behalf" of others or of noble principles—is a key element in any colonialist ideology.

Moreover, with the conversion of nature into a stage-set for the display of human activity, the sun truly becomes the source of illumination for a performance destined to be *judged*. We find Meursault already beginning to experience others as judges during the wake. The blinding, inescapable white light of the lamps in the white-washed room where the wake is held prefigures the sun's oppressive omnipresence in the rest of the story. When he is questioned by the *Juge d'instruction*, the latter sits in shadow, while Meursault is fully and intensely illuminated by a lamp (100). So, the sun is the keystone of many symbolic systems—Camus at least once explicitly identified it with Catholicism (Ohayon 192)—and its power is intensified when it is split-off from the rest of nature in order to make it the essential image of power and hierarchy. Under its light, *presence is guilt*.

The oppressive sun represents the hypertrophy of vision that characterizes modern Western civilization. The sun, then, is a "totalizing eye," penetrating and eliminating murky, mysterious spaces and illuminating individual idiosyncrasies for judgment. It is a structural analogue of both centralized political authority and "panoptical" science. Global illumination from a single center serves both knowledge and power. Whether we emphasize Costes' idea that the sun is a kind of superego or see it as a more traditional sky-god, it is connected with hierarchy and the Law, and thus with guilt. The sun of judgment and knowledge is the modern, comprehensively planned and administered society's insistence on universal transparency. It refuses to acknowledge any unknown, unknowable reality. Things become real only as they are illuminated by the totalizing eye of "knowledge" and Law.

Meursault's mother's death and funeral inaugurate his yearning for the "lost paradise of complete fusion with the all" (Muller and Richardson 22). The sun figures man's authority over nature. This power over nature is basic to Western ethics. At the same time, it serves as the model for authority of man over man. The sun is a father-symbol, and its growing strength in *L'Étranger* emphasizes the loss of the balancing motherly influence and the inexorable isolation of the "individual."

This sun-symbolism can be seen as a model for would-be transcendental subjects (see, for a related point, Bennett 116). In this case, the individual who tries—or is led—to experience the self as a central, transcendental subject is both the sun's imitator and its *rival*. Thus, too, does the child become the father's rival at the moment when he would imitate the father. Meursault imitates the sun, or the father, by participating in Raymond's violence against the Arab woman and by killing the Arab man—by taking, in effect, a dominant position. This dominance is, of course, both inadvertent and illusory. The sun oppresses him, moves him toward the act that will permit definitive condemnation, and fixes and illuminates him as visible to

judgment. He is fuel for the operation of a "mécanique implacable" 'implacable mechanism' (165).

At his trial, Meursault will explain his act by saying it was "à cause du soleil" 'because of the sun' (158). He thus redirects our attention to the fact that his "autonomy," and therefore his responsibility, are derived from the predisposition of the psyche by its constituting symbolism. In other words, he and Camus challenge us to see autonomy within the prevailing model as both mythical and fundamentally unjust. Meursault refuses to cooperate in perpetuating this autonomy-myth, though he will nonetheless be made by the trial to *appear* as a confirmation of it. Camus portrays the "autonomous," individualized self as brought into being in order to be condemned, and in order to confirm by his crime that the established order is both necessary and just. Camus calls Meursault, in the preface to the American edition of the novel, "the only Christ we deserve." Our Law has become so comprehensive and so intolerant of deviation or extraordinariness that we only become functional "individuals" by crucifying or castrating individuality. The Investigating Judge calls Meursault "Monsieur l'Antéchrist" 'Mister Antichrist' (111). This is clearly part of his job, which is to reduce Meursault and his act to comprehensibility within the terms of a set of categories.

Meursault will say that he hopes to encounter a howling crowd at his execution, "pour que tout soit consommé" 'so that everything may be consummated'. It has been noted that this echoes the "consummatum est" attributed to Christ (Ohayon 201). It has not been emphasized, however, that, from the beginning, Camus is preparing us to see Meursault as Christlike in the sense that he is brought into being as a subject in order to be executed. Like all differentiated, "narratable" selves, he is destined for guilt. His story, like those of all narrated "characters," begins with its ending. His fragmented relationship with a mutilated internal and external nature will appear to ratify the fundamentally tautological Law. Visibility will increasingly mean condemnation for Meursault. As language and action *pass through him* he becomes guilty of an *inherited* crime. The sun of judgment is also the sun of the "Enlightenment" (de Certeau 23–24), which seeks out and destroys unilluminated, private, idiosyncratic, non-narrative spaces and makes this universal transparency the medium of power justified as "knowledge."

This conflict with the sun, into which Meursault is initiated by a ceremony, is the literal and symbolic beginning of the conflict with authority—the "parricide"—which will become his crime and the definition of his individuality without ever having been *his* at all. It seems that the subject can exist only as *the one who is guilty*, and narration can only issue from one who has experienced the passage into guilt. Both nature and the individual are appropriated by a symbolic system operating relentlessly to create and

perpetuate a particular civilization's "necessity." Wild, "southern" Algeria (Pratt) "requires" the French civilizing influence. Wild Algeria is inarticulate and unorganized. Similarly, Meursault's interest, immediately after the funeral, in sex, laughter, and the fusion of sun and sea will identify him with the subversive "pleasure principle." He will provide the pretext for a demonstration of authority's power and of its necessity. It is only within an already fragmented world that pleasure can be defined as destructive. The loathing of pleasure built into many social rituals and forms (Horkheimer and Adorno 31) is a powerful force for social cohesion, and also for hierarchy and coercion. Meursault's "parricide" is simply the preference for real pleasure over observing the appearances of formalized grief. He spontaneously, fatally, resists the "disenchantment of the world" (Horkheimer and Adorno 5), which substitutes formula and ritual for felt experience.

We find that Meursault resembles Racine's Phèdre: like Phèdre, he is immobilized by the sun of judgment. He is an individual bound and bounded by the acts and beliefs of previous generations. In Racine's play, the sun—connected with Phèdre's father, Minos, and her grandfather, Helios—represents the deadening, constricting power of preceding generations. Like Meursault's, Phèdre's "crime" confirms her inclusion in a story whose form and meaning her "individual" destiny can only reproduce. Both stories are thus profound challenges to the concept of autonomy when they are seen as recounting ritual repetitions that have been disguised as individual destinies.

This is precisely the kind of process Meursault finds himself involved in, but Camus also challenges our readerly tendency to demand such a process and to see it as truly "progressive." This is, no doubt, why he "gives" us a narrative that is patently impossible. Combined with the idea that separation from the female is the essence of male individuation (Greenblatt 51), Freccero's concept of a fundamentally conflictual, male type of narrative is useful in preparing us to deepen our understanding of Meursault. It should be recalled at this point that refusal to participate in the narrative-building rituals of the society around him had been Meursault's pattern until the composition of the letter. Through the process inaugurated by the letter, Meursault simply takes his place in a chain(gang?) of signifiers which leads to its own consummation in the final ritual of judgment and condemnation. He is caught in a circuit where the messages have already been composed and sent.

The individual, like Meursault, is both the instrument and the victim of this civilization based on fragmentation and guilt. His obedience reproduces the approved patterns, and his disobedience provides pretexts and justifications for public, ceremonial shows of efficient force. The individual is thus the material from which a particular social formation is made, the tool that does the making, and the threat that makes the formation appear necessary.

The spectators in court and, prospectively, at the execution, are the manipulated, passive "collectivity" brought into being and preserved by fear of the "outsider." Camus joins Kafka in suggesting that the individual person is the medium—the flesh, as is literally the case in Kafka's "In the Penal Colony"— in which the Law is inscribed and reproduced, a "cockroach" caught permanently in the light of judgment. Even Meursault's efforts to find his way back to unity—to the source—are steps toward his definitive fragmentation by the guillotine. The guillotine will consummate physically what language has already achieved psychologically and symbolically.

The "sun" of judgment pretends to achieve universal transparency; it actually constitutes the characters whose "truth" it pretends to reveal. It symbolizes, in *L'Étranger*, something much like the disciplinary "knowledge" evoked by Michel Foucault in *Surveiller et punir*. The judgment and sentence imposed on Meursault require developing and publicizing a theory which not only "explains" Meursault's acts and psychology, but also reiterates the necessity and legitimacy of the judgment-ritual itself. Presumably, any members of the social group not persuaded by the theory will be terrorized by the execution. The powerful, panoptical illumination that dominates the story is a kind of enlightenment. The Enlightenment itself emanated from the conviction that knowledge could eliminate surprise and fear. Enclosure of the formerly wild outsider within the light of a domesticating explanation exorcises individuals' fear of their own "wild" potential and dramatizes reduction of the individual to the illustrative, the schematic.

Character/Criminal: Legibility as Decapitation

What is free—"wild" may be a useful synonym for "free" here—does not write (de Certeau 155). It leaves no permanent traces, creates no text. This means, of course, that what is free or wild cannot be *read*. We have shown that Meursault's becoming a narrator or writer is important. Equally important is the fact that this process is also a becoming *legible*. In his arguments to the court, Meursault's lawyer says that he has *read* Meursault's soul (159). The prosecutor makes essentially the same claim, linking coherent legibility with certitude: "J'ai retracé devant vous le fil d'événements qui a conduit cet homme à tuer. . . ." 'I have retraced for you the series of events that brought this man to kill' (153). Initiation into subject-object relations is also conscription into the belief that illuminating the object proves the subject's superiority. Every reduction of experience to a "subject's" comprehension of an "object" is a decapitation.

Meursault's story is an "allegory" of becoming legible in two ways, of course: he is both an example of individuation in a real cultural situation and a character in a novel. Reading always requires a code. As both character

and hypothetical "real" person, Meursault exemplifies the processes whereby an individual comes into, or is reduced to, legibility or commensurability with a code. Both the judicial process and the narrative itself—like all forms of "logic"—reflect the assumption that the subject-object hierarchy is the essence of all relationships. To be legible is to exist as a reproduction and ratification of the code. Trials and traditional novels define an individual—character or criminal—as that which can be understood and elucidated by the judicial or novelistic code. Here we return to the theme of Meursault as originally an "indigestible" outsider—*étranger*—domesticated and reduced to exchangeability within the prevailing marketplace of signs and meanings. His *existence* as an experiencing being must be marginalized and eliminated in this process.

Examining Meursault's "deviant" behavior at the funeral and through-out the story in terms of its relationship with the code of social norms makes us aware of the powerful presence of *ceremonies* in the novel. From the funeral to the trial, and punctuated by the "initiation" at Raymond's home and the "processing" by the judicial system, Meursault is converted gradually into grist for the ceremonial mill. His execution will simply be the final ritual reduction of his body and his person. The ceremonies, like all such rituals, reiterate and reinforce the social code. The *asile* (convalescent home) prefigures the court-room, and both are paradigms of the society. Meursault clearly understands this aspect of his "story," for he wishes for a large crowd at the execution.

From the beginning, Meursault's story is that of an individual who is more difficult than most to read. Because he is not comprehensible—legible—as a conventional son, employee, or lover, he must become the central figure in a different story: that of the parricide. The individual who might exist outside the Law is recuperated as the one who would *overthrow* the Law. This replaces him within the Law's purview and prevents any spread of the idea that the Law is not universal. The "outlaw" thus becomes the monstrous Other, who is actually constituted or "secreted" by the system. His story is then that of the prodigal and outlaw whose crime and whose fate condense and general-ize guilt, making the society's members distrust both external and internal "nature"—both others and themselves, both environment and psyche.

As far as the judicial system is concerned, Meursault's story's most important function is to reiterate the ideological principle that the State is the master reader of signs and legislator of meanings. The administration, social avatar of the sun, is the central subject. All must finally be comprehended within the ruling *coherence*. The individual is thus seen as "writing" his life, but as not being capable or worthy of fully understanding it. I "write" my story; the authorities prove their legitimate superiority by reading-out its true mean-ing to me—or beyond me to a *public*. This is precisely what Meursault evokes

when he describes the experience of hearing his lawyer speak of his, Meursault's, acts in the first person: "A un moment donné, cependant, je l'ai écouté parce qu'il disait: 'Il est vrai que j'ai tué.' Puis il a continué sur ce ton, disant 'je' chaque fois qu'il parlait de moi.... Moi, j'ai pensé que c'était m'écarter encore de l'affaire, me réduire à zéro et, en un certain sens, se substituer à moi" 'At a certain moment, however, I listened to him because he was saying "It is true that I killed." Then he continued in that way, saying "I" each time he spoke of me.... I thought he was, again, leaving me out of the affair, reducing me to zero and, in a sense, substituting himself for me' (159). The lawyer is "reading-out" his preferred explanation as if that explanation were written in Meursault's "soul." This passage also emphasizes, again, the insistence, in this textualizing culture, on the essential *exchangeability* of individuals.

The prominence of cutting-tools in the novel—the knife, the sun's rays as swords, the guillotine—suggest this "Procrustean" aspect of social, and particularly colonial, life. Ultimately, as fodder for the guillotine, Meursault's body *will* serve as ritual matter. Meursault will pay with his blood for having withheld his tears. The bloodstains left after the decapitation, like the trial-record, will be the legible traces substituted definitively for his living experience.

For that is, ultimately, what legibility implies: the substitution of the track for the creature, of the dead traces for the living process. The execution will be the consummation of a *sentence*—in both senses of the word. Meursault's death will end his ability to alter or confuse the "meaning" of his life. It will also make of that life a legible lesson to others. The sun and the blade will have achieved what Michel de Certeau calls the utopia of the modern West: a comprehensive, definitive text inscribed on a cleared, neutral space (135). Our bodies must be disciplined to norms, providing tears and other reactions on cue, and our minds must be disciplined to acknowledge certain horizons by reading certain stories: myths, folktales, novels.

This latter point brings us to another level on which the issue of conscription and inscription into legibility is important in *L'Étranger*: the book we have read *is a text*. There are powerful analogies between the process described *in* the novel and the process *of* the novel—this one, and the novel as a genre. Lennard Davis calls an ideology a novel that a culture writes about itself for itself (24). Like an ideology, a novel presents constructed and disputable meanings as if they were natural and could be apprehended directly (Davis 26). Meursault's inadvertent acquisition of a fate is analogous to his becoming a character. He is written and thus legible. A meaning is assigned to him.

There is a code, or a system of codes, that guides the writing and reading of novels just as there is in the classification of "real" lives. The ideology of

enlightenment and imperialism is as intimately connected with novels as it is with colonialism. The Enlightenment, which penetrates and standardizes all of reality, is the lamp by which all of reality is read. The Great Encyclopedia itself was an attempt to make all of social and natural reality accessible to the "light." Rational exploration of the world created a cosmos unified in principle, and thus accessible to both intellectual and commercial exploitation. The universalizing, levelling ideology of enlightenment—the methodical classification of everything under the sun—has gradually created a modern equivalent of ancient fate.

Camus makes clear, in *L'Étranger*, the way in which inquiry and explanation, whose original purpose was to neutralize the irresistible power of fate, have become a modern *equivalent* of fate. To be made a character in a novel is, like being processed judicially, to be transported into the artificially illuminated space of a discipline, or a kind of ceremony. It is to be submitted to an expert. A novel is thus another Procrustean bed. It is the scene where a necessarily reductive inquiry is conducted. Through the judicial inquiry, Meursault's life is interpreted, retrospectively, as an explanation of the murder—as a novel. The spectators in the courtroom correspond to the readers of a novel. This correspondence is especially clear given the presence of the newspaper writers as mediators in the court. Meursault is processed by the forces of meaning-production.

The final validation of knowledge in the culture of Enlightenment is its ability to generate powerful technologies. The guillotine is the ultimate in explicit technocratic penetration and "trimming into shape." Meursault calls it a work "de précision, fini et éclatant" 'of precision, polished and shining' (170). Writing is, in a much more complex way, the same sort of device. Skilled narration is analogous to the guillotine in that its workmanship gives it an air of unanswerable finality. The trial and the novel emphasize the modern, administrative form of fate in that, once complete, they give the impression that the ending was implicit in the beginning, that it was the real point of departure.

We mentioned earlier Camus' statement that writing is "un déchirement perpétuellement renouvelé" 'A perpetually repeated sundering'. This is true in two ways, both of which are evoked in *L'Étranger*: the writer is initiated into an especially intense experience of fragmentation as he becomes a specialist in symbolic manipulation; he also wields the cutting tools. Like Meursault, the writer becomes an instrument of fragmentation and a fragmented being by the same process.

This is, we believe, the most important reason for the fusion of sun and blade in the murder scene. Meursault's act is a reaction to the slashing, penetrating heat and light of the sun, especially the sunlight reflected by the

Arab's knife. At the same time, the shots are understood by Meursault to have "détruit l'équilibre du jour" 'destroyed the day's equilibrium' (95). He is inhabited and manipulated by the sun, as well as by the disposition of people and forces in colonial Algeria. He is also the one who marks, penetrates, and kills another body. He is the immediate perpetrator of an act which also seems to exist independently, making use of him as if he were merely a puppet. He can, finally, only pass on the old story. He is the intermediary between a reservoir of stories and their repetition for an audience subjected to and by their "lessons."

Virtually everything in the book's second part underlines; Meursault's incorporation—his disappearance—into a discourse of power or mastery. As we mentioned earlier, the *Juge d'instruction* examines Meursault in an artificially heightened light and demands that he ratify what the Judge chooses to regard as the meaning of life. Meursault has become a case, and the case will be *produced* by professional writers posing as mere reporters. The pervasive, powerful lighting imposed throughout the story has now made Meursault's "case" seem like an x-ray. He has become an example of what Max Horkheimer and Theodor Adorno call the "schematization" of men by all-penetrating modern discourses and institutions (35).

The journalists at the trial are like a modern, scriptocratic chorus: they will "explain" the case to a "public" whose existence is constituted largely by the ritual reading of newspapers. In one of the writers, Meursault sees a strange reflection of himself (132). Surely this supports our contention that a writer's split self-awareness has been installed within Meursault. His unfathomably rich, inextricably tangled living experience is going to be reduced, first to a trial transcript and newspaper reports, then to the permanent full-stop engraved by the blade.

The court is like a clubhouse for the police, the court officials, and the newspapermen. As his life achieves full narratability, Meursault as a sentient being becomes irrelevant: "Tout se déroulait sans mon intervention" 'Everything was happening without my participation' (151); "mon affaire suivait son cours" 'my affair was taking its course' (110). He says of the judicial process that it is a "rite implacable" 'implacable ritual' (166), and that "la mécanique écrasait tout" 'the mechanism crushed everything' (171). Moreover, "tout le secret d'une bonne organisation était là" 'that was the whole secret of good organisation' (169). The criminal to be executed is forced into moral collaboration with the process, since he must hope that the guillotine works properly. Any alternative to the prevailing technocracy of light, script, and fragmentation is silenced.

Like a trial or an execution, narration requires fragmentation. Things must be taken apart before they can be reassembled with links deriving from

and confirming a plausible meaning and legitimating a certain discursive organization. Despite the ostensible triumph of the implacable ritual, Meursault's account of his imprisonment clearly states the impossibility of honest narration, of narrative without mutilation. As he uses his memory to kill time, Meursault realizes "qu'un homme qui n'aurait vécu qu'un seul jour pourrait sans peine vivre cent ans dans une prison" 'that a man who had lived only one day could easily live a hundred years in prison' (123). Even a being's own memory cannot exhaustively review his experience. Clearly, narrative is hopeless; it is akin to a decapitation performed to preserve the credibility of a self-referential discourse.

Finally, the test of narrative can never be its "truth." Meursault says of the Prosecutor's version of the events that it "ne manquait pas de clarté" 'did not lack clarity' (153). The theme of illumination culminates in this: the "light" of inquiry, of narration, reveals nothing. It produces plausibility and coherence in accord with pre-existing codes. It is essential to a ritual whose purpose is the reproduction of an ideological "world" through the repetition of stories, but it *erases* experiential truth. Meursault has become the object/creation of a technique, the ritual material permitting the display of an *expertise*.

The process inaugurated by writing is consummated by reading.

NOTE

1. All translations from the French are ours.

BIBLIOGRAPHY

Andrianne, René. "Soleil, ciel et lumière dans *L'Étranger* de Camus." *Revue Romane* 7 (1972): 161–76.

Althusser, Louis. *Lenin and Philosophy and Other Essays*. London: New Left Books, 1971.

Benjamin, Andrew E., ed. *The Lyotard Reader*. New York: B. Blackwell, 1989.

Bennett, Tony, ed. *Culture, Ideology and Social Process*. London: The Open UP, 1981.

Camus, Albert. *Essais*. Bibliothèque de la Pléiade. Paris: Gallimard, 1965.

———. *L'Étranger*. Paris: Gallimard, 1942.

Certeau, Michel de. *The Practice of Everyday Life*. Trans. Steven F. Rendall. Berkeley: University of California Press, 1984.

Crochet, Monique. *Les Mythes dans l'oeuvre de Camus*. Paris: Editions Universitaires, 1973.

Davis, Lennard. *Resisting Novels: Ideology and Fiction*. London: Methuen, 1987.

Foucault, Michel. *Surveiller et punir: la naissance de la prison*. Paris: Gallimard, 1975.

Freccero, John. "Autobiography and Narrative." Heller, Sosna, and Wellbery 16–29.

Freud, Sigmund. *The Standard Edition of the Complete Psychological Works of Sigmund Freud*. Trans. James Strachey. Vol. 21 (1927–31).

Gallop, Jane. *Reading Lacan*. Ithaca: Cornell UP, 1985.

Gassin, Jean. "Camus raciste?" *Revue des Lettres Modernes*. 315–22 (1972): 275–78.

———. *L'Univers symbolique d'Albert Camus. Essai d'interprétation psychanalytique*. Paris: Librairie Minard, 1981.

Greenblatt, Stephen. "Fiction and Friction." Heller, Sosna, and Wellbery 30–52.

Grenier, Roger. *Albert Camus/Soleil et ombre*. Paris: Lacombe/Gallimard, 1987.

Hall, Edward T. *Beyond Culture*. Garden City, NY: Anchor Books, 1981.

Heller, Thomas, Morton Sosna, and David E. Wellbery, eds. *Reconstructing Individualism: Autonomy, Individuality, and the Self in Western Thought*. Stanford: Stanford UP, 1986.

Horkheimer, Max and Theodor Adorno. *Dialectic of Enlightenment*. Trans. John Cumming. New York: Herder and Herder, 1972.

Lacan, Jacques. *Écrits*. Paris: Editions du Seuil, 1966.

Lewis, C. S. *The Abolition of Man*. New York: Macmillan, 1968

Muller, John P. and William J. Richardson. *Lacan and Language: A Reader's Guide to Écrits*. New York: International Universities Press, 1982.

Ohayon, Stephen. "Camus' *The Stranger*: The Sun-Metaphor and Patricidal Conflict." *American Imago* 40.2 (1983): 189–205.

Poster, Mark. *Foucault, Marxism and History: Mode of Production versus Mode of Information*. Cambridge: Polity Press, 1984.

Pratt, Mary L. "Mapping Ideology: Gide, Camus, and Algeria." *College Literature* 8.2 (1981): 158–74.

Ruether, Rosemary Radford. *Sexism and God-Talk: Toward a Feminist Theology*. Boston: Beacon Press, 1983.

Tremblay, V. L. "La Structure mytho-rituelle de l'imaginaire camusien." *The French Review*. 62.5 (1989): 783–92.

ROBERT R. BROCK

Meursault the Straw Man

> ... psychoanalysis and Marxism
> always ended up by interpreting
> everything. They had ceased to
> understand: they explained.[1]

—Jean d'Ormesson

Although d'Ormesson was referring to the critic's approach to literature in general, it should be obvious to anyone reading learned articles on
L'Étranger that he could have had their treatment of Camus' short masterpiece specifically in mind. This desire to explain, rather than to understand,
means that the book will not be discussed as a whole, as an entity, but as
a series of all but unrelated segments. There may well be some discussion
of the story as a manifestation of the *absurde*, as well as arguments over
just what that word entails, but the book will be examined primarily as an
expression of some political, social or psychological cant based on a subjective reading of one or two scenes.

For most critics, the book is either an indictment of the French judicial system that deprives the proletariat of an effective voice by stealing
its language, or it is the case-study of a man with more Oedipal problems
than even Freud ever dreamed of. One doesn't have to spend much time
in a musty library to verify my charge; Ben Stoltzfus has already done the

---

From *Studies in the Novel* 25, no. 1 (Spring 1993): 92–100. Copyright © 1993 University of
North Texas.

essential legwork for his article "Camus' *L'Étranger*: a Lacanian Reading."[2] Perusing it will prove d'Ormesson's point, and mine; some scenes will be "explained," but the basic message of *L'Étranger* will not be noticed, let alone understood.

Stoltzfus's research shows that Meursault is either a nihilistic juvenile delinquent (René Girard) or a man of rigorous honesty (Germaine Brée). He could have been condemned to the guillotine because he won't play the game (Sartre and Robert Champigny) or because he is inept and wants to die (Monique Wagner). The death of the Arab was either an accident (Louis Hudon) or a *crimen ex machina* (Girard). On the other hand, perhaps the judges condemn Meursault in order to "destroy the truth he embodies" (Albert Maquet). Of course, the whole thing might be a *fatum* as in ancient Greek literature (Carl Viggiani).

As to the four extra shots that baffle the judge, J. H. Mathews says they might be the first manifestation of Meursault's will, while Hudon sees them as an expression of exasperation. However, Julian L. Stamm is certain that Meursault was really a homosexual and that the shots on the beach were ejaculations. In his article, Stoltzfus goes on to note that Brian T. Fitch has covered these and various other interpretations of *L'Étranger* in his study; and concludes by citing Alain Robbe-Grillet's comment, "I am the stranger" (L'étranger, c'est moi).[3] Stoltzfus then comes to the very dangerous conclusion that the book is "a work that reads the reader." In other words, "We each read the book with our own unconscious desire."

The unfortunate thing here is that he is right. It is unfortunate in that a too personal identification with the work, or its hero, leads to readings that are then presented to us not as one person's very subjective interpretation of, in this case, *L'Étranger*, but rather as objective, self-evident truth. The book becomes then *not* what the author wrote in fact, but what the critic would have written/meant given his/her personal bent had he/she written it. The critic does not say, for instance, this scene makes me think that Camus may have wanted to supplant his father in his mother's bed, but that it is perfectly obvious that he wished to do so. As Hudon wrote in his essay on *L'Étranger*, "Many put their nickel in the philosophical slot, and existentialism comes out of everywhere, others in the new critical slot, and it rains symbols."[4]

Critics are willing to quote authors on any given subject save one: what the authors think of critics. Stoltzfus, whose article presents a highly personal view of *L'Étranger*, takes Freudians to task and insists that his approach is the only valid one. (For those who do not subscribe to either dogma, the difference between them is not all that obvious.) In any event, perhaps all critics should read, or reread, what Sartre had to say about literary criticism.

When I picked up a book, it made no difference if I opened it and closed it twenty times, I could see that it didn't change. Sliding over this incorruptible surface: *the text*, my sight was only a minuscule surface accident, it disturbed nothing ... I left my bureau, turned off the light: invisible in the darkness, the book continued to glow; for itself alone.

(Quand je prenais un livre, j'avais beau l'ouvrir et le fermer vingt fois, je voyais bien qu'il ne s'altérait pas. Glissant sur cette substance incorruptible: *le texte*, mon regard n'était qu'un miniscule accident de surface, il ne dérangeait rien ... je quittais le bureau, j'éteignais: invisible dans les ténèbres, le livre étincelait toujours; pour lui seul.)[5]

In other words, the reader has no part to play in the work. It exists independently of him and must be approached on its own terms and not as a mirror, or manifestation, of "our own unconscious desire." *L'Étranger*, then, must be seen as a mirror of Camus' soul, not the critic's, a point to which I shall return.

Stoltzfus also quotes Robbe-Grillet's statement, "each of us has a tendency to conceive a history of literature that is his own story" (chacun d'entre nous a tendance à concevoir une histoire de la littérature qui est sa propre histoire.) That is, we tend to see literature as a reflection of ourselves. Stoltzfus gives this quote in order to shore up his argument for a Lacanian reading. He is correct in citing Robbe-Grillet, since this innovative author has based some of his method of writing, not his philosophy, on Camus, as evidenced in his critical essays. However, Robbe-Grillet does not approve of this sort of interpretation. He also wrote that there is no connection between man and things, where Stoltzfus, and others, see the word *lame*, used to describe both the waves and the knife blade, as being highly significant. (Has any such critic seriously wondered what choice of vocabulary items Camus had to describe knife blade and wave, [*lame*], or sea and mother, *mère* and *mer*? As the French say, there aren't thirty-six.) One must also wonder why such psychological interpretations are always predicated on the most morbid and/or prurient readings possible.

Robbe-Grillet, in any case, does not see things the same way that Stoltzfus and the partisans of psychological interpretations do. For Robbe-Grillet, man is man and things are things and things do not have human qualities. This attitude will be seen as antihumanist and therefore criminal and—be ignored.

The crime is to affirm that something exists in the world that is not man, that addresses no sign to him, that has nothing in common with him ... he sees these things, but he refuses to appropriate them, he refuses to enter into any shady understanding with them, any complicity; he asks nothing of them.

(Le crime c'est d'affirmer qu'il existe quelque chose dans le monde qui n'est pas l'homme, qui ne lui adresse aucun siqne, qui n'a rien de commun avec lui ... il les [les choses] voit, mais il refuse de se les approprier, il refuse d'entretenir avec elles aucune entente louche, aucune connivence; il ne leur demande rien.)[6]

This statement is clearly counter to the Freudian and Lacanian approaches to literature.

Moreover, the difficulty of a conventional psychological interpretation of *L'Étranger* was noted by John K. Simon in his article in *Yale French Studies*.[7] He considers the book to be the first successful novel in a contemporary movement that will lead to Robbe-Grillet and Claude Simon, a movement marked by its refusal of conventional social and psychological readings.

Critics who are partial to such interpretations have claimed that the beach scene that leads to the shooting is the first outburst of poetic writing in a book previously most noteworthy for its resolutely pedestrian narration and that it must therefore have special significance. Forgetting the wake, the funeral procession and their *figura*, such critics should at least look at the afternoon and evening Meursault spent on the balcony watching life in the streets. Even students reading their very first novel in French and struggling mightily with the simplest language, are struck by the sheer beauty of Camus' description. As Sunday came to an end, the streets were filled with strutting elegant young men and coquettish women meeting, flirting and joking. There were also the streetlamps and streetcars and their lights reflecting off damp pavement, bracelets and smiles. Camus describes the trees, the paling stars and all "until the first cat slowly crossed the again deserted street" (jusqu'à ce que le premier chat traverse lentement la rue de nouveau déserte). What great psychological horror story are we to make of that?

If the description of the beach scene, the burning sun and the death of the Arab are more emotionally charged, is it really because Meursault is being pursued by some evil Mother? (Just why do critics who insist that he is being so pursued, and identify the Mother as being Meursault's, i.e. Camus', never speak of the loving relationship between Dr. Rieux and his mother in *La Peste*? Or did someone else write that book?) The style that an artist chooses normally corresponds to the events that he is describing. Thus the

beach scene is in a more electrifying style simply because the act that will lead to Meursault's execution is more emotionally, and dramatically, charged than his spending a quiet day on his balcony and then going down to a now empty street to buy bread and pasta.

Robbe-Grillet speaks of *L'Étranger* in *Pour un nouveau roman* because Camus' hero resembles his own "heroes" in *Les Gommes* and *Le Voyeur*, heroes that were inspired, at least in part, by Meursault. Even though the literary goals of the two authors have nothing in common, Meursault embodies much of what Robbe-Grillet feels the new hero should be: a single name, no real, detailed past history, no face or physical description, no clearly defined profession or character.[8] In short, none of the standard literary tactics that allow us to identify with the hero and vicariously share in his trials and tribulations. Comparing Meursault to any hero of Balzac or Stendhal should suffice to convince all but those most incurably wedded to the new criticism that no serious links exist between the two schools of writing and that Camus must have had something else in mind when he wrote this book. In the same way, Robbe-Grillet's affinity for Camus' technique, not for his philosophy, came from his belief that Camus had created a "new" literary hero. He had not, of course; he had simply re-invented the hero of the *conte philosophique*. In any event, Camus' influence can best be seen by comparing Wallas (from *Les Gommes*) and Mathias (from *Le Voyeur*) to Rastignac or Julien Sorel, a comparison that should convince most that Robbe-Grillet also had something other than the conventional psychological novel in mind. If the doubters need further proof of Robbe-Grillet's thinking, they should read what he wrote in *La Jalousie*.

Two of the protagonists, A . . . and Franck, are reading a novel that takes place in Africa. The narrator, who listens and comments to himself but does not speak in the novel, notes that they never talk about the qualities of the text. "On the other hand, they often reproach the heros themselves for certain acts, or certain character traits, as they would for mutual friends" (En revanche il leur arrive souvent de reprocher aux héros eux-mêmes certains actes, ou certains traits de caractère comme ils le feraient pour des amis communs).[9] The same is true for the critics' treatment of *L'Étranger* even though they and Meursault are *not* mutual friends. Some, Girard, for instance, will condemn Meursault for his "crime" even though it is more than obvious that Camus does not. Camus' sympathy, if not affinity, for the accused and against the judges is a constant theme in *L'Homme révolté*. This attitude may well make some of Camus' admirers very uncomfortable. Nonetheless, he did write that if one cannot prove one's own virtue, an impossible task, the prisons must be opened.[10] That statement is a reflection of his soul, his thinking, and his position on the question of punishment.

As such, it is the only opinion that critics should take into account when discussing his works. The critics are free to disagree with his beliefs, but they have no right to falsify or to ignore them.

The major problem with standard political, psychological and sociological interpretations of *L'Étranger* is that they are by literary people who are in the business of seeking, and finding, learned interpretations of literary works. In his novel of student unrest at the University of Nanterre, Robert Merle, who, like Camus, was born in Algeria, presents us with a non-literary person. And an Arab at that.[11] The Arab, Abdelaziz, is a laborer, not a university student. As such, he is interested in mathematics, not literature, since a simple night-school certificate will allow him to get a better job, while studies in literature will not. His would-be helper, a French student, and therefore an intellectual, insists that he read *L'Étranger* and *L'Immoraliste*.

As Abdelaziz knows, and points out, despite all the talk about the "absurd," the only thing that is really absurd is the story itself. As both Camus and Abdelaziz knew, there is simply no possibility that a respectable, gainfully-employed European would ever have been arrested, much less tried, convicted and executed, for having killed an Arab armed with a knife. At least not in the Algeria of 1940. (Let us not forget the Arab prisoners' reaction at finding Meursault, a European, among them.) But since the critics do not live in that place and that period, they have chosen to ignore that simple fact. They should have started by wondering why Camus would base his novel on an impossible situation.

In the same way, the critics have agonized over why he had Meursault kill an Arab. Camus has even been accused of being anti-Arab, an accusation that he probably found too grotesque to bother to refute even though some then mistook his silence for an admission of guilt. He could have cited the articles he wrote attacking the government for its mistreatment of Arabs in pre-war Algeria. But he didn't. Nor did he bother to cite the difficulties he had had with press censors, and the Communist Party, which, for political reasons, backed the government's anti-Arab actions. (How many of the new critics remember that Dr. Rieux refused to cooperate with the journalist, Rambert, when the latter informed him that he could not, or would not, print the whole truth on the Arabs' condition in Algeria?)

Moreover, in a footnote to a discussion of Hitler's Germany and the savage destruction of Lidice, Camus wrote, "We should note that atrocities which could remind us of these excesses were committed in the colonies (India, 1857, Algeria, 1946 etc.) by European nations who obeyed the same irrational belief in racial superiority" (Il est frappant de noter que des atrocités qui peuvent rappeler ces excès ont été comises aux colonies [Indes, 1857, Algérie. 1945, etc.] par des nations européenes qui obéissaient au même

préjugé irrational de supériorité raciale).[12] That statement alone should put to rest all charges of his alleged racism.

But, as some critics continue to look for "proof" of his hatred of Arabs, we are asked to note that there is no Arab culture, such as mosques and souks, in the book. This argument assumes that Camus should have wished to be a latter-day Pierre Loti but I can see no reason for such an assumption. We are also asked to consider the alleged attack on his mother as a motive for the killing of the Arab. If one dares ask the question, "Why, if he hated Arabs to that point, did he not then indulge in language that would cast them in an unfavorable light?", one will simply be ignored, as the student ignored Abdelaziz's objections. The question that should have been asked is not "why did he kill an Arab?" but "Why did he *not* kill a European?"

Sartre was the first one to note that the book is not really a novel since there is no development in the character of Meursault. (He does come to a certain self-knowledge in prison, but that he has changed is very debatable.) He comes to us pretty much a full-blown figure such as we would find in a story by Voltaire. From this, Sartre deduced, logically, that the story is rather a *conte philosophique* in the same way that *Zadig* and *Micromégas* are. This type of literary work does not have as its primary goal the simple telling of a story. Rather, it has a point to prove or at least to demonstrate. Why should Camus have defended himself against those who read the book as an expression of their own unconscious desires or racism? Did Voltaire ever explain what he meant in his *contes*? Of course not. He assumed enough intelligence on the part of the reader to be able to determine that without his further help.

In any examination of *L'Étranger*, one must start with the question, why did Camus write the book? Certainly not for money, since he had no reputation that would lead to serious sales. Just as certainly not to tell a story, since there is no development in Meursault's character or conduct that could lead to a real story. Certainly not, and for the above reasons, to arrive at a philosophical position as Sartre did in *La Nausée*. As with Voltaire, there must have been such a position already determined. Since the one common bond of any importance between this work and, say, *La Peste, Réflexions sur la guillotine, L'Homme révolté*, etc., is the question of the death penalty, let us consider that to be the real subject of the book and see if such a conclusion can be justified. (If we wish to drag his father into the story, let us also remember that his father, who was in favor of capital punishment, witnessed an execution and was sickened by it. As was, finally, Tarrou of *La Peste*.) In chapter five of *L'Étranger*, Meursault thinks about his father who had been, in contrast to Camus' own father, obliged to witness an execution and had also been revolted by it. At the time, Meursault was disgusted by his father's reaction, but now he understands him. "How had I not seen that nothing was more important

than an execution and that, all in all, it was the only truly interesting thing for a man" (Comment n'avais je pas vu que rien n'était plus important qu'une exécution capitale et que, en somme, c'était la seule chose vraiment intéressante pour un homme).[13] Moreover, in *L'Homme révolté*, Camus wrote, "We will know nothing as long as we do not know if we have the right to kill this individual who stands before us or to accept that he be killed" (Nous ne saurons rien tant que nous ne saurons pas si nous avons le droit de tuer cet individu devant nous ou d'accepter qu'il soit tué).[14] It is obvious, at least to me, that these quotes justify my reading of the novel as a pamphlet against the death penalty.

But, since the majority of people, at any given time, are in favor of capital punishment, how can one write a book against it and make it seem a despicable and unacceptable punishment? The answer, I feel, is by setting up a straw man.

As I said, the question that should have been asked is why Meursault did not kill a European. The answer is, because the European would have to be a "real" person and the Arab would not. That is, since Arabs had no real rights, and often no real identity, in the Algeria of Camus' youth, certain weaknesses in his story would go unnoticed if only because other Europeans, not Arabs, would read the book. If this reasoning bothers you, or seems specious, answer the following questions. Why does the Arab have no name? Why does he not have a face or age or profession? Why has he no family, no friends? Who speaks for him at the trial? No one! He simply does not exist other than as a means to get Meursault condemned to the guillotine. Even in *Le Grand dadais*, by Poirot-Delpech, a brilliant novel sometimes compared to *L'Étranger*, the victim had a name, if only Freddy, and two relatives, if somewhat remote. Here, there is nothing. 0. Zero.

Why? Because it forces the reader to concentrate on Meursault, the alleged murderer. It shows him at work, at play. It talks of his friends, his dead mother, his loves, his future both before and after the shooting. He has neighbors, good and bad. (Raymond, too, exists only to get Meursault into a position where he will kill a non-person.) In short, it gives us a "murderer" but no victim, and the reader, Camus hopes, will be properly horrified at his unjust conviction and death sentence. And no one will notice that the Arab doesn't exist because Camus wants it that way. A European "victim" would demand, if not equal time of the author, at least a semblance of existence. Even the most minimal, the lowliest European would have what the Arab does not: family, friends, face, character, social position. A European victim might well have gotten the reader's sympathy and that would have drawn attention away from Meursault and his plight. Camus could not take that chance. A *conte philosophique* must always be played out with a stacked deck.

In a sense, it was the same in *La Peste*, a parable of the Second World War, that has only victims and no guilty. In that book, the rats came on their own, without a leader. There was no evil dictator or his minions to send people to the death camps and the incinerators. In both books, then, there is no one to really hate, no one to blame, no one to castigate, except, of course, the system itself that causes both death by war and death by guillotine. How very tidy.

In *Le Grand dadais*, our hero, Alain, accidentally kills a contortionist who works in a strip-joint. Freddy, as I said, had a name, a job and at least two relatives who testified, falsely it would seem, that his death was an irreparable loss. Poirot-Delpech really doesn't spend any time detailing Freddy's life because it simply is not relevant to the story, even if his death is. It is the same for Camus' treatment, or rather, his non-treatment, of the Arab whose sole contribution to the book is his death. But at least, unlike the Arab, Freddy is there, he speaks and participates, albeit minimally, in the story. Like Meursault, Alain also is tried and convicted, but with a difference. Reflecting on the events that got him into prison, Alain says to himself, "Like all criminals, I deserved a spanking or the guillotine. But these two extreme punishments, the only ones that I could have understood, ran the risk of shocking public opinion" (Comme tous les criminels, je méritais la fessée ou la guillotine. Mais ces deux punitions extrêmes, les seules que j'eusse comprises, risquaient de heurter l'opinion).[15] Instead, Alain got five years and Meursault the guillotine.

Where Poirot-Delpech is not really trying to prove a philosophical point and presents his characters honestly, Camus is, and, in a sense, cheats. After all, had Meursault gotten even an impossible five years in prison instead of the guillotine, can anyone seriously believe that this slim book would have had a second printing? As Judge Orthon put it in *La Peste*, "It's not the law that counts, it's the sentence" (Ce n'est pas la loi qui compte, c'est la condamnation). And Cottard, a criminal, tells Rieux that the judge is public enemy number one.[16]

There is much that is admirable in *L'Étranger*, but this subterfuge is not, because it fails to consider that there are at least two sides to the debate over the death penalty. But then, it didn't really matter since the central question was overlooked in the rush to analyze the hero's non-existent childhood and psyche.

Notes

1. Jean d'Ormesson, *Au plaisir de Dieu* (Paris: Gallimard, Coll. Folio, 1990), p. 516.

2. Ben Stoltzfus, in *Studies in Literature and Language* 31 (1989): 514–35.

3. Brian T. Fitch, *L'étranger d'Albert Camus: un texte, ses lecteurs, leurs lectures* (Paris: Larousse, 1979).

4. Louis Hudon, "*The Stranger* and the Critics," *Yale French Studies* 25 (1960): 59.

5. Jean-Paul Sartre, *Les Mots* (Paris: Gallimard, 1964), p. 152.

6. Alain Robbe-Grillet, *Pour un nouveau roman* (Paris: Gallimard, 1963), pp. 68–69.

7. John K. Simon, "The Glance of Idiots: The Novel of the Absurd," *Yale French Studies* 25 (1960): 112.

8. Robbe-Grillet, p. 31.

9. Robbe-Grillet, *La Jalousie* (Paris: Editions de Minuit, 1957) p. 82.

10. Albert Camus, *Oeuvres complètes*, Vol. 2 (Paris: Gallimard, 1981) p. 451.

11. Robert Merle, *Derrière la vitre* (Paris: Gallimard, 1970), pp. 144–45. I wrote to Professor Merle asking him if Abdelaziz was based on a real person. He answered that *all* (his emphasis) Algerian Arabs who had read *L'Étranger* found it inconceivable that a jury composed of Frenchmen in colonial Algeria would have condemned another Frenchman for having killed an Algerian pimp (his choice of word) armed with a knife. He added that no honest *pied noir* would contest that statement.

12. *Oeuvres complètes*, 2:590

13. Ibid., 1:1203.

14. Ibid., 2:414.

15. Bertrand Poirot-Delpech, *Le Grand dadais* (Paris: Denoël, 1958), reprinted in Folio, p. 143.

16. Albert Camus, *La Peste* (Paris: Livre de Poche, 1966), p. 118.

Meursault and Narrative

I̶t is commonplace to note that the meaning of *L'Étranger* stems from the juxtaposition of two different kinds of narrative, two different renderings of a series of events.[1] The first half of the novel presents Meursault's killing of the Arab from the point of view of the protagonist whereas the second presents the same killing from the point of view of "justice" and society. Indeed, Camus himself drew attention to the "parallelism of the two parts"[2] and his text underlines it repeatedly: senseless (absurd!) gesture or intentional act; accidental murder or premeditated crime; implausible—but true—series of unconnected events (Meursault is the anti-Forster) or plausible—but false—sequence of related actions. More specifically, Meursault finds everything that happened "very simple" (1171) and concentrates on the "how," on the murder and the events preceding it: "Raymond, the beach, the swim, the fight, the beach again, the little stream, the sun, and the five gunshots" (1171–72). Just the facts . . . On the other hand, the examining magistrate (like the judge and the prosecutor after him) favors complexity, wants to know "why," studies the murderer, and focuses not so much on the events as on their interpretation (1171–72). Meursault sees no link between his behavior on the day of his mother's funeral and his killing of the Arab (1171). But even his lawyer does not quite agree (1171). As for the prosecutor, he calls the protagonist a monster (1191), tells the court that it is facing the very

From *Resonant Themes: Literature, History, and the Arts in Nineteenth- and Twentieth-Century Europe*, edited by Stirling Haig, pp. 175–82. Copyright © 1999 by the Department of Romance Languages, the University of North Carolina at Chapel Hill.

same man who, "on the days following his mother's death, indulg[ed] in the most shameful debauchery" (1191), and accuses him of having killed his mother (1195) and even of being guilty of another parricide that the same court is getting ready to examine (1195–96). Meursault states that he had no intention of killing the Arab (1186, 1196) and that he did it "because of the sun" (1196); but the prosecutor claims that Meursault's actions were deliberate (1193, 1194) and successfully argues that the murder of the Arab results from "the workings of a criminal soul" (1193).

If Meursault's (or Camus's!) narrative has been the object of considerable study and if the (essential) traits of his narratorial manner have been well analyzed (the affinity with syntactic parataxis and coordination as opposed to subordination, the preference for the *passé composé*, the refusal of introspection, the terseness, and so on), Meursault's attitude as a narratee, as a receiver of narrative, like his more or less explicit comments on the stories he thinks about or comes in contact with have elicited less attention. If Meursault the narrator and his narrative stance are famous, Meursault the theorist or critic of narrative and his metanarrative positions are not. Yet there are many stories mentioned or reported by the protagonist, even apart from the ones produced during the trial by the judge, the lawyers, or the witnesses: the old janitor's account of funerals in Marengo (1128), for example; the Fernandel movie that Marie would like to see (1137); Raymond's narrative of the conflict with his lover and her brother (1143–46); the story of Meursault's father attending a public execution (1201); and so forth. There are also many direct or indirect comments by the protagonist about these stories. For instance, he finds "correct and interesting" the janitor's tactless remarks about the necessity of burying the dead "very quickly, because it was hot down in the plain, especially in these parts" (1128) and he considers the Fernandel movie "funny in parts but really quite silly" (1137).

Perhaps the most famous story mentioned by the protagonist is "the story of the Czech fellow" (1180) which he reads in an old bit of newspaper. After an absence of twenty-five years, a villager from Czechoslovakia returned to his country and decided to give his mother and sister a surprise. He booked a room under an assumed name in the small hotel that they ran. Failing to recognize him, they murdered him to take his money and, upon discovering his identity, they killed themselves. A similar story was reported in 1935 in *L'Echo d'Alger* and *La Dépêche Algérienne*.[3] Besides, versions of it can be found in many different folk traditions (1780). In any case, Camus used it for the plot of *Le Malentendu* and wrote that the play suggested "an ethics of sincerity. If man wants to be recognized, he has to say plainly who he is. If he keeps silent or if he lies, he dies alone and everything around him is condemned to misfortune. If, on the contrary, he speaks the truth,

he will die, no doubt, but after having helped others and himself to live" (1785). Meursault too, who read the story thousands of times and was characterized by Camus as a man who "doesn't play the game" and who "refuses to lie" (1920) finds that "the traveler had deserved it a little and that one should never play" (1180). Of course, both the traveler's story and Meursault's involve violent deaths and if, in the *fait divers*, a mother kills her son, in the novel, Meursault is accused of matricide. Moreover, both stories feature a "protagonist-as-stranger" and it should be noted that Meursault discusses the Czech traveler just before the famous "recognition" scenes in his cell, when his facial expression first does not correspond to its reflection in a metal dish and then does and when he hears a voice which he identifies as his (1181). In fact, Meursault's critical evaluation of the *fait divers* could be applied to his own narrative. About the story of the traveler, he notes: "In one way, it was implausible. In another, it was natural" (1180). Later on, during his trial, he thinks that the prosecutor's "way of viewing the events [is] plausible" (1194) and he is very much aware that his own explanation of his actions—"it was because of the sun" (1196)—sounds ridiculous. But "le vrai peut quelquefois n'être pas vraisemblable . . ."

At least one other feature of the news item calls for comment. According to the novel's protagonist, the first part of it is missing, though he gathers that the events took place in Czechoslovakia (1180). The beginning of Meursault's narrative is missing too or, at any rate, it is imprecise: "Today, mother died. Or maybe yesterday. I don't know" (1125). So is the end, in a way, since it refers to the future and to the virtual: "For everything to be accomplished, for me to feel less lonely, what remained was to wish that there should be many spectators on the day of my execution and that they should greet me with cries of hatred" (1209–10). More significantly, though Meursault and the prosecutor do not contradict each other with regard to what happened, the beginnings of their accounts differ. As pointed out earlier, in his interview with the magistrate, Meursault began with Raymond (1171–72). The prosecutor, on the other hand, sums up the facts "from [the] mother's death onward" (1193–94). The ends of the two accounts also differ. Meursault mentioned the five gunshots. His accuser points to the murderer's utter lack of regret for his crime— "Not once in the course of the proceedings has this man seemed moved by his abominable offense" (1194)—and he claims that it constitutes further proof of what really happened. For him, the end conditions the beginning just as it is conditioned by it and they both illuminate what comes in between: his narrative is an "Aristotelian" one, a doubly oriented whole with an interacting beginning, middle, and end. For Meursault, on the contrary, whatever links obtain between his being Raymond's friend, his going to the beach, and his killing the Arab are only contingent.

If the protagonist contests teleologically determined narratives and veri-similar ones, it is not because he is incapable of understanding or evaluating them and their effects. Meursault is a stranger, no doubt, but, as he himself would argue, he is not necessarily strange: "I was like everybody else, absolutely like everybody else" (1171). He drinks wine and café au lait, eats fried eggs, bread, and pasta, plays billiards, goes to the races, likes to swim, and has a "girl." He is also a good employee, a good neighbor, and a good friend who "knows what's what" (1146) and is "all right" (1189). Though he may never have had "any real imagination" (1203), he can invent narratives in which a condemned prisoner escapes at the last minute (1200) and he can picture himself getting out of jail and attending an execution (1201). More-over, he can be an effective narrator—"I told Marie [Salamano's] story and she laughed" (1149)—even though he often is an impatient one: "I stayed behind to explain to the women what had happened. Mme Masson was cry-ing and Marie was very pale. It annoyed me to explain to them. I fell silent after a while and I smoked, looking at the sea" (1163).[4] When he goes to the movies with his friend Emmanuel, whose name—like that of Marie or that of Céleste—is so evocative and "who does not always understand what is happening on the screen" (1148), Meursault clarifies things for him. He even seems able to tell the kind of movie that people have seen from the way they look when coming out of the theater: "Soon the neighborhood movie houses disgorged a stream of spectators into the street. Among them, the young men were gesturing with more determination than usual and I thought that they had seen an adventure movie" (1139). He can certainly appreciate the source and function of narratives—desire, memory, killing time, or pedagogy (1178, 1200, 1201, 1208)—as well as their plausibility or lack thereof, their coher-ence or incoherence, their effectiveness, their power. Whereas Meursault con-siders the prosecutor's account plausible and relatively clear, for instance, he thinks that his own defender is much less talented and he finds his speech ridiculous. In particular, he notes that the defender fails to refer to the funeral and he understands that it is a serious omission (1197).

No, what motivates the protagonist's narrative preferences is not a lack of judgment or understanding. What motivates him is a regard for truth. It should be noted that most of Meursault's narratological comments pertain to "true" narratives, purporting to relate what actually happened, what really occurred at some real point in time and space. Not that he has no use for fiction. He seems to enjoy going to the movies and even does it twice with Emmanuel in less than a week (1148); he mentions having read—in some novel?—the description of an examination scene (1169) and also mentions having read "that one ended up by losing track of time in jail" (1180); and, as pointed out above, he invents escape narratives and imagines himself free

again: "it was not reasonable. . . . But, obviously, one cannot always be reasonable" (1201). Still, given his situation, what could be more ordinary—what could be less *strange*—than Meursault's interest in facts and in the adequacy of accounts to what is the case?

Perhaps the very first kind of narrative (implicitly) criticized in the novel is journalistic narrative. Because newspapers are a "little short of copy in the summer" (1183), Meursault's trial is given undue attention and its importance is exaggerated. But Meursault believes that "one should [not] exaggerate" (1178) and he dismisses—narratives conditioned by their (potential) exchange value—like the journalists' but also like the prosecutor's or the defender's (a narrative for money, a narrative for a life)—tendentious accounts in which facts yield to rhetoric. No doubt, it is Meursault's distrust of rhetoric that explains, at least partially, the very quality of his own narration in general and his terseness in particular. The novel repeatedly underlines that the protagonist is a man of few words. The examining Magistrate, for example, speaks of his reputation for taciturnity (1171) and, during the trial, Céleste recognizes that he "doesn't waste his breath for nothing" (1189), Salamano explains that he "no longer had anything to say to [his] mother and that that was why [he'd] fixed her up to enter the home" (1190), and the prosecutor emphasizes that "he knows the value of words" (1194). But if Meursault's reserve is a matter of temperament (the strong silent type) as well as a matter of culture—Céleste, after all, points out that everyone knows what "being all right" or "having a stroke of bad luck" means (1189)—it also springs from his rhetorical convictions and his attempt to provide a minimally distorting representation of what actually took place: the simpler the narrative configuration adopted, the more accurate the results; the less said the better.

The protagonist's "anti-rhetorical" stance intersects—and is underlined by—the motif of "good references" (of adequate acts of referring), which the novel uses insistently. Apart from the title of the novel (who—or what—is *l'étranger?*), apart, too, from the killing of the Arab (accidental murder or premeditated crime?) and from the killer himself (should he be called a criminal and parricide?), there is, for example, the matter of Raymond's real activities (pimp or warehouse-keeper?), the identity of the Czech villager (unknown traveler or brother and son?), Meursault's refusal to address the prison chaplain as "Father"—"I answered him that he was not my father: he was with the others" (1208)—and, above all, his reaction to one of his lawyer's oratorical maneuvers: "At one moment, however, I paid attention because he was saying: 'It is true that I have killed.' Then he went on in that vein, saying 'I' every time he referred to me. I was very surprised. . . . I thought it was a way of excluding me even more from the case, of reducing me to nothing, of taking my place" (1196–97).

Like the other cases in which the problem of reference comes to the fore, the protagonist's "surprise" at his lawyer's flourish can be linked not only to his impatience with rhetoric but also to the Oedipal configuration sketched by Camus's novel. It has often been pointed out that Meursault, who kills a man accidentally and is denounced as a parricide, proves frequently antagonistic to "fathers" (*Perez*, the *patron*, the prison chaplain, etc.) and, of course, the Oedipus myth develops in terms of referential ambiguities (is the best answer to the Sphinx's riddle "Man" or "Human beings" or "Me"? did Oedipus kill Laius or an old man? did he marry Jocasta or his mother? etc.). But there is more (also relatable, no doubt, to Oedipal questions). Commenting on his trial, the protagonist remarks that "it is always interesting to hear oneself being talked about" (1193) but adds that he found one thing rather annoying: whenever he tried to intervene, he was advised not to. He felt excluded from the case, as if his fate was being decided without him and he wanted to remind everyone that he was the accused and that "[it] is important to be the accused" (1193). Soon, however, he came to "recognize that the interest found in being talked about doesn't last very long" (1193). The implicit criticism of "identification narratives," of "relevant" narratives, of narratives telling about their receivers, is notable. But more crucially, and as in the case of the defense lawyer's first-person rhetoric, what is repudiated is speaking for someone, in place of someone, about what happened to someone.

The difficulty (the impossibility!) of speaking accurately about something one has not experienced, of commenting appropriately on situations one has not lived is invoked throughout the protagonist's narration. Céleste, for example, always says that the way Salamano treats his dog "is a crying shame" but Meursault thinks that "no one can really know" (1142). When Raymond asks him what he would do if he were in his shoes, he again says that "one [can] never know" (1145). When Marie wonders whether she loves him, he, of course, cannot "know anything about that" (1154). As mentioned above, he had read that, in prison, "one ends up by losing track of time" but it is only after he is jailed that this actually means something definite to him (1180–81). Similarly, it is only after he realizes he has been talking to himself aloud that he remembers and appreciates what the nurse had said at his mother's funeral: "there [is] no way out" (1181). Later, he also remembers a story his mother used to tell him: although the mere thought of it made him sick, his father had gone to see an execution and, on returning home, he had been violently ill. Meursault had found this behavior a little disgusting; but now he understands: "[i]t was so natural. How had I not seen that nothing was more important than an execution and that, ultimately, it was the only really interesting thing for a man" (1201). It is not unlike Meursault's beliefs about the guillotine. For a long time, perhaps because of the French

Revolution and what he learned in school, he thought that, "to get to the guillotine, one had to go up steps and climb on to a scaffold" (1202). Then, one day, he remembered a picture in the newspaper: the guillotine actually stood flush on the ground: "One always has exaggerated ideas about what one doesn't know" (1202). Finally, in the very last pages of the novel, as he is facing the end of his life, the protagonist understands why, with death so close, his mother had been ready to make a fresh start and he realizes that he too is "ready to start life all over again," that he has been happy, and that he is "happy still" (1209).

The moral seems clear: you've got to have been there (or, even, you've got to be there); and it constitutes more than an indirect plea not to be judged (more than a way of asking who, other than Meursault, can know or understand what happened on the beach). Thematically, it helps to put into question the accuracy of (narrative) representation—after all, the map is not the territory, the story not the event, the word not the thing—as well as the ultimate validity of ethical or epistemological judgments founded on representations, that is, perhaps, the ultimate validity of any ethical or epistemological judgments.[5] From the point of view of characterization, the moral helps to account for Meursault as stranger and, in particular, for his estrangement from himself. The protagonist admits, at one point, that he does not feel much regret for what he has done and he goes on to explain that he has "never been able really to regret anything" (1195). Presumably, he is no longer "there . . ." Later in his narration, as he describes waiting for the day of his execution, he says: "I've never liked being taken by surprise. When something happens to me, I prefer to be there" (1203). But is there a there there and can one ever be—or stay—there? Last but not least, from a narrational perspective, the moral helps to explain why it is impossible to situate in time and space Meursault's act of telling. Does it occur after the killing or also before it? Does it take place in jail or also out of it (1125, 1141, 1200, *et passim*)? Perhaps it is above all because no one is ever quite there that the narrating instance is so elusive and that Meursault is a stranger.

Notes

1. *L'Étranger* in Albert Camus, *Théâtre, récits, nouvelles*. Paris: Gallimard, 1962. All my references are to this edition and the translations are mine.

2. Albert Camus, *Carnets II*. Paris: Gallimard, 1964: 30.

3. Roger Grenier, ed., *Album Camus*. Paris: Gallimard, 1982: 128.

4. The protagonist is also an impatient narratee (1156, 1173, 1193, *et passim*) and his impatience has a bearing on his fate.

5. This may be one basis for Camus' discomfort with "history" as well as for his continued preoccupation with judges and judging.

COLIN DAVIS

The Cost of Being Ethical:
Fiction, Violence, and Altericide

Murder is commonplace in all forms of fiction, so that to tell and listen to stories is to have a taste of what it is like to kill. Oedipus's story is parricidal before it is incestuous. You meet a man at a crossroads and you kill him. Nothing could be simpler. In his novel *L'Étranger*, Albert Camus updates the scenario for the era of decolonization. At the center of the novel is the apparently senseless murder of an Arab on a beach in Algeria. But the murder is not so hard to explain. In an atmosphere of fear, resentment, and simmering violence, a white man confronts an Arab and takes his life. There may be no particular reason to kill him, but neither can Meursault, the murderer, think of any good reason *not* to kill him. Murder, here and elsewhere, is not just one fictional theme among others; rather, fiction is deeply enmeshed with a view of humankind as murderous or, as I have put it elsewhere, altericidal.[1] Killing others is one of the basic things that human beings do, and fiction gives us a glimpse of what we are missing.

It is no coincidence that the story of Oedipus is also a story of detection in which part of what is at stake are the identities of victim and killer. Detective fiction in its modern form distills the tensions of altericidal fiction in general as it revolves around the attempt to identify killers and motives. A murder has been committed and virtually anyone could be guilty. Detective novels and films thrive on twists that illustrate that the net of suspicion

From *Common Knowledge* 9, no. 2 (2003): 241–53. Copyright © 2003 Duke University Press.

can never be thrown too widely; for example, the detective investigating the crime or the judge trying the case may turn out to be the murderer, or the apparent victim of the crime may have faked his or her own death in order to kill someone else.[2] No one is above suspicion, not even the victim or the detective. As Slavoj Žižek puts it, detective fiction shows us "that we *are* murderers in the unconscious of our desire, insofar as the actual murderer realizes the desire of the group constituted by the corpse."[3] But Žižek explains that detective fiction also lets us off the hook by identifying the killer and thereby attributing the dangerously free-floating guilt to a single perpetrator. It could have been us, but it was not. Our murderous desires are barely awake before they are disavowed and plunged back into the unconscious. Fiction fleetingly reminds us that we are beings capable of killing, but then it allows us to forget the fact again.

Fiction, then, may be complicit with the murders it describes. It draws some of its energy from our hostility to others and from our capacity to kill, but it allows us to dissociate ourselves from the desires to which it gives utterance. The lesson to be drawn from this is hardly edifying. If fiction were ethical, literary criticism would not need to be. The various forms of ethical criticism that have flourished in recent years would be redundant if literature were genuinely as subversive, humane, emancipatory, and civilizing as we might wish. For every Jane Austen, there is a Marquis de Sade. More often than not, fiction posits violence as the natural habitat of humankind, and to spare our uneasy consciences, it offers a fig leaf to make us look and feel more civilized. Much fiction is at a far remove from "respect for the other," which in postmodern culture has acquired the status—in place of universal or transcultural principles—of an almost unquestioned moral axiom. Difference or alterity is supposed now to be savored, not eradicated. Emmanuel Levinas is frequently cited as among the major sources of this ethics of otherness. His thought revolves around a primordial encounter between self and other in which the self recognizes the absolute otherness of the other and, rather than responding to it with violence, conceives an infinite responsibility toward it. Oedipus at the crossroads and Meursault on the beach suggest a very different scenario. Confronted with the other, obliged to share the world with someone who is too like me or not enough like me for comfort, I will kill.

There is an age-old bond between fictional and nonfictional violence. The stories that reflect and mold our desires rehearse the same murderous entanglements of self and other—the same intransigent, wounded narcissisms and stubborn reassertions of self—that underpin the monotonous, all too real violence that we see, for example, in the relation of Israel and Palestine. Is there an alternative? To examine that possibility, I want to consider the connection between violence and fiction as theorized in the early work

of René Girard and show how it elucidates what I regard as the archetypal altericidal encounter: the murder of the Arab on the beach in *L'Étranger*. One of Camus's later short stories, "L'Hôte" from *L'Exil et le royaume*, restages that encounter of white colonialist and Arab, but this time murder is avoided. Instead, something resembling Levinasian generosity toward the other is intimated. The intimation does not, however, lead to a happy resolution of conflict, and what is properly Levinasian about the story is its desperate awareness that there is a high price to be paid for being ethical.

In his early book *Mensonge romantique et vérité romanesque*, Girard's account of fictional texts lays foundations for his later work on violence, the sacred, and scapegoating, which would come, in its ambitious theoretical sweep, to include myth, anthropology, and religion. Girard's book appeared in 1961, the same year as Levinas's massively influential *Totalité et infini*, and the two share some concerns—for example, the relation between self and other, and its role in the production of desire. The differences between these texts, though, are more important than the similarities. In Levinas's account, desire is distinguished from need, which can be satisfied because it is directed toward contingent and attainable objects. But for Levinas, desire is desire for the absolutely other and cannot be assuaged, because the other can never be comprehended or possessed. Although what Levinas calls *le tiers*, the third party, will go on to play an important role in his attempt to explain the establishment of social justice, this initial account of desire involves only self and other. Girard argues, on the contrary, that desire is triangular from the outset. What I desire is not inherently desirable or unattainably other. Here, the other is the instigator of desire and not its object. I desire what the other desires, I desire it *because* the other desires it. So there are three figures involved in the Girardian drama of desire: the desiring subject, the desired object, and the prestigious mediator who makes the object desirable to the subject by desiring or possessing it first. This "desire *according to the other*" is not the spontaneous expression of an autonomous subject; rather, it shows the imbrication of self and other, and the essential role of the other in the production of my own desire.

Triangular or mimetic desire can easily turn to violence. By desiring what the other desires, I desire also to be like, even *to be*, that person. But I also establish the other as my rival. The deadlock of desire is that the mediator both makes the object of desire desirable and stands in the way of my obtaining it. The importance of literature in Girard's account is that the triangular nature of desire is understood, and its ramifications explored, only in great fiction. Indeed, the understanding of triangular desire appears to be a defining criterion of great fiction. Moreover, all great literature concludes in the same way: by showing that "desire *according to the other*" may also be renounced.

The protagonists of Dostoevsky, Stendhal, or Proust abandon their mimetic entanglements in order to recover "desire *according to self*"—the ability, that is, to desire outside the thrall of the other and thereby achieve a new, more genuine knowledge of both self and others. Just as, in his later work, Girard would seek instances (in the Christian Gospels particularly) where the logic of sacrifice is suspended, so in this early book, he insists that the potential violence of mimetic rivalries may be avoided. Triangular desire is not the only form of desire, and "desire *according to self*" is, after all, a viable and more authentic alternative to "desire *according to the other*." Girard is categorical and uncompromising in his insistence that all great novels share the same insight into mimetic desire and conclude in the same way by renouncing it: "The conclusions to novels are necessarily banal because they all repeat, literally, the same thing."[4]

Girard does not refer to or use the theories elaborated in *Mensonge romantique et vérité romanesque* in his own compelling reading of Camus's *L'Étranger*.[5] Girard nevertheless makes telling points that can be further amplified by reference to mimetic desire. Like all readers of Camus's novel, Girard puzzles over why Meursault kills the Arab with no apparent motive. Initially, Girard describes the murder as a "structural flaw": Camus needs Meursault to commit a terrible act in order to be condemned by society, but Camus also needs him to be innocent in order to lend pertinence to the attack on the judicial process contained in the second half of the novel. The crime must be both motiveless (so that the reader does not believe in Meursault's guilt) and extreme (so that Meursault cannot escape judgment). Later in the article, however, Girard proposes an explanation of the crime that sketches out a motive for the murder. Meursault, like Camus himself, is a romantic solipsist who seeks total isolation from others while also secretly longing for contact. Despite his attack on the illusions of communication and public success, Camus's literary ambitions are revealed by the very fact that he published a novel at all. The novel reaches out to others even though, thematically, it represents the isolation of the solitary subject. Meursault's crime reflects this tension between the proud rejection of others and the desire for contact and recognition. Because Meursault cannot own up to his desire for contact, the desire is expressed paradoxically through violence. The murder is, as Girard puts it, "really a secret effort to reestablish contact with humanity."[6] Being tried and condemned is not an unfortunate consequence of this crime so much as its hidden purpose. By killing, Meursault imposes his existence and brings himself to the attention of others; he brings himself especially to the attention of the law. Even condemnation, even hatred, are a kind of bond with others. This notion is confirmed in the final sentence of the novel: "For everything to be complete, for me to feel less alone, it remained for me to wish for

there to be a lot of spectators on the day of my execution and for them to greet me with cries of hatred."[7]

Girard's theory of mimetic desire provides a means to amplify this account of Meursault's crime. The episode on the beach is dominated by triangular relations and the desire to reestablish some form of relation with others. At first, Meursault is part of a group of three men, though he feels excluded by the closeness of the friendship between the other two, Raymond and Masson. This prompts him to seek to strengthen his relationship with Raymond. In an encounter preceding the murder, Meursault had taken Raymond's revolver from him and prevented him from shooting the Arab whom subsequently he himself shoots. In this encounter, the possibility of murder is first raised when Raymond asks Meursault if he should kill the Arab.[8] Raymond instigates the desire to kill that Meursault will later implement, so Raymond serves as the prestigious mediator whose desires become Meursault's. Meursault wishes to emulate him, and even to surpass him, by actually committing the murder that he had earlier prevented Raymond from perpetrating. Following the mediator's lead, Meursault wishes first to possess the gun, then to kill the Arab. The situation is further complicated by the implied rivalry between Meursault and the Arab. Meursault perceives the Arab as belonging to a unified group and thus as possessing the sense of companionship that Meursault desires.[9] Feelings of rivalry and hostility may be exacerbated by the fact that the Arab belongs in Algeria in a way that Meursault never can. So the Arab too plays the role of prestigious mediator, in that he is perceived as possessing, and blocking Meursault's access to, the objects of Meursault's desire. The Arab represents the possibility of a sense of community, and at the moment of the crime he occupies the place on the beach that Meursault longs to usurp and that metonymically stands for Algeria (a land in which Meursault will always be an outsider or interloper). The murder is thus doubly motivated. Meursault emulates Raymond's hostility toward the Arab through his desire to kill, and Meursault acts out of rivalry with the Arab by eliminating him in order to claim his place on the beach.

The murder of the Arab illustrates how mimetic desire leads readily to violence. Unable to desire except through mediation of the other, Meursault kills in the place of the other (Raymond). But Meursault kills also in order to destroy the other (the Arab) who instigates and impedes his desire. It may even be that what the other is perceived as possessing is desire itself, so that the murder represents an inevitable impasse, destroying the other in order to become what only the other can be: an autonomous, desiring subject. This application of Girard suggests that, far from being senseless and unmotivated, the murder of the Arab is consistent with patterns of behavior predicted by the theory of triangular desire. The theory serves to show the unity of

disparate phenomena and makes sense of otherwise bewildering data. Girard is out of sympathy with many contemporary theorists in his insistence that his theory has the status of objective truth and is universally applicable. As we have seen, Girard is adamant that great literature always effectively says the same thing as it explores and then renounces the mechanisms of mimetic desire. Girard claims a privileged hermeneutic status for his position—and when he delivers to us the meaning of a text, indeed of all texts, he effectively situates himself (in the terms of his own theory) as the prestigious mediator who possesses and offers us the key to understanding. This desire to possess a truth that draws together disparate experiences is shared by Meursault and by Camus's readers. The murder that Meursault commits, however senseless it may appear, is also a flight from senselessness, in that it causes his removal from the meaningless open spaces he has lived in until that point and subjects him to the enclosed and hence meaningful world of the penal system. That Meursault positively welcomes being taken in hand by a higher authority is confirmed immediately after the murder (in the first paragraph of the second part of the novel). Meursault's initial discussion with his examining magistrate leads to explicit approval of the provisions of the law, for example in supplying him with a defense lawyer: "I found it very convenient that the law took care of these details. I told him [the examining magistrate] so. He agreed with me and concluded that the law was well made."[10]

By committing a murder, and being taken as a consequence under the command of the law, Meursault gives to his life an order and structure that otherwise it would lack. He agrees to be an actor in a story in which the law will have the final word. On this point, though, Meursault deviates significantly from the Girardian model. Girard describes the prestige of the mediator whose desire is not mediated by others. Moreover, Girard places himself in the position of the mediator by claiming to own what his readers desire: the truth. Meursault's actions indicate a more ambivalent relation to the mediator. While acting according to the logic of mimetic rivalry, Meursault also perceives that the mediator is an impostor and that his prestige is unfounded. Neither Raymond nor the Arab actually possess what it is Meursault desires through them. When Meursault kills the Arab whom Raymond had failed to murder, Meursault is simultaneously in rivalry with two mediators, surpassing one (Raymond), by committing the act he himself could not, and destroying the other (the Arab). But Meursault does not surpass or destroy them in order to dispossess them of their prestige and to claim for himself what he imagines is theirs. On the contrary, the murder becomes the paradoxical means by which their prestige can be maintained. Only by excluding himself definitively from possession of what he could never possess (comradeship, Algeria) can Meursault maintain the illusion that it was ever possible to own

it and that the mediators of his desire were not impostors. In other words, Meursault kills the Arab in order to continue believing that a richer, more fulfilled life could have been possible. Girard places himself in the position of the mediator in order to establish himself as the spokesperson of truth; he thereby draws his authority from the mediator's prestige. Meursault kills in order to maintain belief in that prestige, even though he suspects that the prestige is unwarranted. The murder does not enable him to obtain the truth himself, but the murder does make it possible for him to maintain the belief that someone else might know the truth. In the act of murder is encrypted the awareness that the mediator is an impostor and the insight that such knowledge is intolerable. It appears to be better to kill than to live in the knowledge that there is no higher order (or, in Lacanian terms, that the Big Other does not exist).

L'Étranger leads to an ethical and epistemological impasse. It depicts killing as a necessary expedient for maintaining the intelligibility of experience and the intelligibility of the world—and it offers no prospect of securing meaning outside the murderous triangles of desire. The novel does not offer an alternative to Meursault's implicit acceptance that violence is the only means of securing a coherent, patterned universe. In this context, the interest of Camus's later short story "L'Hôte" lies in the way it reproduces elements from *L'Étranger* and combines them in significantly new ways.[11] As in *L'Étranger*, the protagonist of "L'Hôte" is a white Algerian, a schoolteacher named Daru. The story describes an encounter between Daru and an Arab who, as in *L'Étranger*, is referred to only as *l'Arabe*. The background of simmering violence, racial tension, and the forthcoming war of independence is the same. Here, though, it is the Arab who is the murderer. A local policeman, Balducci, has arrested him for killing a cousin. Balducci delivers the Arab to Daru with instructions to take him to the nearby town of Tinguit for imprisonment and trial. Because of the incipient unrest, Balducci cannot leave the area. Daru refuses, but Balducci leaves the Arab with him anyway. Daru prepares food for the Arab and they spend a night together in the schoolhouse; Daru hopes that the Arab will take the opportunity to run away. On the following day, the two men apparently set out for Tinguit, but rather than handing the Arab over to the authorities, Daru gives him food and money, and encourages him to escape. However, Daru later sees that the Arab has continued his journey toward Tinguit and imprisonment. On returning to his school, Daru finds a threatening message on the blackboard: "You handed over our brother. You will pay."[12]

There are so many similarities between "L'Hôte" and *L'Étranger* that the story can be regarded as a rewriting of the novel. Both texts describe a confrontation between a white man and an Arab against a background of

violence, and both are concerned with the authority of the law. The triangular relations of the earlier text are reproduced in the later one. However, in the short story, Meursault's act of violence against the Arab is translated into an act of generosity. Meursault kills in order to submit himself to the law, to reassure himself that there is some higher order even if that order is absurd and arbitrary, whereas Daru rejects the law and refuses to follow the instructions transmitted to him by Balducci. In *L'Étranger*, the operations of mimetic rivalry give a degree of coherence to what takes place; in "L'Hôte," mimetic desire has ceased to govern the actions of the protagonist. Daru is not in thrall either to Balducci, whose law he does not respect, or to the Arab, whose absurd crime infuriates him. In the absence of any mechanism to direct and to explain the action, the story's key decisions remain unmotivated. No reason is given or suggested for why Daru encourages the Arab to escape or for why the Arab chooses instead to hand himself over to the authorities.

The ambiguities of the short story are anticipated in its title. *L'hôte* in French may mean either host or guest. It may refer to Daru as host or to the Arab as guest, or it may suggest that the respective positions of guest and host are themselves insecure.[13] The white man in whose residence the Arab spends a night lives in a land to which the Arab may have a better claim than he himself does, so that the Arab is both his reluctant guest and unwilling host. To confuse matters further, we are told that Daru was born in Algeria and feels exiled anywhere else;[14] he may not belong there in the same way as the Arab does, but neither does Daru belong anywhere else. Like the Arab, he is both host and guest—Daru is both on his home ground and alienated from it. Thus, the title of the story raises and refuses to resolve some of its key questions: who belongs here, who has the right to claim this land as his own, and who is the trespasser? Moreover, echoes of other words can be heard in the title. *L'hôte* is phonetically close to *l'autre* (the other), etymologically linked to *otage* (hostage), and reminiscent of (though not etymologically related to) the Latin *hostis* (enemy). Since, despite Daru's hospitality, the Arab is strictly speaking a prisoner rather than a guest, he is more an *otage* than an *hôte*. Whether or not he should be treated as an enemy is uncertain—as this short exchange between Daru and Balducci indicates: "Is he against us? / I don't think so. But you can never tell."[15] My guest/host may also be my other: my hostage and enemy. These ambiguities are reflected in Daru's treatment of the Arab, which involves fear, resentment, hostility, and anger as well as hospitality and generosity.[16] In *L'Étranger*, Meursault resolves ambiguity by submitting to the coherence afforded by mimetic desire. Murder cuts through the Gordian knot by inviting the intervention of the law. There is, it is suggested, a higher order that I may not understand but that nevertheless underwrites the promise of order. Meursault, then, is like Abraham, who does not know

why God calls upon him to sacrifice Isaac but is prepared to obey, because it is better to put one's trust in a higher authority than to believe that God could be insane or criminal. For Daru, there is no higher order to motivate, to justify, or to make sense of his choices. Killing the other offers no means of restoring sense. When he asks the Arab why he killed, the Arab's reply is, to say the least, uninformative: "He ran away. I ran after him."[17] Meursault kills the Arab in order to preserve the possibility of a higher order of truth and meaning; rejecting any such prospect, Daru chooses instead an act of generosity that puts his own life in danger.

The Arab's apparent decision to hand himself over to the authorities, and the threatening message left on Daru's blackboard, prevent Camus's story from falling into glib moralizing. Daru offends Balducci and tries to help a killer escape from justice; yet his act turns out to be pointless, as the Arab prefers imprisonment to freedom, and Daru may have to pay for his involvement with his own life. Trying to help the Arab results only in embittering others against him. There is no sense here that preferring generosity to enmity will provide any simple resolution to the situation of Algeria on the brink of its brutal war of independence. At the end of the story, Daru is misunderstood and alone. His act has only exacerbated the hostility between whites and Arabs. "L'Hôte," then, is no simple fable about how to become an ethical subject. By the ambiguities of its title, it poses and leaves unresolved fundamental questions about property, ownership, and belonging; and it dramatizes the fraught relations with the other (the other as host and guest, prisoner and enemy). The story offers no certainty that Daru has done the right thing, no reason to think that his actions have had any beneficial effect on anyone, and no prospect that the forthcoming violent conflict between whites and Arabs can be avoided. Indeed, by trying to help a murderer escape, Daru may have succeeded only in making himself his second victim; the Arab's decision to go to prison may result in Daru's death, and we have no way of knowing that this result was not its purpose. Camus's story hints that the attempt to forge any sort of bond with the other may lead only to further racial hatred.

Critics have measured Daru's action by Levinasian ethical standards, and this comparison is worth further exploration for the light it sheds both on Levinas and on Camus's story.[18] Levinas's ideas, of course, have been widely disseminated and discussed in recent years; and although the term *postmodern* is not one that he would have readily accepted, his work has been welcomed in postmodern circles because it provides an ethics that does not rely on imperatives, rules, principles, universals, or absolutes. Levinas's basic aim is to reassert the irreducible otherness of the other against a philosophical tradition that has tended to suppress otherness by assimilating it to sameness.

In Levinas's account, I should not assume that the other is basically like me, that we are all the same "under the skin"; on the contrary, I should endeavor to encounter what is truly other about the other, rather than rejecting or seeking to eradicate what is utterly alien to my understanding of the world. The encounter with otherness is ethical, because ethics is the attempt to remain exposed to the other (including the stranger, widow, and orphan in their vulnerability) and to act on my responsibility for others. I must not succumb to the temptation to repudiate the other. But Levinasian ethics does not impose any particular course of action; instead, it posits responsibility for the other as the condition of our own subjectivity.

Daru's attempt to understand why the Arab killed his cousin illustrates both the attempt and the failure to make the other intelligible in familiar terms. The Arab's explanation ("He ran away. I ran after him.") does not make sense to Daru. The other simply does not think, feel, and act as I do, and that is precisely what makes him other. Levinasian ethics consists in accepting the constitutive strangeness of the other; and in this light, Daru's not questioning the Arab further can be read as a recognition of the impenetrability of the other (rather than as an exasperated renunciation of the attempt to understand him). In showing Daru's openness to the Arab, Camus's story can be said to achieve a Levinasian ethical position. One critic has referred to "L'Hôte" as "the ethical performance in all truth."[19] Another critic has adopted Levinas's vocabulary to describe the story in positive, albeit measured, terms: "While acknowledging the fear, vulnerability and violence constantly at play in human interaction, Camus's "L'Hôte" succeeds, momentarily at least, in dismantling the frontiers which demarcate human relationships, blurring the boundaries between Self and Other and so creating a space where ethical encounter with alterity is possible."[20]

The importance of hospitality in Levinasian ethics, underlined in recent years by Jacques Derrida's work on Levinas, suggests another area of relevance for Camus's story.[21] The scene in which Daru cooks for and eats with the Arab seems as though designed to invite a Levinasian reading.[22] But hospitality, as illustrated in Camus's story and in Levinas's ethical writings, is no easy or comfortable matter. Levinas is now frequently assimilated to a bland, liberal "respect for the other" that entirely misses the exorbitance and distress entailed in his account of responsibility. An ethics of hospitality cannot simply mean that I occasionally invite my friends to my house for dinner. In Levinas's account, my debt to the other is infinite and unconditional, and the other is certainly not just my ally and friend. Hospitality entails an acceptance of risk. The guest may turn out to be a murderer or rapist (and so might the host).[23] In the context of an ethics of hospitality, I can never be entirely sure who or what I am inviting in. I must give the benefit of the doubt, and I must

know that I may regret doing so. When Daru allows a murderer into his house, feeds him, and sleeps alongside him, he knows that he might literally be killed in his own bed.

The extreme nature of Levinasian responsibility, and its difference from weak versions of respect for otherness, become clear in the violent language in which Levinas formulates his ethics; this is especially the case in *Autrement qu'être ou au-delà de l'essence*, which is generally accepted to be, after *Totalité et infini*, his second major work. In *Autrement*, the subject is described as persecuted, obsessed, traumatized, wounded, stripped bare, and exposed. The subject is a hostage accused of a crime it did not commit and is bound to expiate the faults of others. This form of responsibility is nothing like philanthropic altruism. It allows of no calculation of costs and benefits, no happy resolution and no easy conscience. The acceptance of risk is unconditional, as Levinas suggests in a biblical image: "The subjectivity of the subject is the responsibility or being-in-question in the form of total exposure to the offense, in the cheek turned toward him who strikes."[24] The exposure is total, the cheek is not turned to someone who *might* strike it but to someone who we know is certain to strike.

The demand made by Levinasian ethics can never be fully met, because more will always be asked of us.[25] Such an ethics, in sum, requires that we take responsibility for the other in the full knowledge that doing so may cause us harm. The rewriting that "L'Hôte" undertakes of *L'Étranger* offers a glimpse of what it really means to occupy an ethical position. Such a position is not easy and not nice. In *L'Étranger*, there is a direct link between violence and the need to believe in a higher order. By killing, Meursault reaffirms the prestige of the other and submits himself to its guarantor, the law. *L'Étranger* suggests that only senseless violence can put an end to senselessness. The novel does nothing to question the link between fiction and murder that I described at the beginning of this discussion. Girard's account gives a particularly powerful explanation of the link: it characterizes great literature by its understanding of mimetic rivalry, and therefore it situates fiction always on or beyond the edge of violence. Moreover, as Žižek argues, reading murder stories allows us to flirt with and exonerate ourselves from our own desire to kill. We are innocent because others are guilty. "L'Hôte" endeavors to sever the links that bind together fiction, violence, and hostility toward the other. Meursault's act of violence is replaced by Daru's act of generosity, which achieves nothing: there is no law or principle to cut through the ambiguities, to decide to whom the land belongs and who is the interloper. Daru inhabits these ambiguities. He will be estranged from both whites and Arabs, accused of something he did not do, punished when he is innocent, misunderstood. From a Levinasian perspective, these afflictions are what it means to be an

ethical subject. There may be a terrible price to be paid for being ethical, and Daru is prepared to pay.

The link between fiction and violence is long established, and more often than not we will be disappointed if we expect our stories to be edifying. "L'Hôte" nevertheless shows that literature may occupy an ethical space by not knowing and not seeking to know final answers. Its ethics of hospitality consists in leaving unresolved the questions of ownership and belonging, and in its invitation to the reader to share in that suspension of knowledge. Of course, in the context of the violent disputes over territory and sovereignty that are on my mind as I write this article, it is a terrible risk to practice this sort of hospitality, to question one's own right to the ownership of land. Meursault's violence exhibits a yearning for and trust in the higher order of the law, however impenetrable it may seem. That position is much easier to occupy than Daru's: to be ethical in his way means accepting the infinite risk, inevitable failure, and unmeetable cost of welcoming the other. More violence has been committed in the name of certainty than of doubt.[26] Fiction may not save us from ourselves, but in its exploration of ignorance, it will do less harm than the self-righteous claim to say the final word on who is the host and who the guest, who the friend to be welcomed and who the enemy to be expelled.

NOTES

1. See Colin Davis, *Ethical Issues in Twentieth-Century French Fiction: Killing the Other* (Basingstoke: Macmillan, 2000). The present article develops some of the ideas that I present in the closing pages of that book.

2. These sorts of twists are commonplace in crime fiction and films. See, for example, Alain Robbe-Grillet's novel *Les Gommes*, in which the detective ends up killing the person whose murder he had been sent to investigate; the film *Suspect*, in which the murderer is the judge trying the case; and the Agatha Christie story filmed as *And Then There Were None* and *Ten Little Indians*, in which the killer fakes his own murder in order to kill others.

3. Slavoj Žižek, *Looking Awry: An Introduction to Jacques Lacan through Popular Culture* (Cambridge: MIT Press, 1991), 59.

4. René Girard, *Mensonge romantique et vérité romanesque* (Paris: Grasset, 1961), 306. Throughout this article, where French editions are cited, translations are my own.

5. See René Girard, "Camus's Stranger Retried," in *Modern Critical Views: Albert Camus*, ed. Harold Bloom (New York: Chelsea House Publishers, 1989), 79–105.

6. Girard, "Camus's Stranger Retried," 95.

7. Albert Camus, *L'Étranger*, in *Théâtre, récits, nouvelles*, Bibliothèque de la Pléiade 161 (Paris: Gallimard, 1962), 1211–12. All subsequent references to *L'Étranger* are from this edition.

8. Camus, *L'Étranger*, 1166.

9. This perception is suggested in the first sighting of the Arab; see Camus, *L'Étranger*, 1161: "I saw a group of Arabs leaning against a shop window. They were

looking at us in silence, but in that way they have [*mais à leur manière*], neither more nor less than if we were stones or dead trees."

10. Camus, *L'Étranger*, 1171.

11. I am grateful to Jill Beer for helping me appreciate the ethical interest of this short story. See her article "*Le Regard*: Face to Face in Albert Camus's 'L'Hôte,'" *French Studies* 56.2 (2002): 179–92.

12. Camus, "L'Hôte," in *Théâtre, récits, nouvelles*, Bibliothèque de la Pléiade 161 (Paris: Gallimard, 1962), 1623. All subsequent references to "L'Hôte" are from this edition.

13. The only use of the word in the text refers to the Arab; see Camus, "L'Hôte," 1617. Cf. J. Hillis Miller, "The Critic as Host," in *Deconstruction and Criticism*, ed. Harold Bloom, Paul De Man, Jacques Derrida, Geoffrey H. Hartman, and J. Hillis Miller (New York: Seabury, 1979), 217–53.

14. Camus, "L'Hôte," 1613.

15. Camus, "L'Hôte," 1615.

16. On this aspect of the story, see Beer, "Face to Face."

17. Camus, "L'Hôte," 1619.

18. In addition to the article by Beer, see also Elizabeth Hart, "Face à face: L'Ethique lévinasienne dans 'L'Hôte,'" in *Les Trois Guerres d'Albert Camus*, ed. Lionel Dubois (Poitiers: Les Editions du Pont-Neuf, 1995), 172–77, and Jean Sarocchi, "L'Autre et les autres," in *Albert Camus' "L'Exil et le royaume": The Third Decade*, ed. Anthony Rizzuto (Toronto: Les Editions Paratexte, 1988), 95–104.

19. Sarocchi, "L'Autre et les autres," 104.

20. Beer, "Face to Face," 192.

21. See, in particular, Jacques Derrida, *Adieu à Emmanuel Lévinas* (Paris: Galilée, 1997).

22. For a sketch of such a reading, see Hart, "Face à face," 176–77.

23. For discussion of this point in relation to Levinas and Derrida, see Mireille Rosello, *Postcolonial Hospitality: The Immigrant as Guest* (Stanford, CA: Stanford University Press, 2001), 11–13. Rosello's book contains a series of subtle readings of texts and films that stage the tensions and ambiguities involved in the necessary risk of hospitality. The current account here of "L'Hôte" is heavily indebted to Rosello's book, not so much for any particular analysis as for opening up the question of hospitality and its relevance for Camus's story.

24. Emmanuel Levinas, *Autrement qu'être ou au-delà de l'essence*, Livre de Poche edition (The Hague: Martinus Nijhoff, 1974), 176.

25. The difficulty, perhaps even the impossibility, of responding adequately to this exorbitant demand is illustrated by the evasiveness of Levinas's response to questions about the massacres in the Shatila and Sabra camps in Israel-occupied Lebanon in 1982. In a radio discussion broadcast shortly after the massacres, Levinas appeared reluctant to condemn outright those who shared responsibility for the massacres. He suggested that some "others" may be my enemy, such that my debt to them is more limited than my debt to neighbors and allies. This restriction sits uneasily with the unconditional responsibility described in Levinas's philosophical works. For discussion in the context of Levinas's politics, see Howard Caygill, *Levinas and the Political* (London: Routledge, 2002), esp. 182–94; and on the difficulty of translating ethics into politics, see Derrida, *Adieu à Emmanuel Lévinas*.

26. Michael Bérubé makes a similar point more eloquently in his attack on the opponents of antifoundationalism, in "The Return of Realism and the Future of

Contingency," in *What's Left of Theory? New Work on the Politics of Literary Theory*, ed. Judith Butler, John Guillory, and Kendall Thomas (London: Routledge, 2000), 137–56, esp. 149: "You would think, from listening to antifoundationalism's antagonists, that the Crusades, the Spanish Inquisition, the extermination of the native populations of the Americas, the massacre of the Armenians, the Stalinist purges and the Jewish catastrophe are all to be laid at the feet of a handful of jejune postmodern latte-drinking relativists. I find it outrageous, frankly, that foundationalists proceed in this debate as if their side, the side that appeals to objective facts and secure moral grounds, has nothing to answer for in the world's long and sorry history of civil butchery."

ADRIAN VAN DEN HOVEN

Sartre's Conception of Historiality and Temporality: The Quest for a Motive in Camus' The Stranger and Sartre's Dirty Hands

Neither the apparently cold-blooded murder of a complete stranger, the central event in *The Stranger*, nor Hugo's murder of Hoederer in *Dirty Hands*—a political assassination or crime of passion, depending on how one views it—can be considered unusual acts, in literature or in life. The topic of murder has itself created an extremely popular genre: the detective novel or "whodunit," which has become a huge industry and has aficionados everywhere, Sartre being one. In French theater, the topic of political assassination has resulted in such famous plays as de Musset's *Lorenzaccio* (1834), which ostensibly deals with Florence in the sixteenth century and the tyrannical Alexandre de Médicis, who is assassinated by his young cousin, but is in fact "a limpid transposition of the failed revolution of July 1830."[1] It is well known that Sartre was an admirer of Musset and Romantic theater.[2] In 1946, Jean Cocteau, who helped with the staging of *Les Mains sales* (Dirty Hands), wrote *L'Aigle à deux têtes* (The Two-Headed Eagle), which was inspired "by the sad life of Empress Elisabeth of Austria and her tragic death by the hand of the Franco-Italian assassin, Luigi Luchen."[3] Sartre himself, in *Nausea*, has Anny use the engraving in Michelet's *Histoire de France* depicting the assassination of the Duke de Guise as a perfect illustration of "privileged situations."[4]

From *Sartre Studies International* 11, nos. 1 & 2 (2005): 207–21. Copyright © 2005 by Berghahn Books.

In real life, there has been no lack of political assassinations: in 1914, Archduke Franz Ferdinand of Austria and his wife Sophie were assassinated in Sarajevo by the student Princip, which was the immediate cause of World War I; in 1940, Trotsky was murdered in Mexico with an ice pick by his secretary Ramon Mercader, which was one of the inspirations for Sartre's play;[5] in January 1948, Mahatma Gandhi was assassinated by a Hindu nationalist who could not abide political compromise with the Muslims;[6] and more recently, in November 1995, Israeli Prime Minister Yitzhak Rabin was assassinated by Yigal Amir, who claimed that Rabin "intended to give the country to the Arabs."[7] Being a political figure in these turbulent times remains a risky business.

However, Camus' novel and Sartre's play are examples of a particular branch of this genre. The suspense created by the mystery of the true identity of the killer, which is usually maintained to the very end in a murder mystery, and the question in the political thriller of whether the assassin will succeed or fail are replaced in both cases by the quest for the true nature of the motivation behind the act. If there is tension in these works, it derives from the unrelenting quest to find out *why* the characters did what they did and what that might mean to them and to us, the readers/spectators. In addition, both works are largely first-person narratives in which the action is filtered through the main character's perspective. This typically modern device results in the reader/spectator being left with a very partial overview of events; as a result, one cannot help but entertain a certain ambivalent, judgmental attitude toward the final outcome of both works.

Before we try to relate the narrators' specific attitude to their fateful act and to the world in which they perpetrate it and before we illustrate by what specific fictional and theatrical techniques the authors give a distinct meaning to the act, we want to deal with Sartre's theoretical writings of the late 1930s, because in them he stresses the essential relationship between narrative (and dramatic) techniques and the way that the protagonists' act should be viewed. His comments should allow us to see the actions of both protagonists in their proper critical light. Sartre declares in his review article entitled "Temporality and Faulkner's *Sound and the Fury*" that "[a] fictional technique always relates back to the metaphysics of the author."[8] In this article Sartre praises Faulkner's keen sense of the role of time in the characters' destinies, but nevertheless criticizes him for having amputated one of its three dimensions and created characters without a future. As he states, "[T]hese people are impossible" because "their future is blocked," and he adds rhetorically: "[W]hy have Faulkner and so many other writers chosen this particular absurdity which is so un-novelistic and so untrue?"[9] Of course, Sartre very much wants to allow for the possibility of a future, yet he does not want to neglect the past and

its impact on the present. He especially wants to illustrate how the present unfolds in a lived situation and points to an as yet unknown future that normally we can only grasp retrospectively.

In other words, how to render the manner in which a person works out his project in a lived situation in fictional and dramatic terms is already a crucial concern for Sartre in the 1930s. For example, in *Nausea*, published in 1938—but actually the product of seven years of reflection—he faces that vexing question head-on and establishes a radical distinction that is also very much applicable to Camus' novel:

> One has to choose between living and narration ... nothing happens when one lives ... days are added to days without rhyme or reason, it is an interminable and monotonous addition.... But when you narrate a life, everything changes; however, there is a change that no one notices: the proof is that we speak of *true* stories [*récits*]; as if there could be such a thing; events unfold in one way and [in *récits*] we narrate them in the opposite direction. We pretend to begin with the beginning ... but the ending is there and it transforms everything. The guy is already the hero of the story ... instants have stopped piling themselves in a lighthearted fashion one on top of the other, they are snapped up by the end of the story which draws them in and each one of them in turn draws out the preceding instant.... We forget that the future was not there yet....
>
> I wanted the moments of my life to follow and order themselves like those of a life remembered. You might as well try and catch time by the tail.[10]

In the first part of *The Stranger*, Meursault leads an existence in which "days are added to days without rhyme or reason ... [and his life] is an interminable and monotonous addition." It is only in the second part that his life is transformed into a "narration," a *récit* in which causal relations are established retrospectively by the official guardians of the French state in Algeria. These two parts correspond to a distinction made by Fernandez's critique of Balzac and which Sartre makes his own in his article on Dos Passos: "The novel, like life, unfolds in the present.... In the novel the dice are not loaded, for fictional man is free. He develops before our eyes; our impatience, our ignorance, our expectancy are the same as the hero's. The *récit*, on the other hand, as Fernandez has shown, develops in the past. But the *récit* explains. Chronological order, life's order, barely conceals the causal order, which is an order for the understanding."[11]

It goes without saying that much of *Nausea* also corresponds to Sartre's definition of the novel rather than that of the *récit*. In it, Sartre, largely successfully, tackles the problem of how to account for the discontinuous nature of the unfolding of events by using the diary form: it permits Roquentin to describe what has been happening to him on a daily if not hourly basis, and every day seems to bring its own surprises. However, a retrospective analysis quickly reveals that certain parts are in fact composed of set pieces: the visit to the Bouville museum, the dinner with the Self-Taught Man, the discovery of absurdity in the public park, Roquentin's final meeting with Anny, etc. In spite of Sartre's criticism of Mauriac's novels, which in fact correspond more to *récits*,[12] the hand of the godlike novelist remains visible in places. In temporal terms, the ending is quite satisfactory. Roquentin's decision to start composing "a story that can not take place"[13] gives him a fresh start—a future—and, theoretically, this imaginary tale will not add to the superabundance of existing things. But it remains a sleight of hand: a story creates an object and thereby adds to the existing world of objects, regardless of whether it is an imitation of reality or a pure invention.

Not surprisingly, therefore, the question of how to deal with life in open-ended terms continued to haunt Sartre. In the late 1930s, when composing the trilogy *The Roads to Freedom*, he once again had his protagonist, Mathieu, and the other characters attempt to situate themselves in the present and transcend it without losing touch with the lived moment. During the "Phony War," which started in September 1939, Sartre was stationed in northeastern France; he continued to work on his trilogy and kept a diary, which was published in English as *The War Diaries of Jean-Paul Sartre: November 1939–March 1940*.

While reading Emil Ludwig's biography of the last German emperor, William II, Sartre decided to develop a "metaphysics of historiality and to show how historical man historializes himself freely in the framework of certain situations." He defines it as "the unveiling of truth to the absolute subject," i.e., the truth as the subject comes to perceive it for himself. Therefore, he focuses on a fact that is "at once highly personal and exterior to the person of the emperor: the congenital atrophy of his left arm" and quickly establishes a link with his own infirmity: "I have my manner of being [my lazy eye], not only have I turned away from a military career, renounced sports and even despise them, but in addition I have thrown myself beyond this infirmity into study, the liberal professions, the arts, etc. My way of being [my infirmity] reveals itself in my way of wanting to be loved through intellectual seduction.... I am that man with the lazy eye only when I choose to be it freely." And Sartre concludes: "William [also] chose his weakness ... he chose the secret chink in his armor ... his bellicose behavior is his

manner of being-his-own-infirmity ... it becomes a signifying situation. . . . In other words, William is nothing else but the manner in which he historializes himself."[14]

In *The War Diaries*, Sartre summarizes his views of the historian's task as follows: "The historian works on three planes: that of the for-itself, where he has to show how the decision appears to itself in the historical individual; that of the in-itself, where the decision is an absolute fact, temporal but not dated; and, finally, that of the for-others, where the pure event is recaptured, dated, and surpassed by other consciousnesses as being of the world."[15]

If it is noteworthy that in these diaries Sartre establishes a link between William II's and his own infirmity and argues that it shaped their destinies because each freely chose to live it in a certain way, it must also be remarked that he does not deal with the political consequences of World War I, which resulted in the collapse of the German, Austro-Hungarian, Turkish, and Russian empires and led to the rise of ideological conflicts opposing fascism, communism, and bourgeois parliamentary democracies. Nor does Sartre deal with William II's fate. Forced to flee to the Netherlands, William II apparently answered, when asked what he thought of the recent past: "[T]his is not what I had intended, this is not what I had in mind!"[16]—thus illustrating the dictum that "one starts out to make one kind of history, but another one is written for us." Sartre's lack of interest in William's life in exile is due to the fact that he is primarily interested in historialization and much less in mystifying historicity. One could say that after his exile, William II no longer had a project and had already been figuratively "tossed on the trash heap of history." The stress on the "freely chosen infirmity" and the distinct lack of interest in the aftermath of World War I will be echoed in two ways in *Dirty Hands:* Hugo is deliberately painted as a weakling, and the play's conclusion is distinctly abrupt.

Let us now deal more fully with Camus' *The Stranger*. Camus published *The Stranger* in 1943 when Algeria was still a French colony. Meursault, the protagonist, and the other French settlers (*pieds-noirs*) featured in the novel barely seem aware of the Arabs, who are present all around them. However, the colonizer, at least these relatively poor *pieds-noirs*, and the colonized "share" the water, the sun, and the beach together because they come "free," and the one French "tough" in the story has an Arab mistress. The Arab world and its mores continue to hover in the shadows until Raymond, Meursault's neighbor, beats his Arab mistress, and Meursault becomes embroiled with the latter's brother and friends. Meursault ends up shooting one of them, five times, on a blazing hot day on the beach, while his eyes are filled with perspiration and he is blinded by the sun and the glistening blade of the Arab's knife. Hence, even if the colonial situation that Meursault finds himself in

does not appear to be of great significance—the Arabs remain nameless and anonymous threats—that is *significant* in itself. The European minority blithely ignores the overwhelming presence of the Arabs, and in the political and social sense of the word—but not affectively, in the case of Raymond—it can be said that the Arabs barely exist for them. Ultimately, Meursault is condemned not for having killed an Arab but for his inability to express the appropriate sentiments expected of a Frenchman on certain official and ceremonious occasions. If Meursault never expresses remorse for the killing of the Arab, he interestingly *does* evoke sympathy for his mother toward the end of the narration, and expresses approval for her attempt to begin her life again and take Peréz as her "fiancé."

In this context, the trivial local news stories (*faits divers*) featured in the novel assume a particular significance. In jail, Meursault comes upon "a news story the first part of which was missing . . . [a]bout a Czech who had left his village to seek his fortune."[17] He returns after twenty-five years, takes a room in his mother's and sister's inn without revealing his identity, shows off his wealth, and is murdered by them. Meursault concludes: "Anyway, the traveler pretty much deserved what he got . . . you should never play games." When his trial comes up, his lawyer tells him: "[T]he court will be pressed for time. Yours isn't the most important case of the session. Right after you, there's a parricide coming up" (79). Given that during the trial he will be accused of having committed a symbolic matricide, Meursault's "deed" is neatly positioned between a filicide and parricide.[18] The injection into a banal *fait divers* of such themes as the relation of the individual to society and of such deep-seated motives as the role of the mother and of God reminds us that one could apply to *The Stranger* the famous comment made by Malraux about the French translation of Faulkner's *Sanctuary*. "It represents the introduction of Greek tragedy into a detective story."[19]

The relentless quest for a motive makes *The Stranger* extremely similar to Sartre's *Dirty Hands*; in addition, it is also an excellent illustration of what happens to one's acts when they fall into the public domain and are reinterpreted in such a *mystifying* manner that one barely recognizes them. Yet the two works differ altogether in terms of the literary techniques employed by the authors. For an understanding of *The Stranger*, it is crucially important to remain aware of the fact that it is divided in two parts. The first deals with Meursault's narration up until and including the murder of the Arab. It is when contingent factors—the blazing sun, the glistening knife, the perspiration that blinds him—provoke him into pulling the trigger that a Sunday afternoon stroll begins to assume the dimensions of a Greek tragedy. As he states: "[Then] I knew that I had destroyed the day's equilibrium, the exceptional silence of a beach where I'd been happy. Then

I pumped four more bullets into a motionless body in which they disappeared without leaving a trace. And they were like four knocks on the door of disaster" (56–57; trans. changed).

In the second part, Meursault continues the narration of his life, but now he is in prison. In addition, the second part functions as a repetition of the first because, both in jail and in the courtroom, we become acquainted through his narration not just with his reactions to his new surroundings but also, and more importantly, with the comments of all the officials with whom he comes into contact. He narrates faithfully what the prosecuting attorney, the lawyer, the witnesses, and the prison chaplain think of him, his past life, and his crime. The second half could be called an absurd and even mystifying retake of the first, and consequently it is not really possible to reconcile the two halves. Of Meursault it could also be said that in the first part, he was unwittingly living one type of history—like Roquentin, he also leads a life "without any social or collective importance"[20]—and that in the second part, society is writing another one for him. The fact that he smoked during the wake; had a coffee; did not want to see his mother for a final time; went to the beach with Marie, took her to see a comedy, and then slept with her; maintained a friendship with a supposed pimp—all these facts add up in the eyes of the prosecution to a person who is not worthy of being a member of civilized society and must be executed. In the context of Algeria as a French colony, it can also be argued that Meursault, as a member of the occupying and colonizing race, is an abject failure in upholding the values of the official institutional France.

During the trial, one of his friends eagerly proclaims that "he is innocent"; another says that "the whole matter was a calamity"; Marie, his girlfriend, exclaims that "things did not happen the way" that the prosecutor says they did. But the prosecution has verisimilitude and logic on its side. It has rearranged the incidents in Meursault's recent existence in such a manner that he now turns into "Monsieur Antichrist" and "a monster" (68–98). All the same, he cannot adequately explain to the court why he pulled the trigger four more times after he had shot the Arab the first time—his explanation that the sun and sweat got into his eyes is hardly satisfactory in the court's eyes—and his behavior and his associations do allow for the damning interpretation that the prosecution comes up with. Consequently, the jury has no difficulty sending him to the guillotine.

Nevertheless, Meursault does not acquiesce in the judgment of others. When the prison chaplain attempts a final time to persuade him that God is staring at him from the prison wall and that he can't possibly have lost all hope in an afterlife, Meursault reacts angrily and screams out at him: "I was sure about myself, about everything, . . . sure of my life and sure of the death

I had waiting for me. . . . I had been right, I was still right and I would always be right. Sure I had lived my life in one way and I could have lived in some other way. I had not done this while I had done something else. And what of it?" (114–115; trans. changed).

It could be said that at this moment Meursault finally achieves a full awareness of the "unveiling of the truth to [himself as] the absolute subject," and that his refusal to accept any explanation of his acts, other than his own, puts him squarely in the class of persons who refuse any overarching, retrospective interpretation of human behavior. It is as if through him Camus wishes to proclaim that however limited a person's explanation of his past behavior may seem, we must respect it, because his behavior cannot be understood correctly by our retrospective, logical, and probabilistic reconstructions. We are dealing with two worldviews that will always remain incompatible with each other. Meursault sees events unfolding in a consecutive but disjointed fashion. His interactions with others do not go much beyond those that result from basic human needs: food, drink, sleep, work, sex, sun, and the beach. When he becomes trapped in the machinery of the state, he is confronted by a world in which ironclad logic and probability rule. If these rules are inadequate to explain the "true" Meursault as he found himself in a particular, lived situation, it remains equally true that his explanation of his murderous act will seem inadequate to all but himself. Meursault remains unique, an outsider even as he is being ground down by the judicial machinery of the state, which cannot stand such an asocial, amoral individual.

In the context of our discussion, Camus and Sartre are clearly on the same wavelength when it comes to acknowledging an individual's right to his own view of events. But in his play *Dirty Hands*, Sartre goes a step further than Camus. True, Sartre's protagonist Hugo likewise cannot come up with an adequate explanation for his killing of Hoederer, but at the very last moment he suddenly realizes that he would be living a lie and not be giving his own and Hoederer's motivations their proper due if he went along with the Party's wishes. Then he decides that, even if he is confused, he should not acquiesce in the Party's latest strategic twists and turns. Thus, he refuses to accommodate himself to the changed party line, which, ironically, now coincides with the views that the murdered Hoederer had held.

The play is set in Illyria. This is not Shakespeare's imaginary country that provides the backdrop for *Twelfth Night*. Historically, "Illyria is an old name for part of Yugoslavia. . . . [In World War II] Yugoslav resistance to the Nazis consisted of two factions: the royalists under Karageorgevich, whom the Allies supported at first, and the communists under Tito, whom the Allies switched their support to."[21] However, it is more probable that Sartre had Romania in mind: "At the start of World War II, King Carol

II abdicates in favor of his son Michael, who is forced to appoint the pro-Nazi dictator Antonescu to lead the government. The country goes to war on the German side against the Soviet Union. Defeated in 1944, it signs an armistice and declares war on Germany. Antonescu is overthrown and a government of national unity composed of socialists and communists is introduced."[22] In *Dirty Hands*, the PAC, which is composed of Communists, is the minority in a coalition called the Proletarian Party that it has created with the Social Democrats. Opposed to the coalition's political deal-making with "the fascist government of the Regent" and the "bourgeois liberals and nationalists," the PAC is ready to assassinate Hoederer, who is not following the party line.[23]

Because Moscow and the party are portrayed as being willing to indulge in cynical political maneuvers, the French Communist Party viewed the play as a deliberate provocation by Sartre, who in response went so far as to ban performances of *Dirty Hands* so that his "true" intentions could not be misinterpreted by malevolent critics. Ironically, Sartre always maintained that we are responsible not only for our actions but also for their consequences, including those that are not intentional; therefore, logically speaking, he should have allowed the play to continue to be performed. On the other hand, *Red Gloves*, the American adaptation, completely distorted Sartre's original. The fact that the play became a subject of vehement political debate and controversy is a clear sign that Sartre had written a highly topical work that engaged and provoked the public everywhere.

However, since this essay is specifically focused on the manner in which the temporal structure of *Dirty Hands* allows Sartre to juxtapose and balance the intractable conflict between idealism and realism in politics, we shall now turn to his use of temporality to uncover how it allows for this balancing act and contributes to his intention to leave the questions raised suspended in dramatic mid-air. (As Sartre explained in an interview in *Combat*: "I don't take sides. A good play ought to present problems, not solve them."[24]) By framing the events of 1943 within the historical present of 1945, Sartre allows us to live simultaneously in the past *and* the present as each unfolds, to view the main characters as they are living their projects in concrete situations and, paradoxically, to maintain both a *prospective* and a *retrospective* point of view as we evaluate them. Obviously, this structure is altogether different from that of *The Stranger*, in which even in the second part Meursault continues to live life as it unfolds; it is the members of the court who rerun the past, seeing amoral motives and heinous plots where Meursault and his acquaintances see only accidents and basically harmless behavior. Yet at the outset, the intent of the two authors remains similar: they both wish to unveil their characters' behavior as they are "forging the project in a lived situation."

It is for this reason that Sartre employs a "framed" plot, in which the first and the final, seventh tableau—the Vintage translation calls them "acts"[25] but that seems inaccurate—take place in 1945, while tableaux 2 through 6 take us back to 1943 when Hugo is working as a journalist for the party's paper and volunteers to become Hoederer's assassin. Therefore, in the play, unlike in *The Stranger*, it is not others who reconstruct Hugo's past for him; it is rather Hugo who, in a long analepsis (flashback), is allowed to relive the approximately 10 days during which he was employed by the party as a journalist and, subsequently, at his own insistence, became "the useful idiot" who volunteered to kill Hoederer. In other words, theatrical illusion, the suspension of disbelief, allows Sartre to juggle and juxtapose these two distinct temporal "moments": first, in 1945, when Hugo finds himself newly released from prison but unaware of all the military and political changes that have occurred around him in Illyria; and second, back in 1943, in order that the author may illustrate in as much detail as possible the various aspects of Hugo's character—his youthful past, his marriage, his relationship to the other party members and Hoederer—in the hope that the audience may understand what led him to kill Hoederer and to proclaim in the end that he is "unsalvageable." Consequently, our analysis of *Dirty Hands* will of necessity constantly stress the importance of temporality and illustrate how momentary acts and gestures have an impact on Hugo's destiny.

The opening scene functions as a didascalia (a kind of stage direction). It reveals to the audience the rapidly evolving military situation and indicates that time has not stood still during Hugo's incarceration. Significant political changes are in the wind. The radio speaker in Olga's room announces that "the Germans are in retreat along the front [and that] Soviet armies have taken Kirschnar, some twenty-five miles from the Illyrian front. Wherever possible, the Illyrian troops are refusing to fight; many deserters have already gone over to the Allies" (131). At that moment, Hugo knocks on the door. Olga is surprised to see him because he had been given a "five-year sentence" for killing Hoederer, but Hugo explains that he has been "released after two years for good behavior" (132). He makes clear that since his release, he "has not spoken to anyone," and Olga points out that "life has become much more difficult since the Germans' [arrival] . . . three months [ago]" (133). Olga also states that "roughly speaking [the party line has remained] the same" (134). As we have already indicated, the audience will have to wait until the last tableau to discover in an ironic twist that the party has, at the Soviets' insistence, adopted the same line as had been proposed by Hoederer in 1943—and that therefore it has in fact changed significantly. Such final and sudden revelations are typical of the nineteenth-century "well-made play" and "story," which were made so popular in France by, respectively, the *téâtre des boulevards* and

Guy de Maupassant. But this ironic reversal also suits Sartre: his characters require an unknown future so that they may appear to freely undertake their project in an unpredictable situation. When in jail, Hugo had already assessed his own future rather somberly. Now, in a momentary analepsis, which precedes the much longer analepsis yet to come, he assumes Olga's identity and proclaims in her voice: "[W]hen he gets out, they'll shoot him down like a dog for his trouble" (135). As well, some three months ago, he had received a box of poisoned chocolates and reasoned: "[A]t first the party thought I could be used in some way, and then the party changes its mind" (135). Hence, Hugo seems keenly aware of the limited and utilitarian function he performs for the party, and in fact this prepares us for Olga's plea to the other party members that she should be allowed to discover if he is "salvageable" (139).

After Olga insists to Hugo that she "will do as the party tells [her]," he remarks ironically that he was told "to go and kill Hoederer and put three bullets in his gut ... [but] orders leave you alone ... the order stayed behind and I went on alone and killed alone—and I no longer know why" (136; trans. changed). In dramatic terms, it appears that Hugo has already given the entire plot away and that the rest of the play's function is reduced to showing how he went about the business of killing Hoederer. But in fact, the temporal game-playing increases the dramatic tension, achieving its crescendo in the final moments when Hugo decides he cannot go along with the new party line. At no time does he have any difficulty (re-)enacting what happened; but again it is the rationale that remains problematical, and that dilemma is not resolved by Hugo until the very last moment.

Next, three party members—Charles, Frantz, and Louis—arrive, and Louis declares that Hugo "is an undisciplined anarchistic individualist, an intellectual who thought only of striking an attractive pose, a bourgeois who worked when it pleased him and stopped at the slightest whim" (139). Like Meursault's prosecutors, Louis provides a coherent, overarching, logical retrospective explanation for Hugo's behavior. But of course, in prospective terms, Hugo will focus on the discontinuous, accidental, and contingent factors of his behavior, as does Meursault in the first part of Camus' novel. Olga counters that "he is also the guy who at twenty shot down Hoederer despite his bodyguards and managed to disguise a political assassination as a crime of passion." Next Olga presents Frantz with a compromise. It is now nine o'clock; Hugo will be given until midnight to explain why he killed Hoederer. If "they can [still] work with him ... he will be given an assignment tomorrow morning. [If] it turns out that he isn't salvageable," Olga "will let [Louis] in" (140). Thus, Hugo is given a "second chance," and since he has spent two years in jail trying "to understand why [he] did it," at that point he makes an interesting remark that could well be applied to Camus' Meursault: "I know

it by heart, I recited it to myself every day I was in prison. But what it means, that's something else again. It's an idiotic story.[26] If you look at it from a distance, everything holds together, more or less; but if you get up close to it, it falls apart" (142; trans. changed).

At the end of the first tableau, Hugo decides to "begin the story in March 1943 when Louis sent for [him]" (142). Hence, in this long analepsis—the ensuing five retrospective tableaux—he will narrate in the form of a re-enactment in three hours what happened two years ago in ten days, and in the final tableau we will "leap forward" again to the "historical present" of 1945. In temporal terms we are dealing with a total period of two years to which ten days have been added at the beginning. However, it is these ten days that will count as the most important. After we have stepped back in time with Hugo, we will move forward again with him and accompany him step by step as his project unfolds because—to quote Sartre again—"it is in historialization that the concrete absolute, and the unveiling of truth to the absolute subject, reside."

When we meet Hugo again, he is a journalist, and another party member, Ivan, is about to leave at ten to go and blow up the "Korsk bridge." To further emphasize the importance of time, it is indicated that he has but "fifteen minutes" to do the job (145). Next door a vehement discussion is taking place, and afterwards Louis comes out to explain. This explanation is crucial because Sartre wanted to create a theater based on (historical) situations and not on the psychological development of his characters. Louis explains: The Proletarian Party is the result of a fusion of the PAC, represented by Louis, and the Social Democrats. The party has voted four to three to allow Hoederer to negotiate an alliance with the fascist government of the Regent, which has aligned itself with the Axis Powers and the "Pentagon," a party represented by Karsky, which serves as a clandestine rallying point for the bourgeois liberals and the nationalists (148). Sartre has deliberately provided us with a complex political dilemma in order to create a problematics to which there is no easy answer. Either one preserves the purity of the party line or one forges a strategic alliance with the archenemies of the party to save one hundred thousand lives. Louis, Olga, and Hugo opt for the first alternative, but, in order to stop Hoederer and to increase dramatic tension, time is of the essence. Louis explains: "[T]he next meeting is . . . in ten days. That gives us more than a week" (147).

In a vein similar to Roquentin, who proclaimed that "one must choose between living and telling [narrating],"[27] Hugo chooses to become a man of action rather than remain a journalist. At the conclusion of this tableau, in a prolepsis (or a "flashforward," as the French also call it), he momentarily adopts a prospective viewpoint. Hugo can already see himself after he has

accomplished his heroic deed: "[S]omeone will knock on the door and you will smile just the way you are smiling now and you will say: 'he did it'" (152). At this moment, Hugo is still viewing the project at the level of a phantasm. When he actually gets to know his victim, it will become very difficult for him to turn his act into reality.

But we still have four tableaux to go. After Hugo and his wife Jessica arrive at Hoederer's house, matters complicate themselves. The pair turn out to be a typically frivolous bourgeois couple, who immediately run into conflict with the hard-nosed Slick and George, Hoederer's bodyguards, who wish to search their luggage for hidden weapons. After a great deal of playacting, threats by the guards, and Hugo's categorical refusal to let a search take place, as well as the intervention of Hoederer himself, Jessica suddenly agrees to the search, and the guards find nothing. Somewhat improbably, she has managed to hide the revolver in her dress. These scenes may seem oddly out of place but they serve the purpose of underlining Hugo's "infirmities." Not only does he detest his father and turn Hoederer into a father substitute, he is also the weaker partner in the marriage; Jessica frequently outwits him. In tableau four we find Hugo and Jessica in Hoederer's office; she presents Hugo with the gun because "ten days have passed" (185) and still nothing has happened. Next, Hoederer comes in; he is anxious. It is "ten after four" (189), and the regent and Karsky still have not shown up for the meeting. When they do finally arrive, the negotiations initially go badly. Then Hoederer presents them with an ultimatum: "Here are my conditions: a steering committee of six members. The proletarian party is to have three votes; you can divide the others as you see fit. The underground organizations are to remain distinct and separate and will undertake joint action only on the decision of the central committee. Take it or leave it" (198).

The regent appears agreeable but Karsky is not. However, at the very moment when it seems that Hoederer has squeezed an acceptance "on principle" out of him, the didascalia indicate that Hugo *jump[s] to his feet* and begins to protest vehemently. Obviously, the propitious moment for the assassination has arrived: *"he puts his hand in the pocket that holds his revolver"* but *"at this moment a loud explosion is heard. The window panes are shattered, and the sashes of the window are torn off"* (200). Olga has thrown a bomb at the window but has missed, and Hoederer is only slightly injured. Hugo's perfect moment for killing Hoederer has been ruined. Olga's action is meant to represent the introduction of the contingent in Hugo's life, but it is also, of course, carefully timed by the author to enhance the dramatic tension and to defer the dénouement.

Hugo gets drunk because his plans have been spoiled. Olga sneaks into the room: she has "only fifteen minutes" to explain to him that he has

"twenty-four hours" in which to do his deed or they "will get someone else to do it instead" (210). In the following scene, Hugo explains to Jessica that "objectively [Hoederer] is a class traitor" (214), but she does not understand. Then Hoederer enters their room and explains his strategy: the Proletarian Party is weak, and he does not want it to be imposed on the people as the ruling party by the Soviets after they arrive. It is better to let the others govern initially and have them take the blame when austerity measures need to be introduced. Also, a hundred thousand lives may be saved by this strategic alliance with their archenemies (215). Hugo argues in favor of ideological "purity," but Hoederer tells him that he does not mind "getting his hands dirty . . . all means are good when they are effective" (223). In the end, Hoederer puts off the resolution of their conflict until "tomorrow morning" when they will meet again . . . at nine o'clock" (226).

Tableau six is the final installment in this long analepsis, and this time it is Jessica who muddies the waters. She has entered Hoederer's office, [and he] gives her "five minutes" (227) to explain herself. She reveals to Hoederer that "when [Hugo] comes in this morning he'll have his revolver on him . . . [but] he doesn't want to kill you . . . he thinks too much of you for that. It's just that he has his assignment" (229–230). When Hugo comes in, Jessica hides behind the curtain. Hoederer disarms Hugo, casually tosses the revolver on the table (another act that is meant to underline the importance of contingency), and tells Hugo to leave and collect his thoughts before he comes back. Jessica reappears, and they embrace. At that moment, Hugo opens the door and exclaims: "[S]o that's why you spared me . . . but it's all clear now: it was on account of my wife" (239), and he shoots Hoederer three times. Hoederer's last gesture is to cover for Hugo. He yells out to the guards: "[D]on't hurt him. He was jealous. . . . I've been sleeping with his wife" (239). Whatever the truth is, on the surface, the political assassination has been turned into a crime of passion, and contingent factors have obscured the "purity" of Hugo's deed.

In a temporal leap, the final tableau brings us back to the "historical present." Dramatically, less than three hours have passed, but historically we have moved ahead two years and ten days and are again in 1945. Yet Hugo is still no clearer about what precipitated his fateful act. He declares that "it was chance. If I had opened the door two minutes sooner or two minutes later, I wouldn't have surprised them in each other's arms, and I wouldn't have fired . . . it was an assassination without an assassin" (240). With five minutes to go, Olga explains that he is "salvageable" but that he "will have to forget his act" and change his identity again—within the party he had been known under the pseudonym of Raskolnikov, Dostoevsky's mad young ideologue who wanted to be somebody important in history—because "the party has changed its policy . . . last winter the U.S.S.R. informed [them] that for

purely military reasons it favored a policy of reconciliation with the regent" (244). Hugo can guess the rest because in fact the party has adopted the same strategy that Hoederer had favored two years earlier. As Olga explains: "[H]is attempt was premature," but he will be rehabilitated and "have his statue . . . at the end of the war"; thanks to this strategy, "they have probably saved a hundred thousand lives" (245). This ironic reversal opens Hugo's eyes to what *should* be his own line of reasoning now. He may well be "salvageable," but that would make "his crime . . . an error of no significance . . . to be thrown into the trash can [of history]" (246; trans. changed). He concludes: "I don't know why I killed Hoederer, but I know why I *should* have killed him; because his policy was wrong, because he lied to the rank and file and jeopardized the life of the party. . . . I know that I am alone in my opinion, but I won't change" (247; italics mine; trans. changed). And he adds: "A man like Hoederer doesn't die by accident. He dies for his ideas, for his political program; he's responsible for his death. If I openly claim my crime and declare myself Raskolnikov and am willing to pay the necessary price, then he will have the death he deserves" (247). The stage directions then read: "(*Hugo kicks open the door*)" and "(*shout[s]*) 'Unsalvageable!'" (248).

His final suicidal act is both quixotic and meaningful. Meaningful because at a deeper level, we see Hugo identify with the father figure Hoederer and join him symbolically in death, in a narcissistic gesture of self-sacrifice, instead of going out "to play with boys." In fact, he betrays the party members to whom he had earlier professed his "undying" loyalty when he had proclaimed: "Louis, I shall do whatever you want, no matter what . . . Olga and you taught me all I know. I owe everything to you. To me you are the party" (144, 146). His quixotic gesture is also reminiscent of the conclusion of *The Condemned of Altona*: in it, the guilt-laden Frantz joins his cancer-stricken father in a suicidal last ride in the family Porsche.

Hugo's suicide is quixotic because the party will take no notice of his gesture. Neither his real name nor his pseudonym will be featured in the pages of history; at most, his act will be explained to the party members as that of an enemy of the party or perhaps as the gesture of a jealous husband whose brain had been inflamed momentarily by passion. After all, it will be the party that will write the history of this episode, and therefore Hoederer will have his statue and Hugo will be forgotten. Nevertheless, the aftermath of Hugo's life is not dealt with, and the play leaves the future suspended. There is no eighth tableau in which they discuss how to explain Hugo's death to the other party members, nor do we discover whether their newly adopted strategy has been successful.

Since the play ends at the very moment when Hugo shouts his words of defiance—both to the party members, who are waiting for him behind the

door, and to the audience—what we are finally left with is Hugo's desperate attempt to "historialize himself against the mystifying forces of historicity." Even if nobody takes notice, he has succeeded dramatically in making
momentary sense of Hoederer's and his own life. In a flash he has made both
his quixotic gesture and Hoederer's plan seem justified, regardless of how
history will treat either of them. On stage, the "political realist" and the "bourgeois idealist,"[28] as Sartre called them, will forever live and die together, and
the meaning of their fate will be played out endlessly. As the father engen-
dered the son, so will this struggle between realism and idealism continue to
engender real dramatic conflict.

Notes

1. http://romantis.free.fr/Musset/html/lorenza.htm (my translation).
2. Michel Contat and Michel Rybalka, comps., *The Writings of Jean-Paul
Sartre*, vol. 1: *A Bibliographical Life*, trans. Richard M. McCleary (Evanston, IL:
Northwestern University Press, 1974), 184–194.
3. http://raforum.apinc.org/artide.php3?id%20artide=106 (my translation).
See also, Contat and Rybalka, *The Writings of Jean-Paul Sartre*, 188.
4. Jean-Paul Sartre, *Nausea*, trans. Lloyd Alexander (New York: New Directions, 1964), 146–145.
5. Contat and Rybalka, *The Writings of Jean-Paul Sartre*, 186.
6. http://web.mahatma.org.in/last days.jsp?link=Id.
7. http://www.cnn.com/WORLD/9511/rabin/amir/11-06/index.html.
8. Jean-Paul Sartre, *Literary Essays*, trans. Annette Michelson (New York:
Philosophical Library, 1957), 79.
9. Sartre, Literary Essays, 89.
10. Sartre, *Nausea*, 145–146.
11. Sartre, *Literary Essays*, 23.
12. Ibid., 7–23.
13. Sartre, *Nausea*, 178.
14. Jean-Paul Sartre, *The War Diaries of Jean-Paul Sartre: November 1939–
March 1940*, trans. Quintin Hoare (New York: Pantheon Books, 1984), 302–309
(trans. changed). It is interesting to speculate on Sartre's claim that he "turned away
from a military career." His father had chosen just such a career, and it led to his early
death. If the young Sartre indeed aspired momentarily to a similar career, it may
explain why as a writer Sartre compensates for his exclusion from a military career,
owing to his infirmity, by substituting the pen for the sword and regularly adopting
an exceedingly bellicose attitude toward his adversaries, Camus among them. As a
writer, the absence of a father made him also more keenly aware of the untraditional
and even anomalous family situation he had known as a child. As a consequence,
he eagerly exploited the typical, Hamlet-inspired, familial drama in which a young
idealist becomes obsessed with a phantomlike father figure *and* identifies with his
motherly sister figure. In *The Words*, Sartre relates that "a prominent psychologist"
told him that he did not have a superego, and indicates that he was relieved that his
father did not "bestraddle him all life long" (*The Words*, trans. Bernard Frechtman
[New York: Braziller, 1964], 11), as is normally the case for a young man. But he

does admit to having confused his mother with his sister. However, above all, the absence of an imposing father figure may well explain Sartre's eagerness to exploit many forms of expression and impose *himself* on the world as his own creation.

15. Sartre, *The War Diaries*, 314.

16. Ibid., 319.

17. Albert Camus, *The Stranger*, trans. Matthew Ward (New York: Alfred A. Knopf, 1988), 76. All future references to this novel will be incorporated in the text.

18. Camus will deal in dramatic terms with the filicide in *Le Malentendu* (1944) (*The Misunderstanding*, in *Caligula and Three Other Plays*, trans. Stuart Gilbert [New York: Alfred A. Knopf, 1958]). Without wishing to indulge in facile psychologisms, it is not surprising that Camus showed an enduring obsession with his mother. His father was killed in World War I, and as an orphan he knew only his mother, grandmother, and uncle as caregivers. In this connection, it must not be forgotten that when he received the Nobel Prize, Camus, when asked about his attitude toward the war in Algeria, remarked: "I believe in justice, but I shall defend my mother above justice." See Herbert Lottman, *Albert Camus: A Biography* (Garden City, NY: Doubleday & Co, 1979), 618.

19. See the preface to William Faulkner, *Sanctuaire*, trans. R.-N. Raimbault and Henri Delgove (Paris: Gallimard, 1972), 10–11 (my translation).

20. Sartre, *Nausea*, 9. The American translation omits the epigraph borrowed from Celine's play *L'Église*.

21. *Le Petit Robert* (Paris: Société du Nouveau Littré, 1985), 1562.

22. Ibid., 1564.

23. Jean-Paul Sartre, *No Exit and Three Other Plays*, trans. Stuart Gilbert (New York: Vintage Books, 1989), 144–148. All future references to this play will be incorporated in the text.

24. Contat and Rybalka, *The Writings of Jean-Paul Sartre*, 188.

25. It should be noted that two recent French studies of this play also deal with Sartre's use of temporality, but neither draws the same conclusion as this author. See Françoise Bagot and Michel Kail, *Jean-Paul Sartre, Les Mains sales* (Paris: PUF, 1985), and Jean Labesse, *Étude sur Jean-Paul Sartre, Les Mains sales* (Paris: Ellipses, 1997). In addition, two other articles deal with aspects of staging and theatricality similar to those I deal with: Michael Issacharoff, "Éthique et dramaturgie: la théâtralité du théâtre de Sartre (l'exemple des *Mains sales*)," *Éthique et esthétique dans la littérature française du XXième siècle*, ed. Maurice Gagnon (Saratoga: Anma Libri, 1978), 183–190; and Jean Alter, "*Les Mains sales*, ou La clôture du Verbe," *Sartre et la mise en signe*, ed. Michael Issacharoff and Jean-Claude Vilquin (Paris: Klincksieck & Cie; Lexington, KY: French Forum, 1982), 68–82.

26. This is an oblique reference to Faulkner's novel *The Sound and the Fury*. This title was inspired by the following line in Shakespeare's play *Macbeth*, act 5, scene 5: "[Life] is a tale told by an idiot, full of sound and fury, signifying nothing."

27. Sartre, *Nausea*, 145.

28. Contat and Rybalka, *The Writings of Jean-Paul Sartre*, 188.

JOHN FOLEY

The Outsider

> Lying is not only saying what isn't true. It is also, in fact especially, saying more than is true and, in the case of the human heart, saying more than one feels. (*TO*: 118; *TRN*: 1928)

Published, like *The Myth of Sisyphus*, in 1942 in Nazi-occupied Paris, *The Outsider* is a first-person narrative describing the life of a young *pied-noir* or European Algerian named Meursault. The novel is based around three important events: the funeral of Meursault's mother, during which he displays a disconcerting lack of emotion; his killing of an unnamed Arab under fairly obscure circumstances; and Meursault's trial and impending execution. The story culminates in the hero being condemned to death, and concludes with him confronting his fate at the guillotine. The first thing to note in approaching this frequently obscure novel is that *The Outsider, The Myth of Sisyphus* and *Caligula* . . . have an unusual mutual intimacy. Indeed, Camus had originally intended to have them published together in a single volume.[31] Accordingly, although we do not of course read them as a single text, if we are to read *The Outsider* as a novel of ideas, then the severe limits imposed on the meaning of the absurd in *The Myth of Sisyphus* need to be taken into account.

For Camus, Meursault is the absurd hero *par excellence*. His impending execution has nothing whatever to do with his killing of the forever-unnamed

From *Albert Camus: From the Absurd to Revolt*, pp. 14–22, 178–80. Copyright © 2008 by John Foley.

Arab. He was killed because of his social non-conformity, exemplified by his failure to express conventional grief after the death of his mother. Camus insists that at the heart of this non-conformity is a refusal to lie, noting that "lying is not only saying what isn't true. It is also, in fact especially, saying more than is true and, in the case of the human heart, saying more than one feels".[32] This affirmation of Meursault's exemplary honesty is the focus of my consideration of the novel, not only because it is affirmed in the context of the absurd, but also because it is central to one of the most influential critiques of *The Outsider*, that of Conor Cruise O'Brien.

For Cruise O'Brien, far from portraying any kind of philosophical or political truth, the novel in fact promotes a nefarious fiction about colonial Algeria: "What appears to the casual reader as a contemptuous attack on the court is not in fact an attack at all: on the contrary, by suggesting that the court is impartial between Arab and Frenchman, it implicitly denies the colonial reality and sustains the colonial fiction", the "fiction" being that a Frenchman in Algeria who had killed an Arab would be convicted in a court, a fiction that Cruise O'Brien argues is "vital to the status quo", to the legitimacy of the French colonial domination of Algeria.[33] The allegation of dishonesty in this depiction of "impartial" justice in Algeria places Cruise O'Brien in the company of critics such as Henri Kréa and Pierre Nora, for whom Meursault's act is "the subconscious realisation of the obscure and puerile dream of the 'poor white' Camus never ceased to be", and for whom Camus was, like other *pieds-noirs*, "consciously frozen in historical immobility", "unable to confront", adds Cruise O'Brien, "the problem of the European–Arab relation".[34]

However, there is a far greater weight of evidence to support the inclination of his "casual reader" than Cruise O'Brien admits. I hope to show that a very strong case can be made, by a careful reader, in favour of the view that Meursault was indeed convicted and executed for failing to behave in a socially conventional fashion at the funeral of his mother. This becomes immediately clear when Meursault is first arrested after the killing: initially, in fact, "nobody seemed very interested in my case", and it was only later on, once they discovered his behaviour at a time when convention dictated Meursault should be publicly mourning his mother's death, that people began to "eye [him] with curiosity" (*TO*: 63; *TRN*: 1171). Later still, when, in bewilderment at the way that his trial is being conducted, Meursault's lawyer asks whether his client is being accused of burying his mother or killing a man, the prosecution replies that the two cannot be dissociated: "Yes … I accuse this man of burying his mother like a heartless criminal."[35] According to this interpretation, an interpretation supported, as we shall see, by the character of much of his contemporary political journalism, Camus was actually suggesting that a European Algerian was more likely to be condemned to death

for failing to express himself according to social convention than he would be for killing an Arab. It is in this context, too, that we must consider the Arab's continued anonymity.

Cruise O'Brien suggests that it is Meursault's dishonesty rather than his honesty that is proved by close reading of the novel: he argues, for example, that Camus's hero lies when he writes a letter for his neighbour Raymond, designed to "deceive" his Arab girlfriend "and expose her to humiliation".[36] The only thing that Meursault refuses to lie about, Cruise O'Brien insists, is his own feelings. While this observation is in many respects correct, as Joseph McBride has argued, Cruise O'Brien's judgement is undermined by his failure to appreciate the context in which Camus affirms Meursault's honesty (McBride n.d.: 55). Meursault is honest within the context of the absurd; he is as honest as the absurd will allow. He is honest when he feels he can speak in honesty—that is, ultimately, in relation to his own feelings.[37] The absurd disallows him the possibility of constructing criteria for determining good and bad, right and wrong, in other more inclusive or social contexts. Meursault's perceived dishonesty amounts only to his refusal to accept that there are objective criteria for determining a scale of moral values. When Camus spoke of Meursault's honesty, it was this kind of honesty that he had in mind. Furthermore, while Meursault is no more an exemplar of moral behaviour than Sisyphus or Don Juan, he does exhibit a kind of honesty that, as we shall see, is conspicuously absent from most of the other, ostensibly reputable, characters in the novel.

Cruise O'Brien's failure to take Meursault's reasoning into account is exemplified in the very episode in which he argues that Meursault's dishonesty is most apparent: the writing of a letter for his neighbour Raymond, a letter designed to trick Raymond's girlfriend into a humiliating trap. Meursault states: "I wrote the letter. I did it rather haphazardly, but I did my best to please Raymond because I had *no reason not to please him.*"[38] He lacked the moral grounds required for him to refuse Raymond's request. Clearly then, had he refused, he would have done so on the grounds of moral beliefs he didn't actually possess. Such a refusal, Camus implies, would have been dishonest, since lying is "in fact especially, saying more than is true and, in the case of the human heart, saying more than one feels".[39] Once we situate Meursault within the context of the absurd we can begin to see that the "lies" he tells are less a consequence of dishonesty than a consequence of stubborn honesty in the midst of the moral equivalence apparently consequent on the absurd.

Other, more direct, examples of Meursault's honesty can be seen early in the second part of the novel. For example, he notes that when he was first arrested, "I was put in a room with several other prisoners, most of them

Arabs. They laughed when they saw me. Then they asked me what I'd done. I told them that I'd killed an Arab and there was silence."[40] Indeed, Meursault expresses a strong (albeit potentially pathological) sense of honesty when he reads on a piece of paper discovered in his cell of the murder of a man by his mother and sister. The man had been in disguise; his mother and sister killed themselves when they discovered what they had done. Meursault's response is intriguing: "I decided that the traveller had deserved it really and that you should never play around."[41] For Camus, Meursault represents the modern Sisyphus, the authentic man in a world bereft of transcendent meaning.[42] He is the one who lives the absurd in revolt, a revolt that demands not only that he live with a jealous love for physical, sensory existence, but also that he take all actions as morally equivalent (McBride n.d.: 58).

This interpretation of *The Outsider* is further endorsed if we shift our attention from the often obscure psychology of Meursault and consider the novel's depiction of Meursault's confrontation with society as a whole in the context of the absurd (the "absurd" understood primarily as an epistemological claim, a claim regarding the sorts of things we can say we know). Adjusting the focus of our reading of the novel in this way, away from Meursault (whose status as Sisyphean absurd hero Camus affirms[43]) and onto the depiction of his relationship with society in general, our attention is drawn to events surrounding two central points in the novel: the wake and funeral of Meursault's mother and, especially, Meursault's trial (the wake itself at one point seems to take the form of a trial, Meursault noting that "at one point I had the ridiculous impression that [the other mourners] were there to judge me") (*TO*: 15; *TRN*: 1130). In both of these cases, Meursault's lucidity and honesty are seen to come into conflict with the dishonesty of society in general. From the perspective of the absurd, these two events, paradoxically, could be said to have greater significance than the killing of the unnamed Arab. The killing of the unnamed Arab, I suggest, serves both as a formal necessity, so that Meursault *could* stand trial, and as a powerful criticism of the inherent racism of French-Algerian justice, where an individual kills an Arab but is executed for failing to cry at his mother's funeral.

The opening lines of *The Outsider*, "Mother died today. Or maybe yesterday, I don't know", are probably among the most famous in modern literature, and tend to be interpreted as evidence of Meursault's jaded indifference, stoic or not, to normal emotional and moral behaviour. However, although there is certainly some justification to this interpretation, what tends to be overlooked is that Meursault's jarring statement is a direct result of the perfunctory telegram sent by the retirement home where Mme Meursault had lived for the previous several years: "Mother passed away, Funeral tomorrow. Yours sincerely." As Meursault explains, "That doesn't mean anything. It might have

been yesterday" (*TO*: 9; *TRN*: 1125). This subtly constructed passage should make us wary of arriving too quickly at conclusions regarding the character of Meursault. It should also make us wary of arriving too quickly at conclusions regarding those characters with whom Meursault comes into contact. Indeed, if we are to accept Camus's claims regarding Meursault's martyrdom for the truth, then we cannot ignore the degree to which the society that condemns Meursault is constructed upon deceit and lies. This dishonesty, and the extent to which, for Camus, it is associated with religious belief, becomes apparent early in the novel when Meursault arrives at the retirement home, and the home's director tells Meursault that his mother "apparently often mentioned to her friends that she wished to have a religious funeral. I've taken it upon myself to make the necessary arrangements. But I thought I should let you know." Meursault notes, "I thanked him. Though she wasn't an atheist, mother never had given a thought to religion in her life" (*TO*: 11–12; *TRN*: 1127).

This form of dishonesty, and Meursault's confrontation with it, become far more pronounced after his arrest. If we regard the absurd as primarily a claim regarding the severe limits on human knowledge, we shall see that from the perspective of the absurd perhaps the most interesting episode in the novel is that of the judicial process, culminating in Meursault's trial. Heroically absurd, Meursault comes into conflict with the false positivism of both the state and its proxy, the court.[44] The trial stages a confrontation between the simple and direct language of Meursault, who regularly admits to uncertainty and never admits to more than he knows, and the false and bombastic language of the state.[45] As a confrontation between, on the one hand, conventional and institutional law and morality, and, on the other, the absurd, where law and morality rather than the absurd appear to embody injustice, it is worth looking at more closely.

Meursault's claims during his trial that he "hadn't intended to kill the Arab" and that "it was because of the sun" will provoke only laughter in the courtroom, but for the investigating magistrate, who questions Meursault before the trial commences, only one aspect of his confession "didn't make sense" (*TO*: 99, 68; *TRN*: 1196, 1173). Why, he wanted to know, after shooting the Arab once, did Meursault pause and then shoot the lifeless body four more times? It quickly becomes clear that this interests the magistrate (as, indeed, it will interest the state's prosecution) far more than why Meursault shot the Arab the first time. Indeed, it seems to interest them far more than the fact *that* he shot the never-named Arab at all. (Meursault himself seems to hint that these four gratuitous shots, rather than the killing of the Arab itself, are the reason for his own impending execution.[46]) When Meursault replies that the magistrate was wrong to insist on this point, that it didn't matter that much, the magistrate immediately interrupts him and his real concern

is exposed. He is clearly not interested in the crime of which Meursault has been accused, but in his non-conformism, his atheism and, especially, his lack of religiously inspired remorse and guilt:

> he interrupted me and pleaded with me one last time, drawing himself up to his full height and asking me if I believed in God. I said no. He sat down indignantly. He told me that it was impossible, that all men believed in God, even those who wouldn't face up to Him. That was his belief, and if he should ever doubt it, his life would become meaningless. "Do you want my life to become meaningless?" he cried.

For the magistrate, who at one point brandishes a crucifix in Meursault's face, exclaiming "I am a Christian. I ask him to forgive your sins. How can you not believe that he suffered for your sake?" Meursault becomes "Mr Antichrist". For Camus, he represents "the only Christ we deserve."[47]

The state prosecutor, similarly, ignores the actual killing for which Meursault supposedly stands accused, and instead accuses him of being "morally responsible for his mother's death".[48] This compounds the growing sense that Meursault will be condemned to death because of his social non-conformism, and further highlights the sense that the actual killing for which Meursault is supposedly standing trial is of no consequence whatever to the court. Claiming to have "peered into" Meursault's soul, "he said the truth was that I didn't have one, a soul, and that I had no access to any humanity nor to any of the moral principles which protect the human heart". The prosecutor insists that in the case of Meursault "the wholly negative ethic of tolerance must give way to the stricter but loftier ethic of justice. Especially when we encounter a man whose heart is so empty that it forms a chasm which threatens to engulf society." He declares that Meursault had "no place in a society whose most fundamental rules [he] ignored" and calls "with a sense of urgent and sacred duty", with a feeling of "horror ... at the sight of a man in whom I see nothing but a monster" and with "an easy mind", "for this man's head".[49] This febrile reasoning, grounded in "horror at [his] insensitivity", further permits the prosecutor to accuse Meursault of being "guilty of the murder which this court is to judge tomorrow" (a case of alleged parricide), while, it should be noted, neglecting all mention of the actual killing of the Arab for which Meursault was arrested.[50] Certainly whatever the prosecutor may have thought of Meursault's killing of the Arab, it was clearly not *that* crime to which he was referring when he accused Meursault of a crime equivalent to "parricide". As the trial scene progresses, the reader becomes increasingly aware that the prosecutor, sated

with his own self-righteousness, represents a society with the power to send Meursault to his death for his non-conformity, for his refusal to lie, to say "more than is true", and indeed that it will.

Meursault's defence lawyer articulates an attitude essentially identical to that of the prosecution. This becomes evident from their first meeting, in Meursault's prison cell:

> "Let's get straight on with it." He sat down on the bed and explained that some investigation had been made into my private life. It had been discovered that my mother had died recently in a home . . . the magistrates had learned that I'd "displayed a lack of emotion" on the day of my mother's funeral . . ."it matters a great deal. And the prosecution will have a strong case if I can't find anything to reply." (*TO*: 64; *TRN*: 1172)

Initially he is concerned by Meursault's unwillingness to recite conventional platitudes of grief and sorrow, but his attitude quickly turns to contempt when Meursault refuses to lie: "he asked me if he could say that I'd controlled my natural feelings" on the day of his mother's funeral. "I said, 'No. because it's not true.' He looked at me in a particular way, as if he found me slightly disgusting."[51] The lawyer's disgust seems motivated less by Meursault's behaviour at his mother's funeral than by his apparent unwillingness to lie, to follow his lawyer's implicit advice and say what he knew to be untrue in order to improve his chances in court. This sense that the defence is playing the same "game", which Meursault alone refuses to play, is confirmed when, rather than object to it, his lawyer apes the spurious reasoning of the prosecution, claiming that he too had peered into Meursault's soul, and indeed claiming for himself greater talent in metaphysical divination than his colleague: "in fact I read it like an open book". Meursault himself comments at this point: "with all these long sentences and the endless days and hours that people had been talking about my soul, I just had the impression that I was drowning in some sort of colourless liquid" (*TO*: 118, 100–101; *TRN*: 1920, 1197).

In the testimony of the warden from the nursing home where Mme Meursault died we begin to see a more explicit form of dishonesty: "He was asked whether mother used to complain about me and he said yes but that his inmates had rather a habit of complaining about their relatives. The judge asked him to specify whether she used to reproach me for having sent her to a home and the warden again said yes. But this time he didn't add anything."[52] The significance of Meursault's last comment becomes clear when we remember the warden's words of consolation at the beginning of the novel:

You've no need to justify yourself, my dear boy. I've read your mother's file. You weren't able to look after her properly. She needed a nurse. You only have a modest income. And all things considered, she was happier here … you're a young man, a different generation, and she must have been bored living with you. (*TO*: 10–11; *TRN*: 1126)

The warden's testimony in court is clearly motivated by a desire to be seen to be on the side of the society that condemns Meursault, just as his desire to satisfy social convention motivates him to arrange a religious funeral for Mme Meursault, who, as we have seen, "had never given a thought to religion in her life" (*TO*: 12; *TRN*: 1127). Stating that he had been surprised by Meursault's "calmness", the warden goes on to explain that Meursault "hadn't wanted to see [his] mother", that he "hadn't cried once", that he had "left straight after the funeral without paying [his] respects at her grave" and that he did not know his mother's age. This testimony is sufficiently effective for the state's prosecutor to deem it unnecessary to add to it through cross-examination (*TO*: 86–7; *TRN*: 1186–7). However, as effective as it may have been in condemning Meursault in the eyes of the jury, the warden's testimony is false in at least one critical respect. Whereas he claims that Meursault did not wish to see his mother, the careful reader will have noticed that in fact immediately upon his arrival at the home, Meursault makes exactly this request and that, crucially, his request is denied on the grounds that he must first see the warden.[53]

Perhaps the most dramatic of these encounters is with the prison chaplain, who tells Meursault, towards the end of the novel, of his "certainty" regarding the success of his appeal against his sentence (curiously, he also admits to Meursault on the same occasion that he "knows nothing about" his appeal) (*TO*: 113, 111; *TRN*: 1206, 1205). The chaplain informs Meursault that he is "burdened with a sin from which [he] must free [himself]". Meursault replies that he "didn't know what a sin was", that he had "simply been told that [he] was guilty": "I was guilty and I was paying for it and there was nothing more that could be asked of me" (*TO*: 113; *TRN*: 1206–7). Meursault's blank refusal of the chaplain's proffered consolations prompt the priest to add: "I'm on your side. But you can't see that because your heart is blind. I shall pray for you." Meursault responds with an explosion of anger, insulting the priest and telling him that he did not want his prayers: "I was pouring everything out at him from the bottom of my heart in a paroxysm of joy and anger." What Meursault objects to, far more than the religious platitudes themselves, is the certainty they imply: "He seemed so certain of everything, didn't he? And yet none of his certainties was worth one hair of

a woman's head" (*TO*: 115; *TRN*: 1208). Here too, more than ever before, Meursault clearly represents the absurd hero, exhibiting the same wild courage and rebellious scorn in accepting his fate that we saw in Sisyphus.

What is increasingly apparent in each of these cases, from the magistrate to the chaplain, is that beyond their religiously inspired and often violent indignation, beyond even the fact that the actual crime for which Meursault stands accused is almost completely ignored, is a level of certainty that Meursault finds incomprehensible and Camus evidently finds, in the context of the absurd, unjustifiable. This analysis may then lead us to reflect on the differences between the crime that the state commits in executing a man for non-conformity and the crime Meursault commits in killing the unnamed Arab. It seems that the chief difference is that although Meursault is certainly responsible for the death of the Arab, his was a totally unpremeditated act, whereas, in stark contrast, the execution of Meursault is committed by the machinery of the state, by culturally specific mores dressed up as objective moral principles. Nevertheless, although Meursault was executed by the state for not crying at his mother's funeral, Camus nowhere suggests that Meursault was not *responsible* for the death of the Arab.[54] Several critics appear to suggest that the killing of the unnamed Arab was in some way "excusable", and more generally, there frequently appears to be a temptation to interpret Camus's claim that Meursault was killed for failing to cry at his mother's funeral as itself implying that the court had no good reason to try Meursault for killing an Arab.[55] Meursault was condemned to death for not crying at his mother's funeral, but this clearly does not itself imply that he should not have been tried in a court for the killing of the Arab. This point should become clearer when we consider the suggestion in *The Myth of Sisyphus* that to "a mind imbued with the absurd ... there may be responsible persons but there are no guilty ones, in its opinion".[56] Unsurprisingly, then, Meursault's understanding of "guilt" is associated explicitly with the judgement of society, which suggests that for Meursault guilt itself is socially constructed. We note that it is only after the warden and caretaker testify against him, citing his failure to cry at the funeral, his failure to pay respects at his mother's grave, the fact that he slept, smoked and drank coffee during her wake, that Meursault comments, "I stupidly felt like crying because I could tell how much all these people hated me", and "for the first time I realised that I was guilty".[57] Later, during the prosecution's summing-up—a summing-up in which the actual killing continues to be largely overlooked in favour of the events surrounding his mother's funeral—Meursault complains that he cannot understand "how the qualities of an ordinary man could be used as damning evidence of guilt".[58] In contrast, on several occasions Meursault does indicate an understanding of the concept of responsibility. Although

his understanding of responsibility (or fault) is evoked in association with his mother's death, and while he admits to feeling "a certain kind of annoyance" rather than regret for what he had done, I also think that Meursault would have recognized his responsibility for the death of the unnamed Arab (*TO*: 9, 10, 15, 23, 24, 69; *TRN*: 1125, 1126, 1130, 1136, 1137, 1174).

Whereas many critics, such as Conor Cruise O'Brien, perceive a distinct indifference in the character of Meursault, the novel itself repeatedly reminds us of the simple pleasures in which he found joy: "I was assailed by memories of a life which was no longer mine, but in which I had found my simplest pleasures: the smells of summer, the part of town that I loved, the sky on certain evenings, Maria's dresses and the way she laughed."[59] Indeed, far from proclaiming an ethic of indifference, Camus believed that *The Outsider* had, as well as the obvious "metaphysical" or absurd meaning, a "social" meaning.[60] The "social" meaning Camus claimed for the novel relates to its comment on the forces of social conformity, on the death penalty, but also, as I have argued, on the judicial system in Algeria, which he suggests was more concerned with a *pied-noir* not crying at his mother's funeral than with his killing of an Arab. Nevertheless, it seems that to a large extent this social sense was obscured, though perhaps not suffocated, by the sheer metaphysical weight of the novel's pervasive absurdity. This is not to agree with Cruise O'Brien, who claims that the novel may posit Meursault as a metaphysical rebel—a rebel against Christian cosmogony or indeed any idea of the supernatural—but that this "is in no sense a revolt against the values of Camus' culture" (Cruise O'Brien 1970: 31). Quite to the contrary, the novel is about how a fundamentally sincere and honest man becomes a mortal victim of the state judicial system not because he refused to tell the truth, but because he refused to lie. *The Outsider* is a plea for the rights of the individual against social conformity and against the state—in a very profound way, despite its status as absurd novel *par excellence*, it can be seen as a restatement of classical liberalism. *The Outsider* is concerned almost exclusively with constructing a model of what the confrontation with the absurd may look like in a social or political context. Camus is concerned with developing a fictional image of the ontological position dictated by the absurd.[61] Accordingly, although there is a clear dimension of social criticism in the novel, there is no *positive* ethic, no ethic beyond the basic principle of sincerity. The austere dignity of Meursault confronting his death, his complete refusal of hope and despair, is Camus's negative ethic. The question remains, however, whether there is anything to stop Meursault, as the absurd hero *par excellence*, unflinching in the face of the apparent meaninglessness of human existence, from becoming a nihilist. This is the question that is pursued in *Caligula*.

Notes

31. When Camus originally offered the three "absurds" to his friend and publisher Edmond Charlot, he requested that they be published together in one volume, thus wrapping up the "absurd question" (Lottman 1979: 248–9; cf. Camus & Pia 2000: 61).

32. *TO*: 118–19; *TRN*: 1920–21 (from the 1955 "avant-propos" to the American college edition). In what seems to be an earlier version of this text, Camus writes: "One had wanted to see [in *The Outsider*] a new kind of immoralist, which was completely incorrect. The main issue in question here is not morality, but the universe of the trial which is as much bourgeois as Nazi or Communist. . . . With respect to Meursault, there is something positive in him, and that is his refusal, to the point of death, to lie. To lie is not only to say what isn't true, but to say more than one feels, usually in order to conform socially. Meursault is not on the side of the judges, of social rules, of conventional sentiments. . . . If you consider the book from this perspective, you will find a moral of sincerity, and an exaltation, simultaneously ironic and tragic, of terrestrial joys" (*E*: 1611).

33. Cruise O'Brien 1970: 23. There were earlier postcolonial critiques, but Cruise O'Brien's was perhaps the most systematic and least forgiving. For Cruise O'Brien even Camus's journalistic writing on Algeria evinces nothing more than "a painful and protracted failure" to come to terms with "the situation in question" (*ibid.*: 26).

34. Kréa 1961; Nora 1961. Quoted in Cruise O'Brien 1970: 25. Whereas for Cruise O'Brien the trial at which a *pied-noir* is convicted for murdering an Arab is a "historical fiction", for Nora, the condemnation of Meursault is "a disturbing admission of historical guilt".

35. *TO*: 93; *TRN*: 1194. It is worthy of note that not long after beginning his journalistic career with *Alger républicain*, Camus reported on several major criminal trials, including that of Sheikh El Okbi. . . . As Susan Tarrow notes, in each of these cases Camus drew attention to the political motivations behind the proceedings. The title Camus gave one of his articles, "The Story of a Crime; or, How a Crime is Thought Up for the Purposes of a Criminal Charge", Tarrow drily notes, could have been a subtitle for *The Outsider* (Tarrow 1985:53, 203n.2; see *CAC3*: 512).

36. Cruise O'Brien 1970: 20–21. Cruise O'Brien also claims that Meursault "lies to the police" in order to get Raymond, who was prone to what he considered "affectionate" domestic violence, discharged (*ibid.*). This is not quite true: Meursault did tell the police that "the girl had 'cheated' on Raymond", but he did so because, "as far as he could see", this was true (*TO*: 50, 34–5; *TRN*: 1158, 1145).

37. Cruise O'Brien notes this as well. However, and as we will see, the critic fails to recognize *why* this is the case.

38. *TO*: 36; *TRN*: 1148, italics added. The same reasoning that takes place when he "lies" for Raymond is expressed in the following passage: "I then wanted a cigarette. But I hesitated because I didn't know if I could smoke in front of mother. I thought it over, it really didn't matter. I offered the caretaker a cigarette and we smoked" (*TO*: 14; *TRN*: 1129).

39. Reprinted as an "Afterword" in *TO*: 118; *TRN*: 1920. In this brief text, in which Camus insists on Meursault's honesty, he makes no reference whatever to the absurd.

40. Meursault continues: "But a few minutes later it began to get dark. They told me how to lay out the mat I had to sleep on. . . . A few days later I was confined to a cell by myself" (*TO*: 71; *TRN*: 1175).

41. *TO*: 78; *TRN*: 1180. This event constitutes the essence of Camus's play, *Le Malentendu* (translated as *The Misunderstanding* or *Cross Purpose*). Summarizing the meaning of that play, Camus wrote: "It amounts to saying that in an unjust or indifferent world man can save himself, and save others, by practicing the most basic sincerity and pronouncing the most appropriate word" (Camus 1958: vii).

42. At least the Meursault we see after the killing of the Arab, the Meursault who becomes conscious of the absurd, and stays courageously true to its consequences.

43. In the 1955 "avant-propos" to the American "College" edition of *L'Étranger*, printed as an "Afterword" in the Penguin edition of *The Outsider* (*TO*: 118–19; *TRN*: 1920–21). Similarly, although Meursault was an office employee, Camus asserts in *The Myth of Sisyphus* that "a sub-clerk in the post-office is the equal of a conqueror if consciousness is common to them" (*MS*: 66; *E*: 150).

44. It is significant that one of the most powerful of these peddlers of false positivism, the magistrate, should refer to Meursault as "Mr Antichrist" (*TO*: 70; *TRN*: 1174), when, for Camus, he is "the only Christ that we deserve" (*TO*: 119; *TRN*: 1921).

45. A minor instance of this: at first, Meursault did not know to whom the court was referring when they mentioned "his mistress" (*TO*: 96; *TRN*: 1194). For Meursault, Marie was Marie.

46. "And I fired four more times at a lifeless body and the bullets sank in without leaving a mark. And it was like giving four sharp knocks at the door of unhappiness" (*TO*: 60; *TRN*: 1166).

47. *TO*: 68, 70, 119; *TRN*: 1173, 1174, 1921. The magistrate and, later on, the chaplain are bewildered by Meursault's lack of religiously inspired "remorse, and both complain that all previous prisoners in Meursault's position "turned towards Him" (*TO*: 112, 69; *TRN*: 1205–206, 1173).

48. *TO*: 98; *TRN*: 1195. Earlier in the trial, when asked whether Meursault is being accused of burying his mother or killing a man, the prosecution replies that the two cannot be dissociated: "Yes . . . I accuse this man of burying his mother like a heartless criminal" (*TO*: 93; *TRN*: 1194).

49. *TO*: 97–8, 99; *TRN*: 1195, 1196. David Carroll suggests that after his arrest "Meursault loses his privileged place as a French citizen in colonial Algeria and over the course of the second half of the novel is increasingly identified with and put in the place of the colonised Arab, the anonymous, indigenous Other" (Carroll 2007a: 31–2).

50. *TO*: 98–9; *TRN*: 1195. Indeed, through the whole trial proceedings (as reported by Meursault) there are only two references to Meursault's "victim" (*TO*: 91, 92; *TRN*: 1191), and three references to the "Arab" (*TO*: 85, 96, 99; *TRN*: 1186, 1194, 1196), the last of which is made by Meursault himself. In contrast, there are eighteen references to Meursault's mother in the course of the trial (*TO*: 85, 86, 87, 88, 90, 91, 92, 93, 96, 98, 100; *TRN*: 1186, 1187, 1188, 1190, 1191, 1192, 1194, 1195, 1197).

51. "He told me almost spitefully that whatever happened the warden and staff of the home would be called as witnesses and that 'this could make things very unpleasant for me'. I pointed out to him that none of this had anything to do with

my case, but he merely replied that I had obviously never had anything to do with the law" (*TO*: 65; *TRN*: 1170–71).

52. *TO*: 86; *TRN*: 1188–9. The warden's testimony can be usefully contrasted with the honest, though ineffectual, testimony of his girlfriend Marie and his friend Céleste, the two witnesses who best knew Meursault, and whom Camus claimed to be those of his characters (along with Dora from *Les Justes*) who were especially dear to him (in an interview in 1952; Brisville 1970: 188). It is worthy of note that the choice of witnesses at the trial makes it abundantly clear that it is Meursault's behaviour after his mother's funeral, rather than his killing of the Arab, that constitutes the court's concern.

53. *TO*: 10; *TRN*: 1126. The context in which Meursault later declines the offer to see his mother needs to be read in context. At the end of his brief interview the warden says "I expect you'd like to see your mother?" Meursault "stood up without saying anything and [the warden] led the way to the door", and they walked together to the mortuary. When he arrives in the mortuary he meets the caretaker, who tells Meursault: "'We covered her up. But I was to unscrew the coffin to let you see her.' He was just going up to the coffin when I stopped him. He said, 'Don't you want to?' I answered, 'No.' He didn't say anything and I was embarrassed because I felt I shouldn't have said that. After a moment he looked at me and said, 'Why not?' but not reproachfully, just as if he wanted to know. I said, 'I don't know.' He began twiddling his white moustache and then, without looking at me, he announced, 'I understand'" (*TO*: 11–12; *TRN*: 1126–7).

54. It is certainly an act of vengeance, not justice. Meursault at one point states: "In a way they seemed to be conducting the case independent of me" (*TO*: 95; *TRN*: 1195). Also: "I stupidly felt like crying because I could tell how much all these people *hated* me" (*TO*: 87; *TRN*: 1187, italics added). This also, perhaps, suggests that the world of the absurd is perhaps no less murderous than that of the bourgeois state.

55. "[T]his reasonless killing which everything seems to require that we excuse" (Brisville 1970: 58). Similarly Carol Petersen asserts that the Arab "in truth, was murdered by the sun and not by Meursault" (Petersen 1969: 48). Louis Hudon alleges "The muscular contraction which causes the revolver to fire is an involuntary act, most carefully presented as such, an accident. At worst, it is involuntary manslaughter, not murder. The four other shots, those which condemn him, are simply an act of immense exasperation, exercised on what must be presumed at that point, to be an inanimate object" (Hudon 1960:61). "A long time ago I summed up *The Outsider* in a sentence which I realise is extremely paradoxical: 'Any man who doesn't cry at his mother's funeral is liable to be condemned to death'" (*TO*: 118; *TRN*: 1920). The logical confusions that have led some critics to read Camus's claim that Meursault was executed for failing to exhibit the correct emotional responses as in fact meaning that Camus believed Meursault was not responsible for the killing of the Arab is clearly evident in René Girard's "Camus's Stranger Retried" (Girard 2001).

56. *MS*: 65; *E*: 150. Years later, when his wife appeared to have attempted suicide, Camus told his friend and editor Roger Quilliot that he felt responsible but not guilty (Quilliot, interviewed in the television documentary "Albert Camus: The Madness of Sincerity", BBC2, 11 October, 1997). For a brief commentary on various discussions of guilt in *The Outsider* see Henry 1975: 131–2.

57. *TO*: 87; *TRN*: 1187. Close to the end of the novel, thinking of his mother, Meursault declares, "So close to death, mother must have felt liberated and ready

to live her life again. No one, no one at all had any right to cry over her" (*TO*: 117; *TRN*: 1209).

58. *TO*: 97; *TRN*: 1194. Camus seems to associate the sense of guilt (as opposed to the sense of responsibility or fault) with the idea of sin. Near the end of the novel Meursault is visited by the prison chaplain, who told Meursault that although he was certain his appeal against his execution would be granted, Meursault was "still burdened with a sin from which [he] must free [himself]". Meursault replies that he "didn't know what a sin was", that he'd "simply been told that [he] was guilty": "I was guilty and I was paying for it and there was nothing more that could be asked of me" (*TO*: 113; *TRN*: 1206–7).

59. *TO*: 101; *TRN*: 1199. We see here that all of Meursault's nostalgia is directed towards the natural world; it is especially noteworthy that whereas Maria's dresses and smile feature in Meursault's store of fond memories, Maria herself does not. This is a point that will be developed later in relation to "absurd solipsism".

60. "*The Plague* has a social meaning *and* a metaphysical meaning. They amount to the very same thing. It's exactly the same. Such ambiguity is in [*The Outsider*] too" (*NB2*: 36; *C2*: 50).

61. We note here a comment made by Camus to Elsa Triolet in 1943: "you're absolutely right, there can be absurd myths, but absurd thought is not possible" (Letter quoted by Roger Grenier in *Album Camus* (1982): 115–16, quoted in Todd 1996: 328; Todd 1998: 165). Similarly, in "The Enigma" Camus claims that "A literature of despair is a contradiction in terms" (*SEN*: 144–5; *E*: 864–5).

ARTHUR SCHERR

Meursault's Dinner with Raymond: A Christian Theme in Albert Camus's L'Étranger

As most readers of Albert Camus's masterpiece, *L'Étranger* [*The Stranger*] are aware, Camus conceived his protagonist Meursault as a type of Christ figure. In his famous introduction to the 1955 American University edition, he wrote, "[this is] the story of a man who, without any heroics, agrees to die for the truth . . . I had tried to draw in my character the only Christ we deserve." Noting the irony in equating Jesus and Meursault, he reiterated, "I have sometimes said, and always paradoxically, that I have tried to portray in this character [Meursault] the only Christ we deserved. . . . I said this without any intention of blasphemy and only with the slightly ironic affection which an artist has the right to feel toward the character whom he has created ("Preface" 337)." An expert in Biblical exegesis, at the time of writing *L'Étranger* Camus was steeped in early Christian thought. He completed his doctoral dissertation (*diplôme d'études supérieures*) in philosophy at the University of Algiers, a study of the neo-Platonist thinker Plotinus and his influence on St. Augustine titled, "Neoplatonism et pensée chrétienne" in 1936, at age twenty-three (Lottman 91–92, 109). Obviously, he did not draw comparisons between Jesus and Meursault lightly.

At first glance, Meursault bears scant resemblance to Jesus for the average reader. Although Camus evidently conceived of him as a Jesus *persona*, not many scholars have tried to decipher Camus's meaning. By

From *Christianity and Literature* 58, no. 2 (Winter 2009): 187–210. Copyright © 2009 by the Conference on Christianity and Literature.

contrast, numerous critics emphasize how Camus's writing in general combines "humanism" and a strongly religious temperament. They conceive him longing for a God of love, a fraternal but absent Jesus. For example, John Cruickshank, observing that Camus was denounced more often during his lifetime as anti-Marxist than anti-Christian, argues that he sensed the "appetite for divinity" in human beings. For that reason, he rejected blatantly atheistic or anti-religious positions (314–15). As Cruickshank observes, "What makes Camus so significant, and in many ways representative, a figure of his own generation is the fact that he experienced a religious need in its widest sense yet was unable to accept religious belief" (324). The eulogistic religious philosopher James W. Woelfel concludes that Camus was an "agnostic."

Nevertheless, several critics have emphasized the "religious" or "Christian" aspect of *L'Étranger*. In a significant early comparison of the styles of Voltaire and Camus, Patrick Henry observes,

> "The only Christ that we deserve," as Camus enigmatically and ironically referred to his hero, is offered up as a tribal sacrificial victim, not to placate the whims of a revered god, but to insure the validity of the social structure. Both Christ and Meursault epitomize the scapegoat issue, for neither of them is killed for content but for form, the maintenance of the form or structure upon which society is fabricated. Neither attempts to save his life, for each knows that, by doing so, he would lose the validity of that life, its authenticity and its redeeming quality that are only sustained if they are maintained to the end. (162)

Reiterated by many other critics, Henry's standard interpretation echoes Camus's 1955 *avant-propos* to *L'Étranger*.

In an assessment similar to Henry's, Eamon Maher's often-overlooked brief analysis of Meursault's Christ-like characteristics chafes at Camus's analogy to Christ. Attempting to mitigate the force of Camus's statement, the devout Maher observes, "He is careful not to say that Meursault is a modern Christ which would be blasphemous, as he is about as far removed from the lofty position as you could get" (276). Maher interprets Camus's *avant-propos* thusly, "We didn't deserve the real Jesus Christ; maybe Meursault is a more fitting model for us" (277). At the same time, Maher supports Camus's denunciation of a hypocritical society that, living by "appearances," is outraged by Meursault's "brutal honesty" and is less repulsed by Nazi genocide and atrocities than by Meursault's failure to weep at his mother's funeral. He does not think Camus intended to belittle Jesus by indirectly comparing him

to Meursault. In Maher's interpretation, the legal system rejected Christian ethics by its callousness toward Meursault.

Arguing that "people like Meursault make others feel uncomfortable because of the way they openly flout convention and live instinctively," Maher likens the Algerian's worldview to that of Jesus. Like Christ, during his trial Meursault is silent in the face of his accusers: "The court scene evokes many aspects of the last judgment of Christ as Meursault can find nothing to say to defend himself" (Maher 279). Justifying Camus's comparison between Meursault and Jesus, Maher concludes: "When saying that his outsider [Meursault] was the only Christ that we deserved, Camus was not casting any aspersions on his protagonist or on Christ" (280). With regard to Meursault and Jesus, Maher observes, the courtroom rejects both the messenger and the message (280). Noting that the examining magistrate calls Meursault "Mr. Antichrist" after Meursault proclaims his atheism (281), Maher agrees with Camus that the hypocritical judicial functionaries are Antichrists.

Although disagreeing with Camus's assertion that Christianity has failed to explain the prevalence of evil and death in the world, Maher defends him against charges of atheism. Understatedly observing that Camus's sympathetic depiction of the Roman Catholic priest Paneloux in *La Peste* "does not reveal a highly developed anticlericalism" (277), he concludes that *L'Étranger* is "a provocative and spiritual work and I believe that Camus has much to teach the believer and the non-believer alike" (281). Like John Loose and Jean Onimus before him, he asserts that Camus was not so much anti-Christian as non-Christian, more agnostic than atheist. Likewise, Robert G. Cohn's study of Camus's *Exile and the Kingdom*'s short story, "The Growing Stone," tends to minimize Camus's ubiquitous alienation, viewing him as often Christian in temperament. Stressing affinities between Camus and Mallarmé, Cohn argues that both men were obsessed with the figure of Saint John the Baptist: "Like Mallarmé, he [Camus] is giving us a suggestion of how belief is prolonged and modified, even in our indifferent era." He finds that Camus espoused the "perspective of sacred faith, to help right the 'higher balance' of an era which he knew to be frighteningly askew" (160). It seems likely that Cohn would perceive similar currents in *L'Étranger*.

Stephen Ohayon's psychoanalytically-based article in *American Imago* views *The Stranger* as an allegory of Meursault's, and Camus's, repressed guilt over patricidal wishes toward the absent father. (Camus's father was killed at the Battle of the Marne a year after his birth.) Meursault hates the father figure, personified by the sun, but simultaneously desires homoerotic union with him, accounting for his ambivalence toward the sun's heat and rays. By killing the Arab, Meursault deliberately invites his beheading/castration as punishment for repressed patricidal drives. In Ohayon's (201) interpretation,

Meursault realizes his "self-mutilatory project" by being guillotined for murder, tantamount to being "castrated for his crime against the sun-father," although we might add that castration, unlike the guillotine, is not fatal. Ohayon argues that Camus's guilt led him to apologize for Meursault in his *avant-propos*; his words performed "an analgesic function" (191).

Jesus-like, Meursault exhibits "his identification with the sacrificial offering" (Ohayon 201) when he says (like Jesus's "It is finished"), "For everything to be consummated, for me to feel less alone, I had only to wish that there be a large crowd of spectators the day of my execution and that they greet me with cries of hate" (Ward 123).[1] According to Ohayon (201), "The identification with Christ is now complete. 'Pour que tout soit consommé' is the 'consummatum est' uttered by Christ on the cross (John 19: 30)." Ohayon (201) vaguely implies it may be significant that Meursault commits the murder on a Sunday, the day of Jesus's resurrection (on the other hand, as his only day off, Sunday was the only time he could go to the beach), which leads to Meursault's spiritual "rebirth" in prison. However, in light of Meursault's role as a Jesus figure who *submitted* to his Father's will, Ohayon inconsistently argues that Meursault unleashed "patricidal rage" at the Sun-Father by killing the Arab (204).

Perhaps Camus himself identified with Meursault as a Christ figure: Influenced by his study of such predestinarian religious philosophers as St. Augustine and Blaise Pascal, he posited a universal sense of guilt. However, at the *roman*'s end Meursault ironically derides the violent crowds he anticipates will jeer at this "matricide's" execution, unlike Jesus's tragic invocation of his father. In this respect, it is hard to take Ohayon's (and Maher's) analogies between Meursault's palpable disdain when contemplating *his* execution and Jesus's tragic attitude at the crucifixion seriously.[2]

Arguing for an identity between Camus and Meursault, Ohayon points out that as a student in Algiers, Camus, like Meursault, had worked as a clerk (191). In his notebooks, *Carnets*, Camus cryptically observed, in a famous phrase, "Three characters went into the composition of *The Stranger*: two men (one of them me) and a woman" (qtd. in Ohayon 191). Thus, it seems reasonable to conclude that to some extent Meursault represents Camus's thoughts and feelings. Usually, studies of *L'Étranger* confine their analogies between Meursault and Jesus to the murder trial in Part II, chapters three and four. They find Meursault's silence during his trial in the Algiers courtroom analogous to Jesus's silence when Governor Pontius Pilate judges him at his capital trial for sedition in Jerusalem. Apart from the courtroom drama, reminiscent of Jesus's encounter with Pilate, few incidents in *L'Étranger* partake of a biblical cast. This consideration makes an examination of the forensic aspects of *L'Étranger* relevant here.

An article with a uniquely jurisprudential perspective, Mary Ann Frese Witt and Eric Witt's paper on the character of the Algerian-French judicial system at the time Camus wrote *L'Étranger*, unlike Maher's and Ohayon's more directly literary analyses, illuminates implicit similarities between Meursault's response to his treatment at the trial and that of Jesus at his. Their article indicates how the nature of France's judicial processes affected the proceedings. According to the Witts, Meursault's involvement with and murder of the Arab threatened French colonialism. It exposed French imperialism's festering relationship with its indigenous Algerian underclass, as Jesus represented a threat to the Roman Empire's Palestinian dominion. Meursault's responses at his trial, like Jesus's were essentially silent or uncommunicative. The Witts observe, "His [Meursault's] stubborn, paratactic, non-causal and non-rhetorical discourse becomes a formal as well as a substantive threat to the body politic" (12).

The Witts explain that the French trial procedure was inquisitorial and took more consideration of the defendant's personal life than the Anglo-Saxon evidentiary (confrontational) system, which depends more on information about the crime itself. "According to French law, almost anything in the defendant's personal history may be brought into the courtroom," the Witts inform us. Based more on the judge's intuition of the character and personality of the defendant, French law utilizes emotional, subjective factors more than English law, which essentially relies on the evidence. At the novel's conclusion, they note, Meursault is not told precisely what type ("degree") of murder he has been convicted of, cavalier treatment that the legal system generally relegated to Muslims rather than *pieds-noirs* (14–15). In colonial Algeria, the French Supreme Court was the court of last resort; and Algerians were under French legal jurisdiction. In France, most death sentences were overturned or commuted (Witt and Witt 18 n34), making Meursault's fate atypical and unrealistic.[3]

*   *   *

In the following pages, I will depict an instance in which Meursault indeed appears as a Jesus *manqué*, but which critics have not considered from this perspective. The episode I will examine is the unlikely case of his dinner with Raymond Sintès, the upshot of which was that "he wrote the letter for the pimp Raymond, designed to deceive the Arab girl and expose her to humiliation" (Ohayon 189). Students of *The Stranger* generally fail to take the dinner with Raymond very seriously. For example, in a fine brief essay that emphasizes the misadvised nature of Meursault's friendship with Raymond, K. N. Daruwalla (62) merely observes, "He is quite happy to have his black pudding with Raymond so that he does not have to cook dinner."[4]

Meursault's dinner with his neighbor Raymond Sintès at the latter's apartment by his invitation occurs in Part One, chapter three. This is a critical point in the novel. It is during this dinner that Meursault commits his one untruthful, inadvertently "evil" act. At Raymond's request, he writes a deceitful, conciliatory letter under Raymond's name for him to mail to his Arab ex-mistress, designed to lure her to Raymond's room so that he can have sex with her and then beat her up. This is the one instance where Meursault's "innocence" is put to the test, and he is found wanting. He identifies with the *colons*, even to the extent of drinking excessive amounts of alcohol, in order to sacrifice himself for them. Moreover, Camus has provided an excuse for Meursault's "un-Christ-like" behavior: his intoxicated condition.

Alcohol consumption was extremely high in France and in Meursault's Algeria, as a 2004 article by Vincent Grégoire has emphasized. It is well known, as Meursault's conversation with Raymond implies, that drinking reduces our inhibitions so that we generally think, do, and say things we would not do when sober. In addition, the importance of wine in the novel is indicated by Meursault's name—Meursault is a type of burgundy wine, usually white, and produced near Beaune in eastern France (*New Oxford American Dictionary* 1076). This generally unnoticed aspect of his surname conveys Meursault's identity as a pure-hearted ("white") individual, his "white" color as opposed to the darker-skinned Arabs, as well as the significance of wine drinking in his fate.[5]

Ironically, the term *pied-noir*, although it denotes Algeria's créole, native-born white French population, is literally translated, "black foot." The reason for this is that the earliest French Algerians produced wine, one of the country's leading exports, by tramping on the dark-colored grapes with their feet, hence staining their feet with grape juice (Grégoire 25 n2). Thus, by analogy with the type of wine they produce, we can conceive of Meursault's character as pure, or "white," as opposed to that of the "black," or evil *pieds-noirs* who judge and condemn him.

Meursault informs the reader that he had been drinking earlier in the day on the evening of his dinner with Raymond. It was Monday, the day after his mother's funeral, and, cutting short the mourning process, he had gone to work. At lunch, he had "drunk a glass of wine too many" (32), perhaps to escape his unexpressed grief at his mother's death. Afterward, he went home to take a brief nap, and (self-destructively) he was late returning to work. This part of the novel is important insofar as it reveals that Meursault adopts self-destructive behaviors, perhaps acting out guilt about his mother's death; he is unaccustomed to drinking large amounts of alcohol, and is vulnerable to the effects of wine. Thus, it provides a backdrop to what occurs next—the crucial dinner with Raymond later that day, when

Meursault inadvertently gets drunk, and immediately, in his inebriated state, writes the letter for Raymond.

When Meursault arrives home from work, he is annoyed by having to cook dinner. This sets the stage for his dinner with Raymond. He anticipates only boiling some potatoes ("I went straight home, as I had to put some potatoes on to boil" [32]). From the tone of Meursault's apathetic aside to the reader on Salamano's mistreatment of his dog, "This has been going on for eight years. Céleste [Meursault's friend, a restaurateur] is always saying, 'It's pitiful,' but really, who's to say?" (Ward 27), one gains the impression that Meursault equably accepts human nature's ambiguous quotient of violence and evil and concludes that there's not much one can do about it (32–34). At this point, Raymond appears (34), and, like Satan in the Garden of Eden, intervenes irreparably in Meursault's life.

Meursault's dinner and conversation with Raymond, in which he writes the letter, occur on pages 34–42 of Stuart Gilbert's translation of the novel (which remains the most widely available). First, he encounters his elderly neighbor Salamano, who is screaming at his dog, on the staircase while going up to his room. Then Raymond, a suspected pimp, enters from the street. Meursault feels strangely empathetic with him, as something of an alter ego, a *reductio ad absurdum* of his own antisocial tendencies. They chat on the staircase: "He often has a word for me, and drops in sometimes for a short talk in my room, because I listen to him. As a matter of fact, I find what he says quite interesting. So, really I've no reason for freezing him off" (34). As Meursault is about to open the door to his apartment, Raymond says, "Look here! How about having some grub with me? I've a black pudding and some wine" (35). In Matthew Ward's translation (28), he says, "I've got some blood sausage and some wine at my place. How about joining me?" The following sentence conveys how little conscious significance Meursault attaches to Raymond's offer: "I figured it would save me the trouble of having to cook for myself, so I accepted" (Ward 28).

Meursault explains to the reader that he enjoys talking with Raymond despite his unpopularity in the neighborhood. As we have noted, he has spoken with his mysterious neighbor before: "As a matter of fact, I find what he says quite interesting" (34). Raymond's abrupt offer to share his dinner of "black pudding and some wine" seems a caricature of the wine and bread that are Christ's body and blood in the Mass and at the Last Supper. This is the foreground of Meursault's tragic act—his *hamartia* being his unacknowledged post-mortem depression after his mother's death, what Patrick McCarthy calls a condition of being "haunted by death and unable to come to grips with grief and love" (*Albert Camus* 33). His mother's death exacerbates his consciousness of his existing, chronic condition of general friendlessness.

Consequently, he is more willing than usual to assist someone like Raymond, who seemingly befriends him.[6] This dinner ultimately costs him his freedom and his life.

The dinner scene parodies a Last Supper or Black Mass, in which Christ/Meursault is made drunk by Raymond—who, in supplying the wine and sausage (analogous to Christ's blood and body) plays the role of a counterfeit, "Satanic" Christ, the "good Christ" Meursault's alter ego. By writing the letter for Raymond, Meursault provokes the events that culminate in his shooting and killing the nameless Arab woman's nameless brother, leading to his trial and conviction for murder. Thus, it is among the most important events in *The Stranger*. It links Meursault with the concept of the Jesus Christ figure that Camus suggested following the novel's publication.

Those familiar with the New Testament are aware that Satan's Temptation of Jesus Christ before he starts on his preaching mission is one of its most important events. It includes several eloquent maxims. Matt. 4:1–11 and Luke 4:1–13 describe the encounter between Satan and Jesus in nearly identical terms, although the words of their conversation slightly differ in their order. The Holy Spirit leads Jesus into the wilderness to endure hunger and Satan's enticement.

Food plays a major role in Satan's temptation of Christ, as it does in Meursault's dinner with Raymond and his ensuing composition of the letter. After Jesus fasts for forty days and forty nights, he is hungry. Satan comes to him in the wilderness and advises him to convert nearby stones into bread, to which Jesus aptly retorts, "Man shall not live by bread alone, but by every word of God (Matt. 4:4).[7] Satan then takes Jesus to a high mountain, where they may view all the kingdoms of the world, and promises Jesus control over all the kingdoms if he worships him. Jesus, unimpressed, utters the immortal words, "Get behind me, Satan!" (Matt. 4:8). Undeterred, Satan takes Jesus to the Temple of Jerusalem, and suggests he jump off to demonstrate his powers. However, Jesus again rebuffs Satan, asserting, "You shall not tempt the Lord your God" (Matt. 4:12). After this final rejection, Satan leaves the scene, hoping for better luck in the future. In many ways, the dinner between Meursault and Raymond parallels the encounter between Jesus and Satan, although Meursault *succumbs* to Raymond/Satan's request that he write a letter and ultimately sacrifices his life as a result.

During the dinner at Raymond Sintès's apartment (strangely, Sintès was Camus's mother's maiden name, possibly revealing that Camus perceived her as a vindictive or handicapping force in his life), the ordinarily harmless Meursault performs his only malevolent act before the shooting—writing the letter that Raymond sends to his mistress. By this means, Raymond tricks her into coming to his room and assaults her, reviving her brother's

desire for vengeance. This leads to a fight between Raymond and the Arab on the beach, begun by Raymond, during which he is stabbed. Raymond then returns to the beach house to get a revolver, but Meursault persuades him to give the gun to him for safekeeping. Ironically, Meursault, who now has the gun, returns to the beach and commits the murder that he took the gun from Raymond to prevent him from carrying out. Thus, Meursault's dinner with Raymond may perhaps be considered a kind of "Black Mass": "good" Meursault is made drunk by the satanic Raymond and manipulated to do the latter's will, in a mocking satire of Satan's failed seduction of Jesus in the wilderness in the Temptation episode of the New Testament.[8] Unlike Jesus, who refuses to drink wine at the Last Supper (Matthew 26: 29), the "human-all-too-human" Meursault Christ-figure ardently consumes wine during the fateful dinner with Raymond, precipitating his downfall.[9]

In a similar vein, Meursault shows his human-all-too-human frailty as a Jesus *manqué* in composing the letter to Raymond's girlfriend as Raymond's surrogate. By lying and by drinking *alcool*, he distances himself from the flaw-less Christ and seemingly aligns himself more closely with the French *colons*. In effect, he becomes a *human* Christ—with the faults of human beings; but ready to sacrifice himself for them. The "truth" (as Camus calls it in his *avant propos*) that Meursault dies for is to expose the evils of French colonialism and the discord between Muslims and *colons* by means of Meursault's crime and its anomalous capital punishment, which was hardly ever the penalty in Algeria when a *pied-noir* killed an Arab. This is similar to Jesus' fate, in that the Jews, whose laws prohibited capital punishment (John 18:31–32), delivered him to Pontius Pilate, expecting him to be executed according to Roman law.

Although he writes in the preface to *L'Étranger* that it is "the story of a man who, without any heroics, agrees to die for the truth," Camus, cognizant that Meursault's initial prevarication set him on his road to dying for the truth, alludes to the inherent contradiction: "I also happened to say, again paradoxically, that I had tried to draw in my character the only Christ we deserve" ("Preface" 336–37).

Feminist critics and other scholars often point to Meursault's agreement to write the disingenuous letter for Raymond as evincing his cynicism or misogyny.[10] However, a closer look at the circumstances of the event reveals that Camus intended to mitigate Meursault's guilt in the matter, by suggesting that he was intoxicated at the time. The dinner, in which Raymond serves Meursault "black pudding" and wine, caricatures the Last Supper and the Eucharist. The black pudding (which the most faithful translation of *The Stranger*, by Matthew Ward, translates as "blood sausage" [28], thereby making it even more analogous to Christ's blood) and wine represent the body

and blood of Meursault—Camus's Jesus-figure—because it is as a result of the dinner that he loses his life. On a more mundane level, we can say that Raymond, by offering Meursault a slapdash dinner, thereby saving his grateful neighbor from cooking for himself, whatever his motives, is one of the few people who help Meursault.

Another friend, Meursault's coworker Emmanuel, lends him a black tie and mourning band for his mother's funeral. He possesses these things, having recently attended an uncle's funeral (2). Emmanuel has an impish quality. He runs with Meursault to jump on back of a truck so that they can arrive more quickly at Céleste's restaurant for lunch (Ward 25–26). Meursault only mentions him once more in the novel, informing the reader: "I went to the movies twice with Emmanuel, who doesn't always understand what's going on on the screen. So you have to explain things to him" (Ward 34). Thus, unlike Meursault, whose superficial naiveté conceals a passion for truth, Emmanuel is a genuinely simple-minded character. In a sense, he is Meursault's alter ego, despite his relatively minor role. Perhaps Camus intended Emmanuel to represent a satirical depiction of the Messiah or an ironical version of God or Jesus himself. The Book of Isaiah (7:14) predicts "a virgin shall conceive" a son named Immanuel, who, in most interpretations is actually God. However, *The New English Bible* depicts Immanuel more as the Messiah: "For a boy has been born for us, a son given to us to bear the symbol of dominion on his shoulder; and he shall be called in purpose wonderful, in battle God-like, Father of a wide realm, Prince of Peace" (Isa. 9:6, *New English Bible*). Other depictions of Emmanuel include, "his name shall be called Wonderful, Counsellor, The mighty God, The everlasting Father, The Prince of Peace."

The New Testament revives Isaiah's prophecy, referring to the Messiah as "Immanuel" or "Emmanuel" (Matt. 1:23): "Behold, the virgin shall be with child, and bear a Son, and they shall call his name, Emmanuel, which being interpreted is, 'God is with us'" (*New English Bible*). Emmanuel, although he is Meursault's coworker, is not involved in Meursault's and Raymond's encounters with the Arab. Apparently, he is less friendly with Meursault than the restaurateur Céleste, who along with his paramour Marie, Raymond, Masson, and even decrepit old Salamano, testify on Meursault's behalf at the murder trial. Indeed, in light of his name's connotations, Emmanuel's failure to participate in the proceedings and his minor role in the novel suggest that Camus intended him to serve, somewhat ludicrously, as an existential "absent God."

By accepting Raymond's offer of dinner and ensuing friendship (at least, he concurs when Raymond says they are *copains* (breakers of bread together, or "pals") (36, 41), the ordinarily isolated and withdrawn Meursault is sucked into the evil of *pied-noir* male society, whose racial and gender abuses are

epitomized by the reputed pimp Raymond's beating of his Arab girlfriend and his altercation with her Arab male avengers.

It becomes evident that Raymond's motive in offering Meursault victuals was to enlist him in his quest for revenge on his ex-mistress, who he suspects had been unfaithful, and to persuade him to write the letter summoning her to his room, in effect acting as his surrogate. Moreover, in Part I, chapter 6, by seizing the gun from Raymond and putting it in his pocket, Meursault is enabled to accomplish the murderous act that Raymond only contemplated (Ward 56). Acting as Raymond's substitute, he suffers imprisonment and execution as a result. Thus, he martyrs himself for Raymond, who symbolizes Algerian *colon* society.

Among Camus's leading principles is the importance of helping one's fellow human beings, as Meursault helped Raymond by writing the letter for him, albeit with unintended malign consequences for the Arab woman, Raymond, and most of all Meursault. At the end of World War II, referring to himself as a "non-Christian" in speaking of his rejection of Christianity, Camus said:

> I believe I entertain a just idea of the greatness of Christianity; but there are a number of us in this persecuted world who feel that, if Christ died for certain men, he did not die for us. And at the same time we refuse to despair of man. If we do not cherish the unconscionable ambition to save him, we wish at least to serve him. We consent to be deprived of God and of hope, but do not do so easily without man. (qtd. in Peyre 24)

Despite the disastrous results of his dinner with Raymond—including the assault on the Arab girl, her brother's death, and Meursault's conviction for murder—Meursault could not logically be expected to foresee the consequences of such simple acts as eating dinner at a new friend's apartment and helping him write a letter. He was participating in common social activities as a member of *pied-noir* society, with which he showed a renewed eagerness to be involved after his mother's death left him feeling more isolated than before.

Many readers are disturbed by Meursault's general complicity with evil in the course of the novel. Meursault seems complacent about Raymond's beating his girlfriend, both when he tells him about it initially and when it recurs after she returns to his apartment as a result of Meursault's apparently seductive letter (whose exact contents we are never shown). Likewise, Meursault accepts Salamano's brutality toward his mangy dog. When his friend Céleste and even bestial Raymond deplore Salamano's behavior as "pitiful"

and "disgusting," Meursault quietly disagrees (Ward 27–28). This seems similar to Sartre's later observation in *Les Mots* (30) that those who are kind to dogs are often cruel to human beings.

Strangely, Meursault's ostensible apathy concerning Raymond's and Salamano's violent actions toward the weak in some ways reiterates Jesus' teachings. In various immortal phrases, Jesus enjoins us not to condemn others: In the famous instance of the adulteress, he warns the crowd, "Let him who is without sin cast the first stone" (John 8:1). He also instructs his followers to "resist not evil" (Matt. 5:39), and, "Judge not, lest thou be judged" (Matt. 7:1). Jesus's (and Meursault's) resigned attitudes are the result of awareness that all people have been violent and committed evil acts. Jesus himself can be violent, as when he drives the money-changers from the temple (Matt. 21:12–13). And, of course, Jesus voices the ultimate exculpation of the evil and violent, in requesting that God forgive his own murderers, who, like the judge and jury who convict Meursault, have the veneer of law on their side: "Father, forgive them, for they know not what they do" (Luke 23:34). As Paul later declares, "all have sinned and fall short of the glory of God" (Romans 3:23).

Willard Bohn points out, and Monique Wagner even more strongly emphasizes, that Meursault is a victim of his physical sensations. He is also an essentially lonely person, with no intimate friends to whom to confide his inner thoughts and feelings.[11] This inner desolation combined with extreme physical sensitivity helps explain his acute vulnerability to the wine's effects. As students of Camus's religious views point out, his passion for the quantity of experience was a psychological trait that devout Christians usually lack (Loose). But this does not prevent Camus from depicting Meursault as a halo-bearing, ironically saintly figure. In the encounter with the priest at the end of *The Stranger*, Meursault recalls, "The chaplain looked at me with a sort of sadness. I was now completely back up against the wall and the daylight was flowing over my forehead."[12]

There is some similarity between Camus's conception of Meursault in *L'Étranger* and Simone Weil's view of the value of common suffering (she includes criminals' punishment here) and affliction in uniting humanity. In an analysis of the affinity of their ideas, John Dunaway observes, "It is obvious, for example, that the similarities . . . between certain aspects of *L'Étranger* and Weil's ideas on criminal justice and rootedness are not a question of influence, since Camus wrote his first great novel before encountering Weil's writings" (41). In a manner that Weil would appreciate, Meursault takes Raymond's and *pied-noir* evil, in general, upon himself (if we acknowledge that Sintès would have inevitably attacked the Arab). By his conduct after his arrest, he is simultaneously a Christ figure who stoically bears up against judicial assault, and a rebel who refuses to enact social norms such as inordinate

public expressions of grief or to embrace Christianity when the priest comes to his cell. Simone Weil and Camus both want to know, "What does a just man do to contend with evil?" J. P. Little's synopsis of Weil's idea of the "just man" may readily be applied to Meursault, although Camus seems not to have been aware of her thought until after he wrote *The Stranger*: "Taking as her model various mythological and historical figures of the just man, she felt that the only way of dispelling evil was for such a just man to take the evil upon himself, to refuse to pass it on, and by absorbing it into himself, to transmute it into suffering" (46).

At his first—and last—supper with Raymond, hunger tempts the Christ-figure Meursault, like Jesus in the wilderness, but unlike the Nazarene, he fails to resist Raymond's offer of food. The ensuing repast is the equivalent of Christ/Meursault's Last Supper. He drinks wine and eats bloodied sausage. As gifts from the sadistic Raymond, they are ironically the converse of Jesus's benign offer of his blood and body in the form of bread and wine at the Last Supper. By performing a simple favor, writing a letter for another individual, Meursault, perhaps unwittingly, sacrifices himself, unlike Jesus, who, despite some last-minute misgivings ("My God, my God, why hast thou forsaken me?" [Matt. 27:46]), deliberately died for humanity on the Cross. In return, Jesus rose from the dead and a new, powerful religion emerged to honor him. Although the fate of Meursault, the atheistic Christ, is less clear, it seems likely that he will be ingloriously guillotined, rather than receive a pardon, have his sentence commuted, or experience personal resurrection.[13]

Perhaps Meursault's dinner with Raymond left him with an awareness of culpability in the evil of the human condition. Indeed, Camus's remark in an earlier book of aphorisms, *L'Été*, seems to anticipate the dinner's outcome: "At first innocent without knowing it, we become guilty without wanting it" (qtd. in Ohayon 204). At the same time, Camus said, "No cause justifies the death of the innocent" (qtd. in O'Brien, "Camus and Christianity," 159). In their own way, both Meursault and the Arab he killed were innocent men, and there is no convincing way to justify their deaths. As a Jesus figure *manqué*, Meursault murdered the Arab to warn his beloved *pied-noir* society of the errors of its ways: that they should cease persecuting the Arabs, and try to compromise with them, before they lost their Algerian homeland in a civil war. Toward the end of his life, in an appendix to his last, unfinished novel, *Le Premier Homme*, there is even an indication that Camus hoped Algeria would experience peaceful communistic reform in which the land would be divided among the impoverished Arab masses and those *pieds-noirs* who were poor (320–21).

However, instead of executing him for murdering a fellow human being, an Arab whose countrymen would eventually overthrow French domination

unless the *colons* made restitution for their injustice and treated the Arab inhabitants as equals, the prosecuting attorney, judge, and jury are determined to convict and execute Meursault for asocial impropriety, the unrelated "crime" of putting his mother in a nursing home and not showing sufficient grief at her funeral, i.e., not exhibiting the appropriate deference for "white," European social norms. Thus, his efforts to "save" French and Arabs from a bloody Algerian civil war were rendered nugatory. Marie foreshadows the meaninglessness of Meursault's death when she comments on the morning of the Sunday he kills the Arab, that he has a "funeral face" (Ward 47).

Many of Camus's early writings, especially *Noces* and *L'Été*, the exuberant, soulful essays he wrote a few years before *L'Étranger*, expressed his love for French Algeria's *pied-noir*, *colon* society, whose virility, physical uninhibitedness, camaraderie, and closeness to Nature he idolized. He admired the male society's sense of honor and defiance of authority. When Meursault refuses to call the police despite Marie's entreaties, tersely explaining that "I didn't like cops" (Ward 36), he is evoking the *pieds-noirs'* folk morality that Camus writes about so effusively in "Noces" (Thody 86–87): "There are still many of us who observe the highway code, the only disinterested one I know. . . . I have always seen the faces around me take on an expression of pity at the sight of a man between two policemen."

Indeed, Meursault, the *pied-noir* Messiah, seems willing to sacrifice himself, unconsciously serving as a scapegoat if that will lead his *semblables* to act in a more conciliatory manner toward the Muslim majority, who will otherwise ultimately revolt against *pied-noir* persecution and overthrow French rule. Depressed at the thought that the *colons* will one day suffer exile from the beautiful "unity" of "sea and sky" they find in their *patrie*, Algeria, Camus regrets the loss of such "purity," cryptically asserting in "Noces" ("Nuptials"), "It is a well-known fact that we always recognize our homeland at the moment we are about to lose it" (Thody 90).

Meursault commits his one act of lying and deception, that of writing the letter to Raymond's mistress, thereby sinking to the level of his fellow men, the *pieds-noirs* he loves despite their violence and bigotry, and sacrifices himself for them. By lying in pretending to be Raymond, writing the untrue letter *qua* Raymond, Meursault, the invariably honest Jesus figure who, as Camus says, "refuses to lie," paradoxically sets himself up for symbolic "crucifixion" by the guillotine. Like Jesus at his trial, Meursault disdains to lie, not telling the judge, prosecutors and jurors the maudlin, tearful stories about his reaction to his mother's death that they want to hear. Thus, Jesus/Meursault is a God who becomes Man. As the Bible often says, "And the Word was made flesh" (1 John 1:3, 14), and God was "put to death in the flesh" (1 Pet. 8:18). By lying for the first and only time in the novel, and getting drunk as

well, Jesus-Meursault at his dinner with Raymond becomes one with human-kind: and "God becomes Man." The letter's "human-all-too-human" lie, as Nietzsche might call it, provokes the ensuing tragic action: the fight with the Arabs, Meursault's taking the gun from Raymond, and his final encounter with and murder of Raymond's paramour's brother.

Occasionally, Meursault indicates an acute awareness of Arab hostility toward the truculent white minority. At the police station, Raymond is not arrested for assaulting his Arab paramour. The following fateful morning, Meursault, Marie, and Raymond are on their way to the beach when they see Raymond's Arab foes, his ex-girlfriend's brother and a friend, standing across the street from his apartment building. "They were staring at us in silence, but in that way of theirs, as if we were nothing but stones or dead trees," Meursault observes (Ward 48). Meursault's remark on the native majority's festering anger foreshadows the eventual doom of the *pieds-noirs* during the Algerian Revolution, when the French presence in Algeria will be obliterated like dead matter. Sadly, Meursault's society, standing judgment on him in the courtroom, is deaf to his message of fraternity with its Arab neighbors, and instead convicts him for the "crime" of indifference to its hypocritical customs.[14]

In a different context, Patrick McCarthy, adhering to Camus's *avant-propos*, emphasizes the connection between Meursault and Jesus. Paraphrasing Meursault's final remarks, McCarthy writes,

> Christ was God and man, and Camus believed he was chiefly the latter. But Christ is an uninteresting figure unless He retains some tiny trace of the Godhead, and this trace is what lurks behind the "night full of signs." At the very least the absence of God is not to be forgotten or overcome. (*Albert Camus* 78)

Meursault may represent Camus's secularized version of the Holy Spirit. Applying René Girard's methodology in his essay, *I See Satan Fall Like Lightning* to *The Stranger* (although he earlier labeled Meursault a "juvenile delinquent" in a famous, brilliantly iconoclastic article[15]), we may regard Meursault as the *paraclete* or Holy Spirit, which in Greek and Latin means "lawyer for the defense" or "defender of the accused." By contrast, Satan in Hebrew signifies "accuser [i.e., prosecutor] before a tribunal." Confronting his accusers—judge, jury, most of the witnesses, and the prosecutor—the taciturn Meursault, like Jesus and the Holy Spirit, serves as "defender of the accused," both himself and in his persona Raymond and the mass of *pieds-noirs* who oppressed the Arab majority ("Father, forgive them for they know not what they do"), driving them to revolt. The whites convict and execute him, rendering him the scapegoat for their own brutal treatment of the Muslims.

But Meursault's intent was to enlighten them about their secular sin against the *patrie*. As Girard puts it in his book (although not in reference to *The Stranger*, which he does not mention here): "We should take with utmost seriousness the idea that the Spirit enlightens the persecutors concerning their acts of persecution. The Spirit discloses to individuals the literal truth of what Jesus said during his crucifixion: 'They don't know what they are doing'" (*I See Satan* 189–90). While what Alexis de Tocqueville called the "tyranny of the majority" manifests itself in the Algiers courtroom and its desultory procedures, in subdued form constituting a kind of mass hysteria and mob justice, Meursault inevitably realizes, at the novel's end, that his sacrifice has not accomplished anything useful. In a subliminal manner, this may be the reason for his tirade against the priest, who represents the Establishment that has failed to recognize the true meaning of an Arab's murder and instead convicted him for an insufficient display of socially sanctified grief at his mother's funeral.

In Camus's "absurd" world, as he depicted it in the *Myth of Sisyphus*, Meursault, by taking Raymond's—and *pied-noir* evil as a whole—upon himself, only accomplishes his death. He fails in his goal: to achieve increased social awareness by the *pieds-noirs* of the injustices perpetrated against the native Arab majority. On the contrary, he faces execution primarily for not demonstrating enough sorrow after his mother's death, thereby violating hypocritical bourgeois norms that emphasize public displays of grief notwithstanding individual authenticity of feeling or the lack of it. To a certain degree, therefore, my interpretation bears out J. P. Little's view of tragedy in the works of Camus, which requires

> a sense of inevitability, of something which is beyond man's control, of an individual pitted against forces which he cannot match. He may fail because of *hamartia*, or he may do evil unwittingly, but there is always the sense that he is kept ignorant of some vital factor, knowledge of which would have enabled him to avoid tragic consequences. (50)

For Camus, the New Testament's only tragic aspect was the moment that the crucified Jesus viscerally felt human, in perceiving the abandonment by his Father. This was the most authentic moment of his story; much of the rest, for Camus, was mere fantasy. As he said in a speech *sur l'avenir de la tragédie*, possibly influenced by the works of Simone Weil, which he discovered several years after writing *The Stranger*:

> Peut-être n'y a-t-il eu qu'une seule tragédie chrétienne dans l'histoire. Elle s'est célébrée sur le Golgotha pendant un instant

imperceptible, au moment du 'Mon Dieu, pourquoi m'as-tu aban-
donné.' Ce doute fugitive, et ce doute seule, consacrait l'ambiguité
d'une situation tragique. ("Conference" 1706)

Perhaps there is only a single Christian tragedy in the whole
story [of the New Testament]. It celebrates itself on Golgotha in
an imperceptible instant, at the moment of [Jesus uttering], "My
God, why have you abandoned me." This fleeting doubt, and this
doubt alone, sanctifies the ambiguity of the tragic situation. (my
translation)

For Camus, Jesus as an immortal figure cannot be a tragic one, since he
cannot authentically undergo the fear of death. Once he has risen from the
dead, unlike Meursault, he can no longer be considered a tragic representative of humanity: "Ensuite la divinité du Christ n'a plus fait de doute. La
messe qui consacre chaque jour cette divinité est la vraie forme du théâtre
religieux en Occident. Elle n'est pas invention, mais repetition" ("Conference" 1706). ("Afterward Christ's divinity is no longer a matter of doubt.
The mass that daily consecrates this divinity is the true form of religious
theater in the West. It is not contrivance, but redundancy" [my translation].)
Nevertheless, Robert Sutton suggests that Jesus may have shared Camus's
disbelief in the immortality of the soul and the superior significance of the
afterlife (162).

To some extent, Camus mocked the concept of Messianism. On the
secular level, he considered it a hypocritical invention of the postwar super-
powers, the United States and the Soviet Union, part of the rhetoric of their
potentially cataclysmic confrontation. In 1948, in "Helen's Exile" he wrote,
"We are now witnessing the Messianic forces confronting one another, their
clamors merging in the shock of empire" (Thody 151). Camus had become
disillusioned because people no longer respected natural beauty, only the
power and immortality they thought were conferred by Reason taken to
extreme limits, including totalitarianism and nuclear holocaust.

By contrast, writing a decade earlier, he negated the wish for immortality while virtually deifying Algerian *pieds-noirs* sensuality, spontaneity and
love of life. He was almost willing to exempt them from punishment for sin.
"There are some words that I have never really understood, such as sin," he
wrote in 1939 in "Summer in Algiers."

Yet I think I know that these men [the exuberant, working-class
pieds-noirs of his acquaintance] have never sinned against life. For if
there is a sin against life, it lies perhaps less in despairing of it than

in hoping for a better life and evading the implacable grandeur of the one we have. (Thody 91)

Camus similarly exalts the earthiness and physicality of the *pieds-noirs* in his glorified description of amateur boxing matches in Oran. With poignant empathy for the audience, Camus, with a journalist's flair, writes, "In this atmosphere, the announcement of a draw is badly received. It runs counter to what, in the crowd, is an utterly Manichean vision: there is good and evil, the winner and the loser. One must be right if one isn't wrong." When a draw is declared and the competing Parisian and Oranian boxers embrace, the crowd bursts into applause, inadvertently showing its civility, Camus observes ("The Minotaur, or Stopping in Oran," in Thody 123).

As revealed by his "Last Supper" with Raymond and its fateful aftermath, Meursault embodies a human, existential version of Christ. Uncharacteristically, unfeelingly killing the Arab as a brutal *pied-noir* like his friend Raymond might do, Meursault sets himself on a scapegoat's sacrificial course but fails during his trial in his efforts to serve as an exemplar leading sinning fellow men to see the "truth." This is the hidden, Christian meaning of his blundering, needless murder of the Arab, which precipitates his senseless execution. As adumbrated by Meursault's earlier awed, pantheistic, mystical contemplation of Nature when he is on the beach and with Marie, whom he basically treats with respect (Scherr), his tragic fate and culminating self-revelation ultimately reveals to him that the absurdity, what Sartre called "contingency" (see Bourgeois), underlying life's joy and suffering inhered in a *colon* society immune and indifferent to his Christ-like warning and sacrifice. This is one of the undetected meanings of his enigmatic, bitter last words: "For everything to be consummated, for me to feel less alone, I had only to wish that there be a large crowd of spectators the day of my execution and that they greet me with cries of hate" (Ward 123).

Aptly enough, the final words of Meursault, the atheistic Christ, after crucifixes have been menacingly waved in his face by the examining magistrate and an overzealous priest looking for a premature "confession," remind one of the jeering claques ("multitudes") of Jews recruited against Jesus by the relentless high priest Caiaphas. They harassed Jesus after Caiaphas had him arrested, during his brief, improvised "trial" and on the way to the cross, rejecting his healing invocation to "love thy neighbor." In the ultimate humiliation, they called for Pontius Pilate to release the rebel and murderer Barabbas in his stead. (The precise nature of Barabbas's crime is unclear. Mark 15:6–11 identifies him as a rebel who had committed murder during the rebellion, while John 18:40 calls him a robber.) Like Jesus, Meursault is hated by the mob (Mark 15:8–14, 29–32). Like Jesus during his trial and punishment,

Meursault is treated in a degrading fashion in the courtroom, although not to the extent of being barbarically scourged as Jesus was by Governor Pontius Pilate (John 19:1, Mark 15:15, Matt. 27:26). Unlike the judges, jurors and attorneys, Meursault is not given a straw fan on a hot day (87, 88). Always acutely sensitive to his physical surroundings, Meursault "wipe[s] the sweat covering my face" (89), reminiscent of Jesus praying in solitude after the Last Supper, dreading impending death: "And being in agony, he prayed more earnestly. Then his sweat became like great drops of blood falling down to the ground" (Luke 22:44).

There are numerous other affinities between Meursault and Christ in the novel. Ironically, when Meursault asserts that he does not believe in God, the outraged examining magistrate (whose temperament resembles the Jewish high priest Caiaphas) waves a crucifix at him (68), and from that point on seems determined to convict him of murder, while adopting the derisive nickname for him, "Monsieur Antichrist" (71) to mask his anger, similar to the Roman soldiers mockingly calling Jesus "King of the Jews" (Luke 23:36–38). At Meursault's trial, the jurors draw lots (for what purpose is not clear), just as the Roman soldiers drew lots for Jesus's clothing at his crucifixion (Matt. 27:35). After the chief judge incongruously directs incriminating remarks at Meursault, mainly in connection with reports of his conduct at his mother's funeral, Meursault admits to himself, "For the first time in years I had this stupid urge to cry, because I could feel how much all these people hated me" (89–90). He may have found solace in Christ's words to his disciples, "If the world hates you, you know that it hated me before it hated you" (John 15:18).

As this article has argued, Meursault's "last supper" with Raymond is an event of central significance in delineating Meursault's Christ-like role. It is a pivotal circumstance in the unfolding necessity leading to his murder of the Arab, analogous to Jesus at the Last Supper revealing to his disciples that one of them will betray him. This is shortly followed by Judas Iscariot kissing Jesus near the Mount of Olives, thereby exposing his identity to the high priest's soldiers, rendering his crucifixion inevitable. With the similarity of his mission, his persona and his fate to that of Jesus, Meursault in many ways *is*, as Camus said, "the only Christ we deserved."

Notes

1. Except where otherwise noted, citations to *The Stranger* refer to the translation by Stuart Gilbert, which is listed under Camus in the Works Cited list. Citations to the translation by Matthew Ward will be cited as "Ward," and that translation is listed in Ward's name in the Works Cited list.

2. Ohayon provides an occasionally confused discussion of Meursault's similarities to Jesus in his account of the trial. His interpretation of Meursault's final

remarks, when he states that, "For everything to be consummated, for me to feel less alone" (Ward 123; Ohayon 201), as literally akin to Jesus's cry from the cross is moot. Ohayon and Loose both consider this statement as analogous to Christ's calling from the cross, "It is finished." The analogy seems strained in this instance.

3. See also Brock, who argues that Camus wrote *L'Étranger* primarily as a polemic against capital punishment.

4. In one of the best of numerous explications of *L'Étranger*, English Showalter, Jr., does little more than depict Raymond as an unsavory character and impugn Meursault's integrity for befriending him (65–67).

5. For an interpretation of the color "white" as representing purity in *L'Étranger* and linking Meursault's mother's social humiliation when he places her in the Marengo nursing home with that of her alter ego, the cancerous Arab nurse, who is swathed in white, see McCarthy, "First Arab."

6. See Willard Bohn, "*The Stranger* and Kafka's *The Trial*," in Maus's *Readings on The Stranger*, 127.

7. Quotations from the account of Jesus's temptation are taken from the New King James Version of the Bible.

8. "Black Mass" refers to the blasphemous and often obscene burlesques of the Christian Eucharist, allegedly performed by satanic or anti-Christian cults in the thirteenth and fourteenth centuries. Various ritually cannibalistic and sexually perverse rites and worship of animals or idols took place. Naked women's backsides were often used as ersatz altars, and consecrated hosts were supposedly obtained, urinated on and in various ways mutilated. The idea of the Black Mass was most widely disseminated in France, where charges of Satanism and celebration of the black mass were made in the Middle Ages against persons accused of heresy and witchcraft, most notably by King Philip IV against the Knights Templar in 1307, seeking to expropriate their wealth and eliminate their political power by imprisoning them and burning their leaders at the stake. The French novelist Joris-Karl Huysmans described celebration of a Black Mass in late nineteenth-century France in his novel, *Là-Bas* (1891). As part of the Francophone culture, it is likely that Camus was familiar with the concept of the Black Mass.

9. Grégoire provides the most detailed treatment of the role of alcohol and excessive drinking in causing loss of control among Camus's characters, but he does not perceive the episode at Raymond's apartment in the way that is done here.

10. See Conor Cruise O'Brien, Louise K. Horowitz, Anthony Rizzuto, and Christine Margerrison, "Albert Camus and 'Ces Femmes qu'on raie de l'humanité': Sexual Politics in the Colonial Arena." Compare the defense of Camus in Jan Rigaud.

11. Willard Bohn's "The Trials and Tribulations of Josef K. and Meursault" is excerpted in Derek C. Maus's *Readings on The Stranger*, 125–37. For the view that Meursault was essentially sociable, see Robert Champigny, 7–11.

12. *L'Étranger*, quoted in Onimus 113. Ward's translation is: "I now had my back flat against the wall, and light was streaming over my forehead" (119).

13. Elwyn F. Sterling argues that the tone of the novel's conclusion indicates that Meursault will eventually be pardoned, *not* executed.

14. For the argument, questioned in this essay, that Camus in *The Stranger* intentionally depicted Arabs as non-persons without an identity, see Margerrison (2001).

15. For Girard's brilliant, iconoclastic characterization of Meursault as having the personality of a "juvenile delinquent" and a "derelict," and his unfavorable comparison of *L'Étranger* with Camus's *La Chute*, see "Camus's Stranger Retried."

WORKS CITED

Bourgeois, Patrick. "Contingency." *Dictionary of Existentialism.* Ed. Haim Gordon. Westport: Greenwood, 1999. 94–97.

Brock, Robert R. "Meursault the Straw Man." *Studies in the Novel* 25:1 (Spring 1993): 92–100.

Camus, Albert. *Conférence prononcée à Athènes sur l'avenir de la tragédie. Albert Camus: Théâtre, Récits, Nouvelles.* Ed. Roger Quilliot. Paris: Gallimard, 1962. 1699–1709.

———. *Le Premier Homme.* Paris: Gallimard, 1994.

———. *The Myth of Sisyphus and Other Essays.* 1942. Trans. Justin O'Brien. New York: Vintage, 1955.

———. "Preface to the American University Edition of *The Stranger.*" 1955. As reprinted in *Lyrical and Critical Essays.* Ed. Philip Thody. Trans. Ellen Conroy Kennedy. 1968. New York: Vintage, 1970. 335–37.

———. *The Stranger.* Trans. Stuart Gilbert. New York: Vintage, 1954.

Champigny, Robert J. *A Pagan Hero: An Interpretation of Meursault in Camus' The Stranger.* Trans. Rowe Portis. Philadelphia: U of Pennsylvania P, 1969.

Cohn, Robert Greer. "Camus's Sacred: 'The Growing Stone.'" *Stanford Literature Review* 5.1–2 (Spring–Fall 1988): 151–60.

Cruickshank, John. "Albert Camus: Sainthood Without God." *Mansions of the Spirit: Essays in Literature and Religion.* Ed. George A. Panichas. New York: Hawthorn, 1967. 313–24.

Daruwalla, K. N. "The Impact of *L'Étranger*: Oblique Reflections on an Oblique Novel." *Camus's L'Étranger: Fifty Years On.* Ed. Adele King. London: Macmillan, 1992. 59–64.

Dunaway, John M. "Estrangement and the Need for Roots: Prophetic Visions of the Human Condition in Albert Camus and Simone Weil." *Religion and Literature* 17:2 (Summer 1985): 35–42.

Girard, René. *I See Satan Fall Like Lightning.* Trans. James G. Williams. Maryknoll, N.Y.: Orbis, 2001.

———. "Camus's Stranger Retried." *PMLA* 79:5 (Dec. 1964): 519–33.

Grégoire, Vincent. "Le Rôle de l'alcool dans les Oeuvres d'Albert Camus." *Symposium* 58:1 (Spring 2004): 15–26.

Henry, Patrick. *Voltaire and Camus: The Limits of Reason and the Awareness of Absurdity.* Vol. 138. *Studies on Voltaire and the Eighteenth Century.* Banbury, Oxfordshire: Voltaire Foundation, 1975.

Horowitz, Louise K. "Of Women and Arabs: Sexual and Racial Polarization in Camus." *Modern Language Studies* 17:3 (Summer 1987): 54–61.

Little, J. P. "Albert Camus, Simone Weil and Modern Tragedy." *French Studies: A Quarterly Review* 31 (January 1977): 42–51.

Loose, John. "The Christian as Camus's Absurd Man." *Journal of Religion* 42:3 (July 1962): 203–14.

McCarthy, Patrick. *Albert Camus, The Stranger.* Landmarks of World Literature Series. Cambridge: Cambridge UP, 1988.

———. "The First Arab in *L'Étranger.*" *Celfan Review* 4:3 (May 1985): 23–26.

Maher, Eamon. "Camus's Meursault: The Only Christ that Modern Civilisation Deserves?" *Studies: An Irish Quarterly Review* 87:347 (Autumn 1998): 276–81.

Margerrison, Christine. "Albert Camus and 'Ces Femmes qu'on raie de l'humanité': Sexual Politics in the Colonial Arena." *French Cultural Studies* 10:2 (June 1999): 217–30.

———. "The Dark Continent of Camus's *L'Étranger*." *French Studies* 55:1 (January 2001): 59–73.

Maus, Derek C., ed., *Readings on The Stranger*. San Diego, California: Greenhaven, 2001.

New English Bible: The Old Testament. London: Oxford and Cambridge UP, 1970.

New King James Version. Nashville, TN: Thomas Nelson, 1982.

New Oxford American Dictionary. New York: Oxford UP, 2001.

O'Brien, Conor Cruise. *Albert Camus of Europe and Africa*. New York: Viking, 1970.

O'Brien, Edward., Jr. "Camus and Christianity" *The Personalist* 44:2 (April 1963): 149–63.

Ohayon, Stephen. "Camus' *The Stranger*: The Sun-Metaphor and Patricidal Conflict." *American Imago* 40:2 (Summer 1983): 189–205.

Onimus, Jean. *Albert Camus and Christianity*. Tuscaloosa: UP of Alabama, 1970.

Peyre, Henri. "Camus the Pagan." *Yale French Studies* 25 (Spring 1960): 20–25.

Rigaud, Jan. "Depiction of Arabs in *L'Étranger*." *Camus's L'Étranger: Fifty Years On*. Ed. Adele King. New York: St. Martin's, 1992. 183–92.

Rizzuto, Anthony. "Camus and a Society Without Women." *Modern Language Studies* 13:1 (Winter 1983): 3–14.

Sartre, Jean-Paul. *The Words*. New York: George Braziller, 1964.

Scherr, Arthur. "Albert Camus's *L'Étranger* and Ernesto Sábato's *El Túnel*." *Romance Notes* 47:2 (Spring 2007): 199–205.

Showalter, English, Jr. *The Stranger: Humanity and the Absurd*. Boston: Twayne, 1989.

Sterling, Elwyn F. "The Execution of Meursault: A Re-Examination." *Agora: A Journal in the Humanities and Social Sciences* 1:3 (Spring 1970): 13–20.

Sutton, Robert Chester. *Human Existence and Theodicy: A Comparison of Jesus and Albert Camus*. New York: Peter Lang, 1992.

Thody, Philip, ed. *Lyrical and Critical Essays by Albert Camus*. New York: Vintage, 1970.

Wagner, Monique. "Physical Malaise and Subconscious Death-Wish in *L'Étranger*." *Michigan Academician: Papers of the Michigan Academy of Science, Arts, and Letters* 11 (1979): 331–41.

Ward, Matthew, trans. *The Stranger*. By Albert Camus. New York: Vintage, 1989.

Witt, Mary Ann, and Eric Witt. "Retrying *The Stranger* Again" *Literature and Law*. Ed. Michael J. Meyer. Amsterdam: Rodophi, 2004. 1–19.

Woelfel, James W. *Camus: A Theological Perspective*. Nashville: Abingdon, 1975.

Chronology

1913	Born in Algeria in November.
1914	Father killed in Battle of the Marne, World War I.
1918	Educated at grade school and lycée in Algiers until 1930.
1930	Begins to study philosophy at the University of Algiers; suffers first serious attack of tuberculosis.
1933	Marries briefly, divorcing the next year.
1935	Founds and is active in *Théâtre du Travail* (later *Théâtre de l'Equipe*); helps to write *La Révolte dans les Asturies* (*The Revolt in Asturia*).
1936	Receives the *diplôme d'études supérieures* in philosophy.
1937	*L'Envers en l'endroit* (*Betwixt and Between*) published.
1938	Takes a position as a reporter for the *Alger Républicain*. *Noces* (*Nuptials*) published.
1939	Marries Francine Faure in Lyon; returns to Algeria in January 1941.
1941	After the occupation of France by Nazi Germany, joins the Resistance movement.
1942	*L'Étranger* (*The Stranger*) is published.

151

1943	Founds the underground Resistance newspaper *Combat*, which he edits until the end of the war; *Le Mythe de Sisyphe* (*The Myth of Sisyphus*, translated 1955) is published; takes a job as an editor at the Gallimard publishing house in Paris, a position he holds until his death.
1944	Play *Le Malentendu* (*The Misunderstanding*) is produced. Meets Jean-Paul Sartre; play *Caligula*, written before the war, is produced.
1945	Twin children, Jean and Catherine, are born.
1946	Embarks on a yearlong lecture tour of the United States after a translation of *The Stranger* is published.
1947	*La Peste* (*The Plague*, translated 1948) is published.
1948	Play *L'Etat de siège* (*State of Siege*) is produced.
1949	Undertakes lecture tour of South America; *Les Justes* (*The Just Assassins*) is produced.
1950	Publication of *L'Homme révolté* (*The Rebel*, translated 1953), a long statement of his philosophical views, leads to a quarrel and eventual break with Jean-Paul Sartre.
1956	*La Chute* (*The Fall*, translated 1957) is published; adapts William Faulkner's *Requiem for a Nun* (*Requiem pour une nonne*) for stage production.
1957	Receives Nobel Prize for literature; a collection of six short stories, *L'Exil et le royaume* (*Exile and the Kingdom*), is published.
1958	Adapts Dostoevsky's *The Possessed* (*Les Possédés*) for stage production.
1959	Appointed by André Malraux, minister of cultural affairs of the French government, as director of the new state-supported experimental theater.
1960	Dies in an automobile accident on January 4.
1978	*Journaux de voyage* (*American Journals*, translated in 1987), edited by Roger Quillot, published.
1994	*Le Premier homme* (*The First Man*, translated in 1995), the novel he was working on at the time of his death, is published as edited by his daughter Catherine.

Contributors

HAROLD BLOOM is Sterling Professor of the Humanities at Yale University. Educated at Cornell and Yale universities, he is the author of more than 30 books, including *Shelley's Mythmaking* (1959), *Blake's Apocalypse* (1963), *Yeats* (1970), *The Anxiety of Influence* (1973), *A Map of Misreading* (1975), *Kabbalah and Criticism* (1975), *Agon: Toward a Theory of Revisionism* (1982), *The American Religion* (1992), *The Western Canon* (1994), *Omens of Millennium: The Gnosis of Angels, Dreams, and Resurrection* (1996), *Shakespeare: The Invention of the Human* (1998), *How to Read and Why* (2000), *Genius: A Mosaic of One Hundred Exemplary Creative Minds* (2002), *Hamlet: Poem Unlimited* (2003), *Where Shall Wisdom Be Found?* (2004), *Jesus and Yahweh: The Names Divine* (2005), and *Till I End My Song: A Gathering of Last Poems* (2010). In addition, he is the author of hundreds of articles, reviews, and editorial introductions. In 1999, Professor Bloom received the American Academy of Arts and Letters' Gold Medal for Criticism. He has also received the International Prize of Catalonia, the Alfonso Reyes Prize of Mexico, and the Hans Christian Andersen Bicentennial Prize of Denmark.

DAVID SPRINTZEN is a professor emeritus of philosophy at Long Island University and also served as chairperson of the department at C. W. Post College. He founded the Institute for Sustainable Development at Long Island University and served as its codirector for seven years. His publishing history includes being an editor and translator of *Sartre and Camus: A Historic Confrontation*.

JACK MURRAY is a professor emeritus at the University of California, Santa Barbara. He is the author of *The Landscapes of Alienation* and other titles.

LARRY W. RIGGS is a professor in French at Butler University. He has published texts on Molière and Camus.

PAULA WILLOQUET-MARICONDI is an associate professor and chairperson of the media arts department at Marist College. Her work includes editing *Framing the World: Explorations in Ecocriticism and Film*.

ROBERT R. BROCK is an associate professor emeritus at the University of Montana. He has published *Lire, Enfin, Robbe-Grillet*.

GERALD PRINCE is a professor of romance languages and chairperson of the French section at the University of Pennsylvania. He is the author of several books, including *A Dictionary of Narratology* and *Narrative as Theme*.

COLIN DAVIS is a professor of French at Royal Holloway, University of London, where he also is director of research for the School of Modern Languages, Literatures and Cultures. His publications include *Ethical Issues in Twentieth-Century French Fiction: Killing the Other* and *French Fiction in the Mitterrand Years: Memory, Narrative, Desire*.

ADRIAN VAN DEN HOVEN is a professor emeritus in the French studies department at the University of Windsor. He is the executive editor of *Sartre Studies International* and coeditor of *Sartre Live*, among other publications.

JOHN FOLEY has been a postdoctoral researcher at the National University of Ireland, Galway.

ARTHUR SCHERR has taught history. His work includes *Thomas Jefferson's Haitian Policy: Myths and Realities*.

Bibliography

Abecassis, Jack I. "Camus's Pulp Fiction." *Modern Language Notes* 112, no. 4 (September 1997): 625–40.

Amoia, Alba. *Albert Camus*. New York: Continuum, 1989.

Baker, Richard E. "Camus's Existentialist Hero." In *The Image of the Hero in Literature, Media, and Society*, edited by Will Wright and Steven Kaplan, pp. 528–38. Pueblo: Colorado State University, 2004.

Bartlett, Elizabeth Ann. *Rebellious Feminism: Camus's Ethic of Rebellion and Feminist Thought*. New York: Palgrave Macmillan, 2004.

Beauclair, Michelle. *Albert Camus, Marguerite Duras, and the Legacy of Mourning*. New York: P. Lang, 1998.

Braun, Lev. *Witness of Decline; Albert Camus: Moralist of the Absurd*. Rutherford, N.J.: Fairleigh Dickinson University Press, 1974.

Bronner, Stephen Eric. *Camus: Portrait of a Moralist*. Minneapolis: University of Minnesota Press, 1999.

Chaitin, Gilbert D. "The Birth of the Subject in Camus' *L'Etranger*." *Romanic Review* 84, no. 2 (March 1993): 163–80.

———. "Confession and Desire in *L'Etranger*." *Symposium: A Quarterly Journal in Modern Literatures* 46, no. 3 (Fall 1992): 163–75.

Champigny, Robert. *A Pagan Hero, an Interpretation of Meursault in Camus' The Stranger*. Translated by Rowe Portis. Philadelphia: University of Pennsylvania Press, 1969.

Combs, Robert. "Camus, O'Neill, and the Dead Mother Society." *Eugene O'Neill Review* 26 (2004): 189–98.

155

Cordes, Alfred. *The Descent of the Doves: Camus's Journey to the Spirit.* Washington, D.C.: University Press of America, 1980.

Curtis, Jerry L. "Thorns and Thistles: The Weltanschauungen of Voltaire and Camus." *Proceedings of the Comparative Literature Symposium* 8 (1975): 83–98.

Davison, Ray. *Camus: The Challenge of Dostoevsky.* Exeter, Devon, UK: University of Exeter Press, 1997.

Ellison, David R. *Understanding Albert Camus.* Columbia: University of South Carolina Press, 1990.

Fitch, Brian T. *The Narcissistic Text: A Reading of Camus' Fiction.* Toronto; Buffalo: University of Toronto Press, 1982.

Gaillard, Pol. *Albert Camus.* Paris: Bordas, 1973.

Girard, René. "Camus's Stranger Retried." *PMLA* 79, no. 5 (December 1964): 519–33.

Hansen, Keith W. *Tragic Lucidity: Discourse of Recuperation in Unamuno and Camus.* New York: P. Lang, 1993.

Henry, Patrick. *Voltaire and Camus: The Limits of Reason and the Awareness of Absurdity.* Banbury, England: Voltaire Foundation, 1975.

Hughes, Edward J., ed. *The Cambridge Companion to Camus.* Cambridge; New York: Cambridge University Press, 2007.

Kamber, Richard. *On Camus.* Belmont, Calif.: Wadsworth/Thomson Learning, 2002.

Keefe, Terry. *French Existentialist Fiction: Changing Moral Perspectives.* Totowa, N.J.: Barnes & Noble, 1986.

Kellogg, Jean. *Dark Prophets of Hope—Dostoevsky, Sartre, Camus, Faulkner.* Chicago: Loyola University Press, 1975.

King, Adele, ed. *Camus's L'Étranger: Fifty Years On.* New York: St. Martin's, 1992.

Knapp, Bettina, L., ed. *Critical Essays on Albert Camus.* Boston: G.K. Hall, 1988.

Lazere, Donald. *The Unique Creation of Albert Camus.* New Haven: Yale University Press, 1973.

Lehan, Richard. *A Dangerous Crossing; French Literary Existentialism and the Modern American Novel.* Carbondale: Southern Illinois University Press, 1973.

Longstaffe, Moya. "A Happy Life and a Happy Death: The Quest of Camus's Etranger." *French Review* 64, no. 1 (October 1990): 54–68.

Maher, Eamon. "Camus' Meursault: The Only Christ That Modern Civilization Deserves?" *Studies: An Irish Quarterly Review* 87 (Autumn 1998): 276–81.

Margerrison, Christine, Mark Orme and Lissa Lincoln, eds. *Albert Camus in the 21st Century: A Reassessment of His Thinking at the Dawn of the New Millennium.* Amsterdam; New York: Rodopi, 2008.

Margerrison, Christine. "The Dark Continent of Camus's L'Etranger." *French Studies* 55, no. 1 (January 2001): 59–73.

Masters, Brian. *Camus: A Study. London: Heinemann Educational*; Totowa, N.J.: Rowman and Littlefield, 1974.

McCann, J. "The Verdict on Meursault." *Nottingham French Studies* 29, no. 1 (1990): 51–63.

Morot-Sir, Edouard. "Camus, Reader of Melville: Recognition of a Fraternal Model." *The French-American Review* 6, no. 2 (Fall 1982): 328–41.

O'Brien, Conor Cruise. *Albert Camus of Europe and Africa*. New York: Viking Press, 1970.

Orme, Mark. *The Development of Albert Camus's Concern for Social and Political Justice: "justice pour un juste."* Madison, N.J.: Fairleigh Dickinson University Press, 2007.

Oxenhandler, Neal. *Looking for Heroes in Postwar France: Albert Camus, Max Jacob, Simone Weil*. Hanover, N.H.: University Press of New England, 1996.

Rizzuto, Anthony. *Camus: Love and Sexuality*. Gainesville: University Press of Florida, 1998.

Rysten, Felix S.A. *False Prophets in the Fiction of Camus, Dostoevsky, Melville, and Others*. Coral Gables, Fla.: University of Miami Press, 1972.

Sagi, Avi. *Albert Camus and the Philosophy of the Absurd*. Translated by Batya Stein. Amsterdam; New York: Rodopi, 2002.

Sherman, David. "Camus's Meursault and Sartrian Irresponsibility." *Philosophy and Literature* 19, no. 1 (April 1995): 60–77.

Showalter, English, Jr. The Stranger: *Humanity and the Absurd*. Boston: Twayne Publishers, 1989.

Solomon, Robert C. *Dark Feelings, Grim Thoughts: Experience and Reflection in Camus and Sartre*. Oxford; New York: Oxford University Press, 2006.

Stoltzfus, Ben. "Camus's *L'Etranger:* A Lacanian Reading." *Texas Studies in Literature and Language* 31, no. 4 (Winter 1989): 515–35.

Thody, Philip. *Albert Camus: A Study of His Work*. London: Hamish Hamilton, 1957.

Vasil, Dean. *The Ethical Pragmatism of Albert Camus: Two Studies in the History of Ideas*. New York: P. Lang, 1985.

Acknowledgments

David Sprintzen, "*The Stranger.*" From *Camus: A Critical Study*. Copyright ©
1988 by Temple University.

Jack Murray, "Closure and Anticlosure in Camus's *L'Étranger*: Some Ideological
Considerations." From *Symposium* 46, no. 3 (Fall 1992): 225–40. Copyright ©
1992 by the Helen Dwight Reid Educational Foundation.

Larry W. Riggs and Paula Willoquet-Maricondi, "Colonialism, Enlightenment,
Castration: Writing, Narration, and Legibility in *L'Étranger.*" From *Studies in
Twentieth and Twenty First Century Literature* 16 (1992): 265–88. Copyright ©
1992 by Kansas State University and the University of Nebraska-Lincoln.

Robert R. Brock, "Meursault the Straw Man." From *Studies in the Novel* 25, no.
1 (Spring 1993): 92–101. Copyright © 1993 by the University of North Texas.

Gerald Prince, "Meursault and Narrative." From *Resonant Themes: Literature,
History, and the Arts in Nineteenth- and Twentieth-Century Europe,* edited by
Stirling Haig. Copyright © 1999, Department of Romance Languages, the
University of North Carolina at Chapel Hill.

Colin Davis, "The Cost of Being Ethical: Fiction, Violence, and Altericide."
From *Common Knowledge* 9, no. 2 (2003): 241–53. Copyright © 2003 by Duke
University Press.

Adrian van den Hoven, "Sartre's Conception of Historiality and Temporality: The Quest for a Motive in Camus' *The Stranger* and Sartre's *Dirty Hands*." From *Sartre Studies International* 11, nos. 1&2 (2005): 207–21. Copyright © 2005 by Berghahn Journals.

John Foley, *"The Outsider."* From *Albert Camus: From the Absurd to Revolt*. Published by McGill-Queen's University Press. Copyright © John Foley 2008.

Arthur Scherr, "Meursault's Dinner with Raymond: A Christian Theme in Albert Camus's *L'Étranger*." From *Christianity and Literature* 58, no. 2 (Winter 2009): 187–210. Copyright © 2009 Conference on Christianity and Literature.

Index

Characters in literary works are indexed by first name (if any), followed by the name of the work in parentheses

161

ML